Reporting Dangerously

Reporting Dangerously

Journalist Killings, Intimidation and Security

Simon Cottle

Richard Sambrook

and

Nick Mosdell

Simon Cottle
Cardiff University
School of Journalism,
Cardiff, United Kingdom

Nick Mosdell
Cardiff University
School of Journalism,
Cardiff, United Kingdom

Richard Sambrook
Cardiff University
School of Journalism,
Cardiff, United Kingdom

ISBN 978-1-137-40672-9   ISBN 978-1-137-40670-5 (eBook)
DOI 10.1007/978-1-137-40670-5

This Palgrave Macmillan imprint is published by SpringerNature.

The registered company is Macmillan Publishers Ltd. London.

Contents

List of Figures

About the Authors

Simon Cottle is Professor of Media and Communications, School of Journalism, Media and Cultural Studies (JOMEC) at Cardiff University where he was Deputy Head and Head of School (2008–2015). Previously he was Inaugural Chair and Head of the Media and Communications Program at the University of Melbourne, Australia. He is Director of a new Research Group at Cardiff: 'Communications, Human Security and Atrocity in Global Context'. Cottle is the author of many books on media, globalization and the communication of conflicts, crises and catastrophes. Most recently these include *Mediatized Conflicts* (2006); *Global Crisis Reporting* (2009); *Transnational Protests and the Media* (Ed. with L. Lester, 2011); *Disasters and the Media* (with M. Pantti and K. Wahl-Jorgensen, 2012); and *Humanitarianism, Communications and Change* (Ed. with G. Cooper, 2015). He series edits the Global Crises and Media Series. He is thinking about the history of violence and communications and the possible leverage that global communications can help secure in contexts of human insecurity and imminent atrocity.

Nick Mosdell is Deputy Director MA International Public Relations and Global Communications Management in the School of Journalism, Media and Cultural Studies at Cardiff University, UK. He teaches research methods modules to master's students and has written research methods textbooks. He has also contributed to a variety of research-based publications including media and military relations, for example *Too Close for Comfort? The Role of Embedded Reporting in the 2003 Iraq War* (2004); *Embedded Reporting in War and Peace* (2006); and *Shoot First and Ask Questions Later: Media Coverage of the 2003 Iraq War (2006)*. He was involved in the International News Safety Institute's Global Inquiry into journalist deaths that resulted in *Killing The Messenger* (2007), and has produced casualty reports for INSI every year since then.

Richard Sambrook is Professor of Journalism at the School of Journalism, Media and Cultural Studies (JOMEC) at Cardiff University. He is Deputy Head of School and oversees the practice-based vocational training. Previously, he worked in BBC News for 30 years as a producer and editor, culminating in a decade on the board of management as Director of News and Director of Global News and the World Service. His publications include *Are Foreign Correspondents Redundant* (2010) and *Delivering Trust: Impartiality and Objectivity in the Digital Age* (2012) both written for the Reuters Institute for the Study of Journalism at the University of Oxford. He is also Chair of the International News Safety Institute.

1
Introduction

Journalism is becoming a more dangerous profession. Reporters and editors are being targeted, murdered, and intimidated more regularly and in increasing numbers. Yet it is not an issue which in itself is often reported. Occasionally, there is an event, such as the murder of the Charlie Hebdo cartoonists in Paris, which brings to the fore the violent opposition journalism and free speech can face even in the West. And once a year the free speech and journalism non-governmental organisations such as the Committee to Protect Journalists (CPJ), the International News Safety Institute (INSI), or Reporters Sans Frontières (RSF) report their annual tally of journalists and media workers killed. But the underlying facts and trends behind these figures are little discussed, and the wider impact on society little considered.

This book is an attempt to place into a wider context the dangers journalists face in conducting their work.[1] We will consider the statistics and look at the trends behind the rise in journalist killings and intimidation, consider what factors have led to this rise, and place them in an historical and global context.

We will look at specific case studies and draw upon first hand interviews to understand the different pressures faced by journalists around the world. We will look at the industry and political responses to these pressures. Finally, we will cast forward to the current international policy initiatives to consider what hope there is for addressing the problem.

Above all, we will argue that journalism has historically contributed an indispensable if under-recognised and insufficiently theorised role in the formation and conduct of civil societies – and continues to do so. This is why reporting from un-civil societies matters.

According to INSI, on average two journalists a week have lost their lives doing their job – week in, week out – over the last dozen years or more. Most of those killed are not the international reporters who can make global headlines. They are local journalists investigating crime or corruption – seeking to stand by a professional commitment to free speech and inquiry.

Headlines from the first few months of 2015 give a sense of the problem:

'Kidnapped TV crew reported executed by ISIS'

'Kidnappers murder journalist in Mexico'

'Prominent pro-Russian journalist murdered by masked gunmen in the streets of Kiev'

(INSI 2015a)

But behind each headline there is a personal story. Take, for example, Daud Omar, who was shot dead together with his wife in their home in Baidoa, Somalia when their killer broke into their house. The local police commissioner blamed armed group Al Shabaab which had previously claimed responsibility for attacks meted out against journalists. Or Nerlita Ledesma, who wrote for one of the Philippines' biggest newspapers and was shot dead by a gunman on a motorcycle on her way to work in January 2015. Or Robert Chamwami Shalubuto, a journalist for state media in the Democratic Republic of Congo, whose body was found in a grocery store close to his home after he had been shot in the chest. There are too many others to list.

As the BBC's Chief International Correspondent, Lyse Doucet, has written:

Never have we lived in a time when journalists, their editors, and media organisations ... spend so much effort and care trying to assess the dangers. But never has there been a time when journalists have faced such odds of being in the right place at the wrong time. In all too many places, we are no longer just taking calculated risks to report on the front line. We are the front line. Unresolved murders, kidnappings for ransom, beheadings are now happening at an alarming rate. Now, all too often, we are also the story. That's not the way journalism should be.

(INSI 2015b)

Journalists, by the nature of their work, have always put themselves in harm's way, and some have had to pay the ultimate price for doing so.

However, a number of factors have significantly increased the risks they face through the last years of the twentieth century and early years of the twenty-first.

First, the ending of the Cold War led to a different character of global conflict. At the peak of the Cold War, many conflicts were proxies for the East–West stand-off. As such, journalists worked clearly on one side of the line or the other, often alongside the military. Afterwards, frontlines became harder to identify; armed groups had uncertain or changing affiliations; journalists were left to fend for themselves. There were advantages to such independence – but also risks in operating in conflict zones with no clear affiliation or protection. And with the breakdown of societies in Libya, Syria, parts of Africa and beyond, journalists became more exposed.

Thirty years ago, journalists were acknowledged as neutral observers, with civilian status. Today, as Lyse Doucet described, they are too often targets. The increasing reach and status of the media and the rise of non-state violence has made journalists useful pawns in the asymmetrical conflicts following the September 2001 terrorist attack on New York and the West's military response in Afghanistan, Iraq and the wider Middle East. This has been accompanied by changing, and at times increasingly tense, relations between the military and the media.

From the murder of American journalist Daniel Pearl in Pakistan in 2002, through to the murders of James Foley and Steven Sotloff in 2014, it is clear that terrorist groups now see journalists as useful targets. Their graphic murders are a way to command global attention and horrify the wider public.

Increasing competition in the media has in some areas led to increased stridency. The advent of social media has promoted opinion over factual reporting – again contributing to a perceived loss of neutrality. In states such as Egypt, attempts to report the views of the opposition are no longer accepted as necessarily legitimate – as illustrated by the arrests of journalists reporting the views of the Muslim Brotherhood. Political instability and extremism can lead state actors to move against independent journalism in the interests of maintaining influence. Today, political divisions can mean there is a battle for minds as much as for territory, which means independent journalists can be regarded as, or confused for, political opponents.

With the decline in perceived neutrality has come a rise in impunity for attacks on journalists, the blatant intimidation of journalists and the craft of journalism. When journalists and their sources are seriously threatened and there is no adequate protection, self-censorship is inevitable. If violence and intimidation are intended to silence awkward journalism, they work.

The growth of organised crime in Asia, South and Central America and the Caucasus placed local journalists at significant risk in reporting drug cartels or corruption. Mexico has become one of the most dangerous countries in which to report as the drugs trade has moved north from Colombia towards the US border. As crime and corruption hollow out the democratic institutions of some states, the rewards for organised crime grow – and the level of threat to anyone seeking to report it increases too. With very few murders of journalists ever solved or prosecuted, it has become an effective form of censorship in some societies.

Finally, the development of technology has allowed journalists to reach more places than ever before – but that has included places with significant risk. Today, with a mobile phone and laptop, journalists can report from anywhere. But their movements can also be tracked and they can be targeted – which seems to have happened with Marie Colvin, the *Sunday Times* correspondent killed by targeted mortar fire in Homs, Syria, in 2011 after a series of powerful reports about civilian casualties. Technology increasingly allows reporters to be live on air on the front lines – but with a commensurate increase in risk alongside frontline fighting. In addition, digital technology allows journalists and citizens to report more openly – but also leaves them more publicly exposed. And the technology of reporting is subject to widespread surveillance by states and other actors inhibiting investigative journalism. Digital security is increasingly important in journalism safety. Often, weak digital security can compromise journalism. Occasionally, it compromises the safety of the journalist.

Further, the widespread availability of media technology means armies or terrorists are no longer dependent on the media to report their side of the story. They can do it for themselves. So Israel's Defence Force (IDF) has its own YouTube channel where it posts training videos, and reports and explanations of operations – no longer reliant on local or international media's interpretation. Equally, terror groups like the Islamic State of Iraq and Syria (ISIS) have used social media to influence media coverage of their cause, and to recruit new members.[2] In these circumstances, where media were once afforded some protection in order to ensure accounts reached a wider public, they are no longer seen as essential to military, or terrorist, communications.

The changing backdrop of societal violence, political and technological change, is therefore important for a deeper understanding of the risks and dangers confronted by journalists and media workers around the world.

The killing of journalists is clearly used not only to shock, but also to intimidate. As such, it has become an effective way for groups and even governments to reduce scrutiny and accountability, and establish the space to pursue non-democratic ends.

Civil Society and the conduct of daily, ordinary 'civil life' can only flourish within recognised, democratically organised and protected societies. Journalism's 'responsibility to report' places journalists and their craft at the centre of established, emerging and collapsing societies around the world. Journalists witness and communicate conflicts, injustices, and social and democratic failure. As such, journalism and civil society are indivisible and mutually constitutive, mutually dependent.

This means all of us, journalists or not, have a stake in the ability to report freely and openly, and in ensuring journalists can continue to do so. The protection of journalists reporting in and from dangerous places cannot be regarded as simply a matter to do only with them or as only about journalism. It implicates us all. This is even more the case in an interconnected, interdependent, globalised world. If there are territories or issues which become effectively unreported or unreportable, it affects all of us, not only those directly involved.

In a globalised world, in which the UN's 'responsibility to protect' doctrine urges the international community to recognise its shared responsibility to protect the lives of those confronting genocide, atrocity and mass killings, the world's journalists also deserve increased international recognition and protection when throwing a spotlight on collective injustices. Indeed, there is a case for the current lexicon shifting from 'protection' and 'security' (practically aimed at keeping individual journalists safe) to 'safeguarding' and 'prosecution' (seeking to create legal contexts and international conditions) designed to counter the seeming impunity with which so many murders of journalists are carried out. Wider institutional and legal frameworks must be brought into play and robustly enforced if journalists in the future, as well as those currently reporting form uncivil societies, are to be properly recognised and safeguarded. Journalists need this not only when seeking to alert the world's conscience to gross acts of inhumanity around the world, but also when reporting on the everyday violence, intimidation, crime and corruption that insidiously threatens and undermines their own and other people's 'civil society'.

This issue also sits at the heart of global concerns about freedom of speech and whether governments, aid funders and the development community should recognise it as a primary right (from which it follows that independent journalism must be protected) or a secondary right (behind the right to life or the right to health) by which the media are simply a tool to support other aims.

This book argues for a wider social and political responsibility for the protection of independent journalism. It does so in the context of the rapid changes to the field of journalism itself, including globalisation, corporate and competitive restructuring, casualisation and the rise of the so-called 'citizen journalist', and the continuing revolution in social media and news technologies.

These have all given rise to debates about what exactly counts as 'journalism', who can be classified as a 'journalist' and therefore who is counted as a 'journalist casualty'. These are not easy matters to resolve. We seek to provide a clear overview of the differences in play and what's at stake.

We set out the latest statistical findings on journalist killings and intimidation collated from around the world, and place them in a broader context of trends and themes. We also give voice to journalists who have experience in reporting from conflict zones and uncivil societies, hearing their experiences and candid reflections on why they do it and how they seek to protect themselves.

We look at how the news industry has responded to the changing risks run by its staff and what has motivated the changes introduced over the last 25 years to how news organisations operate in hostile environments Finally, we discuss the evolving institutional frameworks and initiatives designed to keep journalists safe, including UN Security Council 1738 and the UN Plan of Action on the Safety of Journalists and the Issue of Impunity.

Too often, academic studies of journalism have sought to critically interrogate the nature of reporting from war and disaster zones, examining perceived deficiencies or distortions but failing to recognise the professional motivations and practical dangers for those undertaking such work. Similarly, the response from journalists and news organisations has often lacked a broader social or political context, seeking only to draw attention to the immediate casualties or risks.

This study therefore deliberately takes a different, more integrated approach set out below. It seeks to recognise that journalism and its 'responsibility to report' are inextricably bound up with the constitution and conduct of civil societies. We hope it will support a better understanding of the unacceptable price increasing numbers of journalists now pay for an historically forged commitment to reporting from dangerous places, and that it will contribute to the broader moves within civil society to ensure they can safely continue to do so for the benefit of us all.

Approach

Reporting Dangerously: Journalist Killings, Intimidation and Security sets out with the aim to better understand some of the multifaceted complexities and changing dynamics involved in journalist killings and intimidation around the world today, as well as the policies and initiatives designed to keep them safe(r). We hope that some of the views and discussion in this book may open up new insights, deepen understanding or even help to identify possibilities for keeping journalists (if not entirely safe) at least considerably safer. Most within the news industry would probably agree that attaining zero risk when setting foot into some of the most deadly places and hostile reporting environments, unruly and uncivil by definition, is an unrealistic prospect, and could only be achieved by failing to get close enough to the story and its human consequences. This would pose its own risks and dangers not only to local populations situated *in extremis* but also to the well-being and responsiveness of global civil society. Nonetheless, all would probably also agree that the chances of protecting and safeguarding journalists could be considerably improved and that it is now imperative that every opportunity be taken to ensure that this happens.

This book draws deliberately on six different voices, each bringing into play distinctive but complementary views from different vantage points on this most pressing of issues. The first three voices are those of authors. Though we are all based in the School of Journalism, Media and Cultural Studies at Cardiff University, each of our separately authored chapters brings different perspectives and expertise to the problem. Richard Sambrook, Professor of Journalism at Cardiff, was formerly Director of Global News at the BBC where he worked as a journalist for 30 years as a producer, editor and manager. He has first-hand managerial experience of grappling with the difficulties and dilemmas of trying to ensure the safety of BBC and other journalists working in dangerous places around the world, and has researched and written on, among other subjects, the changes and challenges facing foreign correspondents (Sambrook 2010). He has also been closely involved in the work of INSI since its inception and other initiatives aimed at reducing risks and keeping journalists safer in the work that they do.

Simon Cottle, Professor of Media and Communications, has conducted ethnographic research into the world of news production and professional practices, and has written extensively on journalism, conflict and crisis reporting. He has a strong interest in the history of violence and communications, and in how contemporary processes of globalisation often converge in today's global crises. The latter are highly dependent on media and communications, both in respect of wider processes of world recognition and also policy interventions and public responses (Cottle 2009, 2011, Cottle and Cooper 2015). He is particularly interested in how today's new media ecology affords new reporting challenges as well as progressive possibilities in the advance of world society (Cottle 2013, 2014), and in the part played by journalism as part of this. He is the Series Editor of the *Global Crisis and Media* series for the publisher Peter Lang, that includes *Humanitarianism, Communications and Change* (Cottle and Cooper 2015).

Nick Mosdell is Deputy Director MA International Public Relations and Global Communications Management at Cardiff, and an expert on research methodology. He has researched and written on war journalism and co-authored, with Richard Sambrook, and Dr Kenneth Payne, *Killing The Messenger: Report of the Global Inquiry by the International News Safety Institute into the Protection of Journalists* (Sambrook et al. 2007). He continues to support the work of this monitoring and advocacy group through collating and interpreting trends in journalist killings and intimidation around the world each year, and advocating changes to keep journalists safer.

This variety of experience and expertise converges productively, we hope, in our approach to journalist killings and intimidation, and to the associated problem of impunity – whether found within a wider culture of indifference or state complicity and connivance. All the voices contributing to this book, its narrative and exposition, are of one mind insofar as we all seek to secure increased traction on the nature of these disturbing trends and better fathom and propose what can be done about them. The imperative to do so is underlined by our fourth voice in *Reporting Dangerously*, an absent voice but one that silently and insistently echoes throughout the entire book.

This is the voice of those journalists who have been killed in the course of their reporting, and whose deaths we here recount to remind ourselves and our readers of the terrible human costs and tragic consequences involved for the journalists, their families and colleagues – as well as for wider society. These silent voices from the grave underline the dreadful reality of those colleagues who continue to report in similar circumstances, and who endure similar physical threats and/ or psychological duress when doing so. By detailing the individual circumstances and fate of just some of the many journalists who have lost their lives in recent years, we pay testimony to all those journalists killed around the world as well as their colleagues now working in similar unruly, uncivil places.

Our fifth voice is also granted deliberate prominence throughout the book. This concerns the perspectives, experiences and views of practising journalists, correspondents, editors and managers working for different news organisations around the world. We include their accounts and testimonies, and hear them speak (often at unusual length) about what motivates them to carry out this dangerous work, their perceptions of the dangers involved, and how changing communications, political and social realities on the ground, as well as new safety initiatives, all impact upon their reporting practices and efforts to keep themselves and their colleagues safe – and why some of them calibrate their threshold of acceptable risk quite differently.

Finally, a sixth voice also informs our approach and efforts to grapple with this dreadful problem. This is the voice of those organisational, industry-based and wider national and international political entities that have sought to recognise the worldwide problem of journalist killing, intimidation and kidnapping, doing so through the formulation of policies and frameworks designed to keep them safe(r). Across recent years, news organisations and related professional bodies have sought to introduce or extend safety training, hostile environment and first-aid courses as well as other protective measures to minimise risks when reporting in dangerous, hazardous places. Important as these are, wider institutional and political initiatives are also required at national and international levels, be they the implementation and enforcement of legal-judicial frameworks and prosecutions or the sought-after cultivation of a prevalent and normative culture challenging indifference and actively condemning state complicity as well as involvement in the killing of journalists with impunity.

Book structure

Reporting Dangerously: Journalist Killings, Intimidation and Security is organised around four principal sections and nine sequenced chapters. Following this Introduction, Part I, 'What's Happening and Why it Matters', comprises two complementary chapters that provide an informed overview of what is happening to too many journalists around the world in terms of the dangers confronted and the unacceptable human costs that this now entails. Chapter 2, 'Reporting in Uncivil Societies and Why it Matters' by Richard Sambrook, profiles individual cases of journalist killings and intimidation to underline the unacceptable human costs borne by journalists working in difficult, often violent contexts. It also reflects on the civil and societal costs incurred by communities and wider collectives when they are unable to recognise themselves or their democratic aspirations because of the chilling effect that violence and intimidation can exert on journalists' reporting; and on how this disempowers people's capacity to intervene within the lifeblood of their own societies. Violence and intimidation prove not only antithetical to journalism's historically forged and normatively proclaimed mission of informing publics and acting as a critical watchdog in respect of political elites and the corporate powerful, but also places a dead hand on the democratic impetus of both formerly vibrant as well as formatively emergent civil societies.

Chapter 3, 'Mapping the Parameters of Peril' by Nick Mosdell, then provides a systematic, up-to-date and clear overview of the statistical patterns and trajectories of journalist killings and intimidation across recent years, and documents the sorts of conflicts and places that are the most deadly, and the sorts of journalists who are most at risk. These collective findings make for reading every bit as disturbing as the detailed cases of journalist killing presented in the preceding chapter. In addition, the chapter reflects methodologically on the changing and increasingly elastic conceptualisation of who and what exactly counts as a 'journalist' and 'journalism'. It considers whether this extends from full-time, paid professionals to part-time amateurs as well as to so-called citizen journalists and social activists, or even belligerents and, on occasion, states when all are seeking to get their particular message across and/or further their cause. Taken together, these two chapters serve to paint a disturbing picture of the patterns and consequences of journalist killing and intimidation in the world today.

Part II, 'Approached in Context: History, Violence, Journalism', comprises two further complementary chapters written by Simon Cottle. These follow on from the previous section by aiming to provide deeper contextualisation for understanding the changing nature and increased preponderance of violence encountered by journalists in today's world society, as well as for why exactly growing numbers of them volunteer to put themselves in the eye of the storm and thereby in harm's way. Chapter 4, 'On the Violent History of the Globalised Present', reviews and reflects on the historically changing nature of violence in human society, and how such trends have paradoxically positioned more journalists at risk at a time in human history when war and violence are thought to have undergone a distinct and measurable decline. The chapter points to how many of today's conflicts and crises around the world are either spawned by or are otherwise intimately interconnected with processes of globalisation, and argues that this needs to be better understood when trying to understand recent trends in journalist killing and intimidation. As a way of better understanding global crises and conflicts today, the discussion focuses on the changing nature of warfare, and discerns three, distinct, contemporary forms of waging collective violence: the new Western way of war; new war; and mediatised, image wars. Each of these, it is argued, impacts directly on journalists, and increasingly positions them at risk.

Chapter 5, 'Journalism and the Civil Sphere', follows up on the conceptual and theoretical debates about the history of violence and how the latter now converge in global crises and conflicts in today's interconnected and inegalitarian world. It does so by thinking through a little more theoretically the indispensable roles and responsibilities of journalism within civil societies and those discernible historical processes of democratic deepening. Here, the emergence and subsequent performance of journalism are situated in respect of the considerably longer-term, historical trajectories unfolding over centuries. These include processes of individualism, democratisation, humanitarianism and the institutionalisation of human rights, as well as the growing moral repugnance exhibited towards public displays of violence and deliberately inflicted pain and punishment, and an increasingly observed empathetic disposition towards human suffering. It is in relation to these historically deep-seated trajectories that we can begin to explain the seeming paradox of increased journalist killings in a time of reducing world violence; and, importantly, why it is that more and more journalists feel obliged to report in and from dangerous places.

Part III, '"We are the Frontline": Journalist Voices', promotes the voices of the journalists themselves as we hear their views and perspectives on the dangerous work that they do. Chapter 6, 'Reporting from Unruly, Uncivil Places: Journalist Voices from the Frontline' by Simon Cottle, canvasses the views of journalists, specialist correspondents, editors and senior managers working across different media and located in different parts of the world. It outlines and reflects on why they do this dangerous work, how risks have changed over time, and how they are unevenly distributed with regard to employment status, age, gender and location. The chapter further provides first-hand experiential accounts and reflections on reporting dangerously.

Chapter 7, 'Keeping Safe(r) in Unruly, Uncivil Places: Journalist Voices in a Changing Communications Environment' by Simon Cottle, listens to the accounts and experiences of reporters who have worked in some of the most dangerous parts of the world and how they have sought to keep themselves safe(r) and minimise risks when working in the field. We also hear different views expressed about journalists' calculus of risk and to what extent and why they variously follow policies and practices designed to keep them safer when reporting in or from hostile and hazardous environments. We further hear their views about and experiences of working within today's rapidly changing global communications environment, and how this enters into dangerous reporting – sometimes helping to minimise reporting risks, sometimes exacerbating them, and often doing both simultaneously.

Part IV, 'From Protecting to Safeguarding', follows on from these 'frontline' views and experiences in twinned chapters written by Richard Sambrook. Chapter 8, 'Protecting Journalists: An Evolving Responsibility', sets out the organisational history of initiatives and schemes that have sought to improve journalism safety over the years. It includes some of the key voices and makes reference to some of the most important documents and policies that have been enacted at news organisation level and which have been implemented with the aim of protecting journalists. However, as we have stated earlier, there is much more to protecting journalists and keeping them safe(r) than the immediate policies of news organisations or working practices of journalists.

In order to tackle the apparent impunity that surrounds so many journalist killings and threats, as well as the unacceptably high numbers of journalist deaths, it is the responsibility of the wider international community and its representative bodies to ensure legal prosecutions and the propagation of a culture that normatively seeks to challenge indifference or, worse, connivance and complicity in journalist killings and intimidation. This geopolitically broader and culturally deeper commitment to journalist 'safeguarding' forms the focal point of Chapter 9, 'Safeguarding Journalists: the Continuing Responsibility to Report'. Here we look at some of the most recent initiatives and developments at this wider institutional level, reproduce some of the key documents and protocols, as well as offer reflections and further commentary on their effectiveness and limitations.

Finally, Chapter 10, 'Conclusion: Ways Forward', offers a summary rehearsal of some of the key findings and arguments outlined across the course of the book as well as an assessment of where we are and what is yet required to help ensure the enhanced safety of working journalists around the world. Here we offer some views on what could yet be done, notwithstanding remaining structural difficulties, political stumbling blocks and professional concerns about an overcompensating culture of journalist risk-aversion, and what is now most urgently needed. The indivisible link between journalism's 'responsibility to report' conflicts and injustices around the world and the 'responsibility to protect' not only those directly involved in such circumstances, but also the journalists themselves who put their lives on the line to report from such dangerous places, is underlined one last time.

Notes

1. For the purposes of this discussion it may be helpful to define the general sense in which three key recurring terms are used throughout this book and in the context of journalists reporting dangerously. 'Dangers' refers to those present and generally known conditions, people or other agents that can cause harm. 'Hazards' refer to those remaining dangers that have yet to be fully mitigated or contained through means of avoidance or other measures. 'Risks' refers to those efforts to calculate or calibrate the likelihood of something bad happening. Journalists often know the dangers that they are presented with when they enter into a war situation for example, and they will try as far as possible to minimise these in practice by adopting sensible avoidance practices, making use of material resources to try and keep themselves safe – fixers, protective armour, communication systems – or by tactically withdrawing from the most dangerous circumstances. But not all dangers can be controlled or rendered less dangerous by such means, and those that remain do so as hazards. Efforts to calibrate these dangers and hazards seek to reconstitute them as 'risks'; that is, as calculated possibilities or anticipated likelihoods which then afford an improved basis for decisions and actions and responses when things go badly wrong. Unfortunately, unpredictability, contingency and a myriad of other 'unknowns' can all confound the best efforts to minimise dangers and keep journalists safe by seeking to reconstitute them as hazards or acceptable calibrated risks; which is not to suggest that such efforts have not and cannot save lives, simply that the field of dangers, hazards and risks frequently overruns journalism's capacity to contain, much less control, them.

2. The Islamic State of Iraq and Syria (ISIS), also known as the Islamic State of Iraq and the Levant (ISIL), or the Islamic State of Iraq and ash-Sham, or simply Islamic State (IS), is a Salafi, jihadist, extremist, militant group and self-proclaimed Islamic state and caliphate. We refer to this group throughout as ISIS.

References

Cottle, S. (2009) *Global Crisis Reporting: Journalism in the Global Age*. Maidenhead: Open University Press.

Cottle. S. (2011) 'Taking Global Crises in the News Seriously: Notes from the Dark Side of Globalization', *Global Media and Communication*, 7(2): 77–95.

Cottle, S. (2013) 'Journalists Witnessing Disasters: From the Calculus of Death to the Injunction to Care', *Journalism Studies*, 14(2): 232–248.

Cottle, S. (2014) 'Rethinking Media and Disasters in a Global Age: What's Changed and Why it Matters', *Media, War & Conflict*, 7(1): 3–22.

Cottle, S. and Cooper. G. (Eds) (2015) *Humanitarianism, Communications, and Change*. New York: Peter Lang.

International News Safety Institute (INSI) (2015a) *Casualties*. Available from http://www.newssafety.org/casualties (last accessed 10 June 2015).

International News Safety Institute (INSI) (2015b) *Under Threat*. Available from   http://www.newssafety.org/underthreat/under-threat-the-findings. html#Foreword_by_Lyse_Doucet (last accessed 10 June 2015).

Sambrook, R. (2010) *Are Foreign Correspondents Redundant? The Changing Face of International News*. Oxford: Reuters Institute for the Study of Journalism, University of Oxford.

Sambrook, R. J., Mosdell, N. and Payne, K. (2007) *Killing the Messenger: Report of the Global Inquiry by the International News Safety Institute into the Protection of Journalists*. Working paper. Belgium: International News Safety Institute (INSI).

Part I
What's Happening and
Why It Matters

2

Reporting in Uncivil Societies and Why It Matters

Richard Sambrook

> The link between independent journalism, democracy and economic development is one that is frequently acknowledged, but less frequently explored.

At a basic level, journalism serves to provide the public with sufficient information to make informed choices about their lives. It can further act in the interests of transparency, supporting good governance and ethical standards, in a watchdog role through investigation and scrutiny, and it can support social cohesion through hosting public debate at a level beyond the capacity of individual citizens.

Civil society relies upon information to provide citizens with the opportunity to build political representation, grow economic capacity, improve public health and education, and strengthen the quality of life. In providing that information, journalism can oversee the formation and implementation of policy, and shine a light on corruption, human rights abuses or poor governance.

The link between strong independent journalism and healthy democratic and economic development has been set out in a number of studies sponsored by the UN, UNESCO and the World Bank among others (World Bank 2002, Norris 2006, Henrichsen et al. 2015). These underline ways in which ethical journalism can have a constructive social role not only in identifying and exposing corruption or poor governance, but in building social cohesion through civic debate and providing an outlet for public concern.

A 2013 policy briefing from BBC Media Action – the BBC's development charity – suggests that media can help create or help undermine sustainable political settlements in fragile states. Specifically, commercial media alone may not be sufficient to support healthy democratic and economic ends – some element of public media with a clear ethical framework may be required. More specifically, public interest media can either intensify or help to transcend the dangerous politics of identity which can feed hate speech and unrest as seen in Rwanda in the 1990s or in Kenya around the 2007 elections (Thompson 2007, Deane 2013). Not everyone sees free media and independent journalism as a first-order right or requirement for civil society. Many in the development community argue that it is merely an instrumental good – valued for its ability to deliver other more pressing needs such as health information or education. However, as Joseph Stiglitz argued in a World Bank paper in 2002, greater openness and the benefits for political and economic stability and development should be seen as a fundamental requirement for a civil society. Plurality of media is instrumental, indeed essential, for delivering such openness (World Bank 2002, p. 27).

The media's roles as watchdog, as a forum for civic debate and in providing a channel for citizens concerns all directly, and impacts in different ways on sound government and economic development. More recently, the moves towards Open Government and the provision of public data by which citizens can gauge the efficiency and effectiveness of government performance also rest on the ability of the media to interpret data and hold governments to account (Sambrook et al. 2013).

It clearly follows that societies that are closed to scrutiny, which impede or in which it is impossible to undertake independent journalism, will suffer as a consequence. It also follows that, to the extent journalism has a public responsibility, that responsibility must be to pursue independent journalism even in uncivil societies where conditions are hostile towards it. Shining a light into dark corners has therefore always been a core motivation for publicly motivated journalists. In doing so, they place themselves at risk.

By seeking to report from uncivil societies, journalists act in the interests of both local citizens and the wider international community, strengthening public accountability and helping to establish stable conditions for development.

Uncivil societies can take many forms. They include: dictatorships where a ruling elite seeks to exercise power by disenfranchising citizens; war zones where conflict prevents normal social, political or economic activity; fractured societies with insufficient political or social strength to hold a country together; and hollow states where the normal framework of social, political and economic activity is severely compromised by crime or corruption.

We should recognise therefore that the journalists' impulse to place themselves in danger is not simply, or even, a question of seeking professional exclusivity or personal fulfilment through the exercise of courage. In venturing into dark and difficult places, and attempting to report back, their motivation is rooted in the core mission of journalism to hold others to account on behalf of the public, and in so doing fulfil a vital public-interest role. Sometimes that role may be conducted locally, within their own society. Sometimes it is conducted globally, by international correspondents reporting to the world.

On whichever scale, there is little question that doing so is becoming more complicated and more perilous.

In recent years, there have been at least three key drivers of the increase in violence towards journalists: the loss of neutral status; the growth of global organised crime; and the use of technology and compromised digital security. To some extent they overlap and support each other – in other ways they impact on journalists entirely differently. This chapter will look at examples as case studies of how these three issues impact on the killing and intimidation of journalists.

The loss of neutral status

In the wake of the Second World War, journalists working overseas were still regarded as neutral observers, entitled to a degree of protection as civilians in harm's way and useful for communicating a just cause or military success to the wider public. During the years of the Cold War, this status endured as global conflicts were carried out largely as proxies for the East–West standoff. Following the collapse of communism in Europe (and equally in satellite states), this framework broke down and, with it, the notion of journalistic neutrality.

As the spectre of mutually assured destruction between two global superpowers shrank, other conflicts grew and became more sharply defined around ethnic nationalism or regional imperialism. So reporters in the Balkans in the 1990s found themselves caught in an ethnic conflict with no clear front line and no clear protective affiliation. And as war in the Middle East developed, first with the 1991 Gulf War, then the 2003 Iraq War and the collapse of order in countries following the 2013 'Arab Spring', participants increasingly saw conflict in stark binary terms: 'you are either with us or you are against us'. In these circumstances, journalists were not 'with' any side, so were more and more treated as being 'against' them. Warfare had moved from being concerned with control of territory, to control of information, to control of media. The physical battlefield had metastasised into a battle for hearts and minds – what some analysts have called 'information war' (Tumber and Webster 2006).

This translated itself into what many saw as governments or agencies adopting an 'anti-media' position – including US forces in Iraq in and after 2003 (Paterson 2014) and the increasing vulnerability of journalists to jihadist groups either for kidnap and ransom or for kidnap and murder for publicity purposes. The first prominent example of this was Daniel Pearl, the *Wall Street Journal* reporter captured and then murdered in Pakistan in 2002. But by 2015, seven journalists were captured and beheaded by jihadist groups between January and June alone.

It was clear Western military authorities first saw the media as a target with the bombing of Serbian TV headquarters in Belgrade by NATO forces in 1999. Officers said it was a legitimate attack because the station was broadcasting propaganda. The international media community saw this as crossing a line where communications and media openly became military targets.

Later, in the 2001 Afghanistan conflict, the US forces deliberately bombed Al Jazeera's Kabul office. Again, in 2003, US forces for the same reason bombed the Al Jazeera bureau in Baghdad. Also that year, US forces targeted the Palestine Hotel in Baghdad, where most of the international news journalists were staying (Paterson 2014). No explanation for these attacks was offered.

As the British broadcaster Nik Gowing has written, this suggests:

> at best a culture of military indifference and inefficiency to the business of explaining the deaths of media personnel. At worst it suggests a policy of endorsing and covering up firstly the targeting, then either the maiming or killing, of media personnel. (Gowing 2003)

Equally, in the last decade, a number of media personnel appear to have been targeted by the Israeli Defence Force (IDF) with little explanation or open accountability (Paterson 2014, p. 103); and in Egypt, journalists seeking to report the views of the Muslim Brotherhood were arrested and imprisoned from 2013 onwards.

The attitude of 'you're either with us or against us' denies the legitimacy of independent journalism. It allows a culture of impunity to develop and, at worst, a conflation of legitimate journalism with terrorism or enemy action. This loss of neutrality for independent journalism is now a major factor driving violence against newsgatherers.

The murders of US journalists James Foley and Steven Sotloff and Japanese journalist Kenji Goto by members of the ISIS jihadist group in 2014 were graphic and startling illustrations of how journalists can become political pawns. Their execution on camera, distributed via social media, was used as a publicity tool by the group in an attempt to exercise asymmetrical power against Western countries and the Syrian government. Foley had been abducted in northern Syria in 2012, Sotloff in 2013. Their abductions were part of a growing pattern of kidnapping of Western journalists attempting to report the civil war there. Many of these abductions were purely for criminal purposes, with gangs demanding high ransoms in order to help fund their activities. Some countries and families complied. Both US and UK governments, however, went on record saying they would not deal with terrorists or pay ransoms to groups associated with terrorist groups – and as such, US and British journalists became higher profile. At one point, it is believed IS held as many as 23 foreign hostages – most of them freelance journalists or aid workers.

Although it is thought Foley and Sotloff were initially taken by gangs with criminal intent, they were passed on to ISIS who, unable to obtain a ransom, used the murders of the two journalists for political purposes. *New York Times* reporter Rukmini Callimachi spoke to former ISIS hostages to understand what they endured. She recounts:

> The story of what happened in the Islamic State's underground net-work of prisons in Syria is one of excruciating suffering. Mr Foley and his fellow hostages were routinely beaten and subjected to waterboarding. For months, they were starved and threatened with execution by one group of fighters, only to be handed off to another group that brought them sweets and contemplated freeing them. The prisoners banded together, playing games to pass the endless hours, but as conditions grew more desperate, they turned on one another. Some, including Mr Foley, sought comfort in the faith of their captors, embracing Islam and taking Muslim names.
>
> (Callimachi 2014)

The result of these graphic murders and the high level of abductions was that many news organisations pulled back from attempting to report the Syrian conflict. The risks seemed too high. This left much coverage to freelance journalists, prepared to take those risks on their own account, and to local journalists. However, they too are vulnerable.

The cultural chasm between independent journalism and ISIS applies equally to Muslim journalists.

Suha Ahmed Rahdi

An Iraqi newspaper journalist, Suha Ahmed Rahdi was murdered by ISIS fighters in July 2015. She worked for a newspaper in Mosul. Local reports said the fighters entered her home and abducted her for several days before her body was handed back to her family. A statement from ISIS said it had charged her with spying and executed her. Reports of her murder varied between being shot and being decapitated. She was the 14th journalist to be executed in Mosul after ISIS took over the city in June 2014, according to a regional media watchdog, the Iraqi Journalists Syndicate (Rudaw 2015).

Cyrenaica TV crew

In Libya, five members of a TV crew working for Cyrenaica were captured in 2014, held for nine months, and then murdered through beheading. The crew were seized at a fake checkpoint near Ajdabiya on 5 August 2014. They were on their way back to the town, travelling on the desert road, after filming the inauguration of the House of Representatives in Tobruk. The bodies of the five men – Abdussalam Al-Kahala, Younis Al-Gamoudi, Khaled Al-Hamil, Younis Al-Sal and Mohamed Galal – were found following the arrest at the Libya-Egyptian border crossing at Musaid of an Egyptian said to be a member of ISIS. According to a lawyer representing Cyrenaica TV, the man confessed to involvement in the murders. No explanation for the killings has been offered (INSI 2015).

There are many other examples of the brutal murder of both local and foreign journalists in the failed states of the Middle East. The expansion and high profile of the media – with the Internet providing immediate global reach – coupled with deep ideological divides means there is no neutrality for international or many local reporters in these conflicts. As a consequence, the world knows less about what is happening within parts of Syria, Iraq and Libya than it should. The emergence of ISIS as a significant force in 2014 appeared to take Western leaders by surprise. At least one reason for this was that independent reporting had been compromised and limited by the extreme physical threats which journalists faced. These relative gaps in scrutiny arguably allowed extremism to gain a tighter grip.

The brutal attack on the offices of the satirical magazine *Charlie Hebdo* in Paris in 2015 illustrated that media in Western countries and cities are now regarded as legitimate targets by extreme groups. The extent to which members of otherwise peaceful countries can now unexpectedly inflict terror on their fellow citizens means the threat to media (as well as to the public) now has no clear boundaries. The fact that the motivation for inflicting violence can be silently embedded within a culture makes it all the more threatening and difficult to confront.

Conflict in a region, and the extreme politics it produces, can also compromise state actors. The Pakistani journalist Hamid Mir wrote in 2012:

> In the past year I have received numerous phone calls from senior government officials informing me that I face serious threats to my life and that I should be careful while speaking on television and writing for newspapers. There was a time when believed I could be provided with protection against threats by the law enforcement agencies. But I have lately realised that nothing can be done to protect media persons when state agencies themselves decide to bully them.
>
> Dozens of daring journalists have been kidnapped and killed in my country by the state and non-state actors in the name of 'national interest'. I am lucky to be still alive, maybe because I live in Islamabad, the capital, and not in the Baluchistan or Khyber Pakhtunkhwa provinces or Karachi, which are considered to be dangerous places for journalists. (Mir 2012)

In such circumstances, self-censorship becomes a significant issue. Whether by agents of the state or armed gangs, intimidation can silence independent journalism as successfully as murder. The Secretary of the Pakistan Press Foundation, Oswais Aslam Ali, put it this way:

> For every journalist who has been deliberately targeted and murdered, many others have been injured, threatened and coerced into silence. The increase in threats and violence has forced many of my colleagues to resort to self-censorship, relocation or even to leave the profession altogether. As a consequence, news reports from conflict areas are based on press releases, not on observations by independent

journalists, so they often lack credibility and do not inform the public in an objective manner. Incidents of threats, attacks and killings of journalists are also clear evidence of the entrenched culture of impunity enjoyed by those who attack and murder journalists, which seriously undermines freedom of expression in the country. (Ali 2015)

This loss of neutrality is no longer a threat limited to those in conflict zones or a perception limited to those waging conflict. State agencies in otherwise peaceful countries, or in ones compromised by conflict on their borders, can also see independent journalism as a problem to be shut down. Sometimes it is for political expediency, sometimes as a symbol of power or repression. Both war and politics are now as much about control of minds as control of territory – which places journalists on the front line.

When state actors are involved, holding those responsible to account is more difficult. However, impunity can be tackled, even when the state may have been behind killings. During and after the Balkan wars, a number of journalists were murdered in Serbia after criticising the government of Slobodan Milosovic: reporters like Radoslava Dada Vujasinovic, who investigated corruption in Milosovic's Government, and was found shot dead in her apartment in 1994. Her death was reported as suicide.

In 2014, with a new government elected, and following pressure from colleagues of those killed, the Serbian Commission for the Investigation of Murders of Journalists (SCIMJ) was established (CPJ 2014a).

The SCIMJ consists of representatives of the journalism community, the ministry of the interior and the security services. They oversee teams of police and security officials investigating the previous murders of journalists. Within a year, four suspects linked to the state had been charged with the murder of Slavko Curuvija, another influential journalist, shot dead in 1999. His criticism of the government was cited as the motive for the crime.

In times of extreme politics, journalists simply doing their work in holding power to account can find themselves enemies of the state, with their lives at risk as a consequence. Yet it is precisely at such times that independent journalism may be of most civic value. The SCIMJ is a rare example of how a now stable society can reach into its past and put right the crimes of an earlier uncivil period; and, by so doing, make clear the obligation of the state towards independent journalism.

By such a process, they set an important precedent which indicates no-one can assume they will escape justice in future.

The increase in global organised crime

As Misha Glenny has argued, the collapse of communism in 1989 brought many democratic benefits to Eastern Europe and beyond. But it also fed, through market liberalisation, the parallel development of the Internet and greater freedom of movement, a significant growth in international organised crime (Glenny 2008). He estimates that the criminal black economy is now worth up to 15 per cent of global GDP. As the opportunities for greater production and distribution of illicit goods into the developed markets of Europe and the US became apparent, the opportunity for enormous wealth drove violence, intimidation and murder.

Today this is seen in countries like Mexico, a major centre of distribution for the drugs trade, in Africa and in eastern Europe with prostitution, and central Asia with both drugs and people trafficking. So for journalists investigating crime – and the corruption of governments and agencies which accompanies it – the risks have grown in parallel over the last 25 years. Equally, as Glenny outlines, in some states government and law enforcement are corrupt and significantly compromised by large, powerful crime syndicates. In such an environment, criminal interests can hollow out the democratic and institutional heart of the state. With no independent or reliable rule of law or justice to depend upon, investigative journalism can become additionally perilous.

It's clear from the annual figures produced by the International News Safety Institute (INSI) that, as a consequence, it is local journalists undertaking these kinds of investigations and reporting who are most at risk of violence or murder. Unlike international reporters, they are part of the society they report, fixed in place, and therefore more exposed to threats and intimidation. And equally, the size and power of international criminal gangs and the complicity of governments and law enforcement in some countries means most perpetrators remain unidentified and unpunished. Impunity is the overarching issue for the international community concerned with the levels of violence towards reporting and the intimidation of free speech.

The intimidation of local journalists is clearly used by gangs and corrupt agencies to compromise independent journalism and create a chilling effect on any further investigation.

Murders by criminal gangs or mafia occur in many parts of the world. They share a common brutality.

Georgiy Gongadze

As an investigative reporter in Ukraine, Georgiy Gongadze had published numerous articles about corruption in the country's ruling elite. He went missing in the summer of 2000, and his headless body was found in a forest two months later.

Shortly after his body was discovered, audio tapes were revealed by an opposition politician which appeared to record then President Leonid Kuchma and two other men – one of them, Yuriy Kravchenko, the country's interior minister – talking before Mr Gongadze's death about how to get rid of the journalist.

Attempts to prosecute Mr Kuchma – who denied any wrongdoing – failed when the tapes were rules as inadmissible evidence, having been recorded illegally. Their authenticity has never been fully established.

The former chief of the Ukrainian interior ministry's surveillance department was arrested in 2009 and confessed to the killing. He said he was told to carry out the assassination by Mr Kravchenko. The Interior Minister was found dead at his dacha outside Kiev in 2005, on the same day he was due to be questioned about Mr Gongadze's murder. It appeared he had committed suicide, although the fact he had two gunshot wounds to his head led to speculation he may have been murdered (CPJ 2014b).

John Kituyi

On 30 April 2015, a Kenyan newspaper editor, John Kituyi, was walking home from his office in the town of Eldoret when he was attacked and bludgeoned to death. The attackers took his phone – but left his cash and watch – before escaping by motorbike.

Kituyi's weekly news magazine had recently reported the prospects of a successful prosecution of William Ruto, the country's deputy president who faces charges of crimes against humanity at the international criminal court related to the mass killings and displacements that accompanied Kenya's disputed 2007 presidential election.

The journalist's colleagues said they saw his murder as part of a growing pattern of intimidation of journalists in Kenya (Mutiga, Guardian 2015).

Sandeep Kothari

In June 2015, Indian investigative journalist Sandeep Kothari was riding his motorbike towards a village in the province of Madhya Pradesh when he was hit by a car. He was bundled into the vehicle and driven off.

Kothari was a 40-year-old freelance journalist who worked for a number of daily papers in the Jabalpur area. He had been reporting on illegal mining and had filed a court case against individuals to highlight the activities. It is a mineral-rich area and sand mining is a lucrative local activity – although much is done illegally by local mafia. After he was abducted he was beaten to death, his body burned and dumped near a railway line. Three men were later arrested – one a director of a company Kothari was investigating.

Kothari's family say he was frequently intimidated by the authorities and falsely accused of crimes which he did not commit and which were never investigated. His sister Sandyha told the Indian press she had frequently pleaded with her brother to leave journalism as it was too dangerous. His brother Rahul said:

> He was in jail for 17 months, 15 days back, he sent notices to 27 people who had acted as false witnesses against him. My deceased brother has been complaining of and writing about the mafias for five years now. His murder was a result of that. In these five years, some 20–25 false cases have been registered against him. (DNAIndia.com 2015)

His was one of a series of unrelated attacks on Indian journalists in early 2015. Journalists frequently face harassment and intimidation by police, politicians and officials in India.

Earlier in the same month, police registered a murder and criminal conspiracy case against a ruling party politician over the death of freelance journalist Jagendra Singh. Mr Singh published an article and posted allegations of corruption on Facebook against Ram Murti Singh Verma.

Djalma Santos de Conceição and Evany José Metzker

In May 2015, two Brazilian journalists were murdered in a week for their outspoken work on drug trafficking and on corruption. Violence against journalists in Brazil is rising sharply, and –

according to the Committee to Protect Journalists and INSI who ana-lyse casualty figures – it is now among the most dangerous countries in which to work as a journalist.

Djalma Santos de Conceição was a 53-year-old radio journalist known for speaking out about drug trafficking and cartels. He pre-sented the daily morning programme 'Acorda Cidade' on RCA FM, a community radio station in Conceição da Feira, a town of about 22,000 people, 128km northwest of Salvador, the state capital of Bahia.

One Saturday night, three armed men barged into a small private party in a bar in the town. Santos de Conceição was dragged out. His mutilated body was found the next day in a rural area. Police said he had been tortured – his right eye had been gouged out and his tongue had been hacked off. He had also been shot in the leg, chest, abdomen and face.

Earlier in the same week, the decapitated body of Evany José Metzker, an online journalist known for denouncing corrupt politi-cians, was found in a rural area of the Minas Gerais state. Metzker, who was 67, had often received death threats. When his body was found, his hands were tied behind his back and his body showed signs of torture. He appears to have been abducted five days earlier. Police believe his investigations into child prostitution and drug dealing were the motivation (Tavares 2015).

Armando Saldana Morales

Mexico is one of the few countries recognized as more dangerous than Brazil.

In May 2015, the body of Armando Saldana Morales was found in a car near Cosolapa in Oaxaca. He had been shot in the head four times after being stopped by gunmen as he drove home. The 52-year-old journalist wrote for a local newspaper in Veracruz, *Crónica de Tierra Blanca*, and appeared on a regional radio show, 'La Ke Buena 100.9 FM'. He had been reporting a number of stories about organised crime, including the alleged theft of petroleum products from pipelines belonging to Petróleos Mexicanos, or Pemex, the state oil company (Attanasio 2015).

Investigating pipeline thefts has previously led to the murder of journalists in Mexico. In August 2014, freelance journalist Octavio

Rojas Hernández, who worked for two months for the Veracruz newspaper *El Buen Tono*, was shot dead. Two days earlier, the paper had published a story on the army and Oaxaca state police breaking up a local ring accused of siphoning gas from pipelines belonging to Pemex.

According to the CPJ, Veracruz is one of the most dangerous states in Mexico for journalists. Four other Veracruz journalists have been killed and at least six other Veracruz journalists died in unclear circumstances. At least three journalists have disappeared in the state in the same time period. The CPJ say there have been more than 50 journalists murdered in Mexico since 2007 – and 90 per cent of the killings are unsolved (CPJ 2015).

The case studies above are merely a sample of the deaths of local journalists attempting to fulfil a public-interest role in their societies. In most cases, the response of the state is inadequate in pursuing and prosecuting the perpetrators – leaving the path clear for similar violence to follow. What's clear is the intimidation of independent journalism and the failure of state institutions go hand in hand.

Technology and digital security

As the BBC correspondent Andrew Marr noted in his book *My Trade*, the development of journalism has always been closely aligned to developments in technology.

Transatlantic cables, airmail, wired photographs from the front. ... there has always been a new development to exploit. The Second World War was the first radio war, with correspondents sending back vivid sound despatches; Korea saw the arrival of lightweight cameras and television footage from the front line; by Vietnam there was colour. The two Gulf wars were widely described as video-arcade conflicts because of the eerie green footage of missiles homing in and obliterating targets. The modern impact of satellites, electronic news gathering, sat-phones and digital cameras. (Marr 2004, p. 332)

The growth of satellite and Internet technology has greatly aided journalism, allowing reporting from places that were previously unreachable and at a far lower cost than in the past. But it has brought with it new dangers that the profession was slow to recognise.

Many of the issues surrounding digital security compromise independent journalism but are not life-threatening. However, there is no question that online journalism has increased threats and intimidation towards journalists, placed bloggers and citizen journalists at greater physical risk, and the technology behind digital news allows the identification and targeting of journalists in ways which most are still too inexpert to recognise. In other words, the technology which supports modern reporting also endangers it.

In 2012, the *Sunday Times* correspondent Marie Colvin and French photographer Remi Olchik were killed by what's assumed to be Syrian government shelling in Homs in Syria. She had been filing graphic reports of civilian casualties via satellite phone, and it's suggested that her broadcasts had been monitored and allowed her position to be deliberately targeted. Colvin was one of the most experienced and respected international correspondents, frequently reporting from conflicts around the world. Her death was noted by presidents and prime ministers as well as her many friends and readers.

The French correspondent for *Libération*, Jean-Pierre Perrin, was with them in Homs before the attack. He told his paper, 'The Syrian army issued orders to "kill any journalist that sets foot on Syrian soil"' (Ramdani and Allen 2012).

According to the Electronic Frontier Foundation, there are a number of ways that satellite phones can be monitored and locations detected. As security researcher Jacob Applebaum put it:

> Satellite phone systems and satellite networks are unsafe to use if location privacy or privacy for the content of communications is desired. These phone protocols are intentionally insecure and tracking people is sometimes considered a feature. (Timm and York 2012)

Colvin's death was a high-profile example of a more widespread problem. For some years, governments have used technology, often provided by Western governments, to track and identify journalists and activists. This was the case in Iran after the 2009 post-election uprising – leading to a number of journalists and bloggers being arrested – and again in Egypt, Syria and elsewhere following the 2013 Arab Spring uprisings.

We now know, after the revelations by Edward Snowden about the extensive levels of US and UK government surveillance, that any unencrypted communications can be easily monitored – risking both physical exposure of journalists working 'behind the lines' but also a public exposure of sources assisting journalistic investigations. Further, the

Internet has allowed so-called citizen journalists and others to report and contribute to public debate in ways which may expose them unwittingly to risks.

As the UNESCO report 'Building Digital Safety for Journalism' put it:

> The danger emanates from various sources ranging from State-based actors to third parties. There is digital surveillance that goes beyond international standards on privacy and freedom of expression. There is hacking of data and disruptive attacks on websites and computer systems. More extremely, some media actors are being killed for their online journalism. From 2011–2013, 37 of the 276 killings of journalists condemned by the UNESCO Director General were killings of journalists whose primary platforms were Internet-based. Many, if not most, of the other journalists who were killed also used digital tools in their daily work, which may have exposed them in various ways. (Henrichsen et al. 2015)

A recent survey in the United States by the Pew Research Center and the Tow Center for Digital Journalism at Columbia University found two-thirds of investigative journalists assumed the government had collected data about their phone calls, emails or digital communications. And 70 per cent believed being a journalist made it more likely their communications would be monitored (Holcomb et al. 2015).

Some 50 per cent of those surveyed said they used some tools for digital security – but only 9 per cent used a full suite of security tools. Alan Rusbridger, the former editor of the *Guardian*, who was at the forefront of the Edward Snowden revelations, told a university conference:

> Every journalist should understand that there is no such thing as confidential digital communication. None of us have confidential sources. Peer to peer encryption is difficult for most journalists and it is quite time consuming and most journalists don't do it. We are all going to have to work on this in this world where people can intercept everything. (Ponsford 2014)

Clearly this raises significant risks when some governments are hostile to journalists – and at least some of the technology is almost certainly available to terrorists or criminals. This applies as much to 'citizen journalists' or bloggers as it does to those working for mainstream media organisations. Increasingly, there is little discrimination made between activists, citizen journalists and professional journalists in the online environment. Those working independently have the benefit of Internet access to a global public space – but it can also leave them exposed and unsupported.

Take, for example, Mo'az al-Khaled, a 23-year-old journalist and third-year student at Damascus media college, who was originally from the Golan Heights. He was expelled for his activist reporting. In June 2012, Syrian security officials arrested him at his home in Damascus because of his reporting of demonstrations in the Barzeh and neighbouring Qaboun districts. After being held in Sednaya prison, he was transferred to Adra central prison, where he was placed in solitary confinement. Physically and psychologically tortured for two years, he finally died in detention in February 2014. His family learned of his death when they received his personal effects from the prison authorities (FreeSyrianVoices.org 2015, p. 8).

Or, again in Mexico: a report from an International Center for Journalists Knight International Journalism Fellow, Jorge Luis Sierra on digital security for Mexican journalists and bloggers found 70 per cent of them had been threatened in some way. One example cited:

> In September 2011, two bloggers who reported frequently on local crime, including drug trafficking and related gang activity, were tortured and hanged on a bridge in Nuevo Laredo, a town near the U.S border. The town is run by the Zetas, one of Mexico's most active and dangerous criminal organizations. A note near the scene signed 'Z' warned that other Internet users could meet the same fate. Later that month, the body of a decapitated woman was found in the city with a message saying she was killed for her posts on the social media forum 'Nuevo Laredo en Vivo.' (Sierra 2014, p. 1)

Digital journalists may not have to travel to front-line conflicts to be at risk. Their online profile alone can draw attention from those who would prefer their voices silenced.

There are now multiple guides to digital security available for journalists. However, the more technical aspects of encryption are not yet widely adopted and some of the risks of surveillance and monitoring are little understood. We can expect aspects of weak digital security to continue to contribute to deaths of journalists and citizen journalists for some years to come.

Technology has also contributed to the perceived loss of neutrality of journalists. Whereas generals or armed groups once saw journalists as a useful conduit to the public, they are now no longer needed.

National armies, armed groups, terrorists all have their own social media channels by which they can communicate directly to the public or their supporters.

Increasingly, the low cost and ease of use of media technology means that these channels can offer highly sophisticated media accounts – influencing the public and mainstream media alike, and indeed the conduct of the conflict when images are as graphic and iconic as the ISIS beheading videos (Molin Friis 2015).

Journalists are no longer a constituency to be offered protection as the only means of wider communication. An Internet account and camera phone can do the job more directly, and without intermediation of the message.

These few examples of journalists being murdered are a fraction of those which could be cited. They are not exceptional by the standards of such deaths, but are offered as illustrations of the human stories behind the casualty numbers and illustrations of some of the major issues driving the increase in risk.

They also illustrate how, for an international correspondent reporting on a global conflict or a local journalist representing the concerns of the community about crime or corruption, these increased areas of risk undermine a core purpose of journalism: to provide an informed society, supporting political representation and social and economic development.

References

Ali, O., 2015, 'Under Attack and Afraid – Pakistani Journalists Leaving Profession', International News Safety Institute (INSI) blog. Available from: <http://www.newssafety.org/news/insi-news/insi-news/detail/blog-under-attack-and-afraid-pakistani-journalists-leaving-profession-1608/> (last accessed 12 August 2015).

Attanasio, C., 2015, 'Armando Saldaña Morales, Mexican Journalist, Murdered In Oaxaca After Reporting on 'Chupaductos' Oil Thefts', LatinTimes.com. Available from: <http://www.latintimes.com/armando-saldana-morales-mexican-journalist-murdered-oaxaca-after-reporting-313945> (last accessed 6 June 2015).

Callimachi, 2014, 'The New York Times Recreates ISIS Captivity of Foley, Sotloff', Columbia Journalism Review. Available from: <http://www.cjr.org/darts_and_laurels/the_new_york_times_recreates_i.php> (last accessed 10 July 2015).

Committee to Protect Journalists (CPJ), 2014a, 'A New Start on Old Murders in Serbia'. Available from: <https://cpj.org/reports/2014/10/the-road-to-justice-curuvija-murders-serbia.php> (last accessed 12 August 2015).

Committee to Protect Journalists (CPJ) 2014b, Georgy Gongadze. Available from: <https://www.cpj.org/killed/2000/georgy-gongadze.php> (last accessed 12 August 2015).

Committee to Protect Journalists (CPJ) 2015, Mexico. Available from: <https://cpj.org/americas/mexico/> (last accessed 10 July 2015).

Deane, J., 2013, *Fragile States: The Role of Media and Communication*. London: BBC Media Action.

DNAIndia.com, 2015, 'MP Scribe Killing: I Told my Brother – Leave Journalism or You Will Die Says Sandeep Kothari Sister', Available from: <http://www.dnaindia.com/india/report-mp-scribe-killing-i-told-my-brother-leave-journalism-or-you-will-die-says-sandeep-kothari-s-sister-2097799> (last accessed 6 June 2015).

FreeSyrianVoices.org, 2015, 'Death of the Journalist Mo'az al-Khaled'. Available from: http://free-syrian-voices.org/death-of-the-journalist-moaz-al-khaled/ (last accessed 10 July 2015).

Glenny, M., 2008, *McMafia: A Journey through the Global Criminal Underworld*. London: Vintage.

Gowing, N., 2003, 'Aiming to stop the story?', *Gulf News*. Available from: <http://m.gulfnews.com/news/uae/general/reporting-conflict-aiming-to-stop-the-story-1.372376> (last accessed 15 June 2015).

Henrichsen, J., Betz, M. and Lisosky, J., 2015, *Building Digital Safety for Journalism: A Survey of Selected Issues*. Paris: UNESCO.

Holcomb, J., Mitchell, A. and Purcell, K., 2015, *Investigative Journalists and Digital Security: Perceptions of Vulnerability and Changes in Behavior*, Pew Research Center. Available from: <http://www.journalism.org/2015/02/05/investigative-journalists-and-digital-security/> (last accessed 10 July 2015).

International News Safety Institute (INSI), 2015, *Casualties*. Available from: <http://www.newssafety.org/news/newsletter-signup/detail/kidnapped-tv-crew-reported-executed-by-isis-1566/> (last accessed 10 July 2015).

Marr, A. (2004) *My Trade*. London: Macmillan.

Mir, H., 2012, 'Reducing the Dangers of Journalism: a View from Pakistan', BBC Academy blog. Available from: <http://www.bbc.co.uk/blogs/collegeof journalism/entries/499fcf9f-61f6-3a26-8547-5aefbc1f6531> (last accessed 12 August 2015).

Molin Friis, S., 2015, 'Beyond Anything We Have Ever Seen': Beheading Videos and the Visibility of Violence in the War Against ISIS', *International Affairs*, 91(4). London: Royal Institute of International Affairs.

Mutiga, M., 2015. 'Journalist's Murder Prompts Fears for Press Freedom in Kenya', *the Guardian*. Available from: <http://www.theguardian.com/world/2015/may/03/journalists-prompts-fears-for-press-freedom-in-kenya> (last accessed 12 August 2015).

Norris, P., 2006, 'The Role of the Free Press in Promoting Democratization, Good Governance, and Human Development', Paper presented at the Midwest Political Science Association Annual Meeting, 20–22 April, 2006. Chicago, IL: Palmer House.

Paterson, C., 2014, *War Reporters Under Threat*. London: Pluto Press.

Ponsford, D., 2014, 'Rusbridger on How No Journalist's Sources are Safe, Joining IPSO and Why He Would Have kept *News of the World* Open', *Press Gazette*. Available from: <http://www.pressgazette.co.uk/rusbridger-how-no-journalists-sources-are-now-safe-joining-ipso-and-why-he-would-have-kept-news> (last accessed 10 July 2015).

Ramdani, N. and Allen, P., 2012, 'Marie Colvin: Britain Summons Syria Ambassador over Killing', *Daily Telegraph*. Available from: <http://www.tele graph.co.uk/news/worldnews/middleeast/syria/9098511/Marie-Colvin-Britain-summons-Syria-ambassador-over-killing.html> (last accessed 21 August 2015).

Rudaw, 2015, 'ISIS Executes Woman Journalist in Mosul'. Available from: <http://rudaw.net/english/middleeast/iraq/070720152> (last accessed 10 July 2015).

Sambrook, R. 2013, *The Media and Open Government*. London: Open Government Partnership. Accessed July 2015 via <http://www.opengovpartnership.org/sites/default/files/OGP-Media-Council-Report.pdf>.

Sierra, J.L., 2014, *Digital Security for Mexican Journalists and Bloggers*. Freedom House. Available from: <https://www.freedomhouse.org/sites/default/files/Digital%20and%20Mobile%20Security%20for%20Mexican%20Journalists%20and%20Bloggers.pdf> (last accessed 10 July 2015).

Tavares, F., 2015, 'Brazil: Journalist Evany José Metzker Murdered While Investigating Drugs and Child Exploitation in Minas Gerais', *Upside Down World*. Available from: <http://upsidedownworld.org/main/brazil-archives-63/5378-brazil-journalist-evany-jose-metzker-murdered-while-investigating-drugs-and-child-exploitation-in-minas-gerais> (last accessed 6 June 2015).

Thompson, A. 2007. *Media and the Rwanda Genocide*. Pluto Press.

Timm, T. and York, J., 2012, *Satphones, Syria, and Surveillance*, Electronic Frontier Foundation. Available from: <https://www.eff.org/en-gb/deeplinks/2012/02/satphones-syria-and-surveillance> (last accessed 10 July 2015).

Tumber, H. and Webster, F., 2006, *Journalists Under Fire*. London: Sage.

UNESCO: The International Programme for the Development of Communication, 2014, '*Why Free, Independent and Pluralistic Media Deserve to Be at the Heart of a Post-2015 Development Agenda*'. Available from: <http://www.unesco.org/new/fileadmin/MULTIMEDIA/HQ/CI/CI/pdf/news/free_media_ post_2015.pdf> (12 August 2014).

World Bank, 2002, *The Right to Tell. The Role of Mass Media in Economic Development*. Available from: <http://elibrary.worldbank.org/doi/pdf/10.1596/0-8213-5203-2> (last accessed 10 July 2015).

3
Mapping the Parameters of Peril

Nick Mosdell

Between 1996 and 2014 over 2,100 journalists and media personnel have died while doing their work, according to the International News Safety Institute (INSI). More than half of them were murdered.

This chapter aims to use the figures produced by INSI to unpack some of the trends over the past 19 years and to provide some statistical evidence for the themes of this book. Firstly, we highlight the dangers of reporting from countries that are unstable as a result of national and international conflicts. We then look at societies that are uncivil as a result of widespread corruption and organised crime, where journalists are murdered with little or no legal consequences, and the effect that this has on the local and global news agenda (and the subsequent information deficit). Finally, we outline some of the issues in compiling these kinds of statistics in a world where the definition of a journalist is blurred and the global digital media can potentially be subverted to further the interests of terrorist or other criminal organisations.

INSI was officially formed in 2003, partly as a result of increasing concerns within the industry about the safety of journalists in the changing geopolitical landscape following the Balkans conflicts in the 1980s and 1990s. The dangers highlighted in these situations have been discussed earlier in this book, in particular the changing nature of warfare following the collapse of the Soviet Union, the subsequent loss of perceived neutrality for reporters in war zones, and the ability to transmit live or near-live with lightweight kit that places correspondents closer to the front lines – and to bear witness to the scenes of atrocity that characterised these conflicts.

On World Press Freedom Day 2005, INSI launched its Global Inquiry into journalists' deaths around the world. The output was branded as

Killing the Messenger, first published in 2007, and annual update reports have been published by INSI under this name every year since. During the inquiry, the United Nations Security Council recognised the dangers faced by correspondents in war zones, and passed Resolution 1738 that specifically refers to journalists covering war and conflict situations. This was partly a result of the work done by INSI, alongside many other agencies (Committee to Protect Journalists [CPJ], International Federation of Journalists, Reporters Sans Frontières among others), and this work continues with increasing efforts to lobby international agencies and governments to act on a culture of impunity where journalists' murders are concerned, in countries that are not explicitly engaged in conflict as well as those that can clearly be classified as war zones.

The Global Inquiry, and subsequent *Killing the Messenger* reports, include all media staff who have died as a direct result of their work, and record accidental deaths as well as violent deaths, initially with a view to identify trends and hotspots for safety training recommendations – whether they be hostile environment courses in preparation for conflict zones or training in advanced driving for areas where road accidents appear to be prevalent.

The figures include staff and freelance journalists, across a variety of platforms, and crucially also include all support staff who help them in their work:

> For all types of media activity, ancillary staff such as drivers, translators and security personnel are a vital part of the news gathering process. (INSI 2007, p. 13)

More discussion about the methodology and the difficulties of counting these cases will follow later in this chapter, as will a discussion of why, currently, there are no citizen journalists among the INSI figures produced for *Killing the Messenger.*

The findings from the Global Inquiry were surprising, and unveiled new concerns that many had not realised or considered. In the Foreword to the initial report, former editor of UK newspapers *The Sunday Times* and *The Times* Sir Harold Evans wrote:

> The first shocking thing about this report is to learn just how many are dying ...
> The second shocking thing is to learn how many of them were murdered, most of them local beat reporters whose names do not

resonate in the media. This is different from the sadly familiar fact that by-lined war correspondents, who knowingly risk their lives, get fatally caught in the crossfire of a battlefield, they walk on a land-mine, they hitch a ride on a fated combat plane, they are mistaken for combatants. Every conflict claims its press victims. Kosovo, for instance, is thought of as a sanitized affair, an air campaign with mass briefings away from the action, yet at least 25 journalists and media workers were among the hundreds of civilian fatalities. (INSI 2007, p. 2)

Figure 3.1 demonstrates a rise over time in the number of deaths, and there is little prospect of these numbers diminishing.

We have already stated that war and conflict reporting is not neces-sarily the most dangerous situation, but the sharp rise in numbers from 2003 is obvious from this graph and, alongside Figure 3.2 showing the top ten most dangerous countries, coincides with the war in Iraq. The numbers from there give a useful illustration of the complexities that we discuss within this book.

Conflict and post-conflict reporting

During the period of 'official combat operations' in Iraq in 2003, March to May, INSI recorded the deaths of 16 media staff (INSI 2003). Inevitably, given the nations involved in the war, these casualties, some of whom were high-profile international correspondents, gave rise to much debate about the dangers of war reporting and the system of 'embed-ding' where journalists were assigned to specific military units. Much has been written about the impact of this arrangement on the freedom to report (see, for example, Lewis et al. 2003, Tumber and Palmer 2004) and on whether perceived neutrality was compromised by it.

It is important to note, however, that the risks were far greater for local media staff, and that this increased dramatically in the chaos that followed the capture of Baghdad (see Figure 3.3).

As the country descended rapidly into a quasi-civil war where rival militias competed for territory and power, media outlets and their work-ers became deliberate targets.

They were singled out for a variety of reasons – in reprisal for their coverage, because of the affiliation with Western news organisations, and as a means of undermining the formation of Iraqi civil society. (Simon 2015, p. 71)

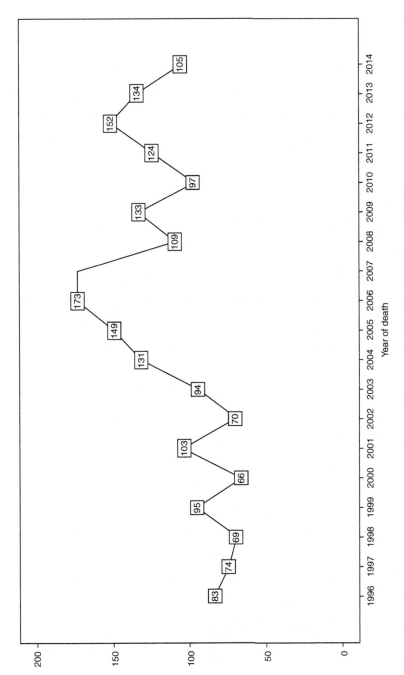

Figure 3.1 Number of fatalities between 1996 and 2014: Total = 2,134 (Cardiff University/INSI)

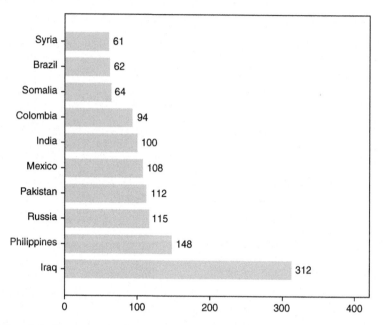

Figure 3.2 Top ten most dangerous countries between 1996 and 2014 (Cardiff University/INSI)

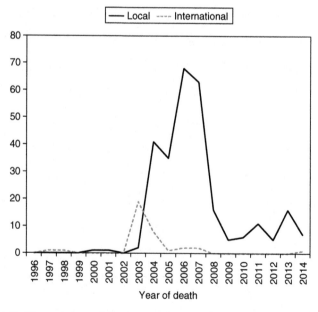

Figure 3.3 The number of local and international journalists killed in Iraq (Cardiff University/INSI)

In 2007, for example, The Royal Television Society in the UK honoured all Iraqi camera operators who had put themselves at 'extraordinary risk' in providing footage of the aftermath of the war. A representative group gathered at the BBC bureau in Baghdad and took part in a live satellite link-up to the awards ceremony. For the group's safety, the images were not broadcast outside the UK. They spent the night at the bureau to avoid being followed home.

Former ITN and current NBC News veteran Bill Neely suggests:

> We are very aware that we come into these countries and stay for a while, and then we walk away and move on to the next conflict. And the people that we work with, who help us, usually have to stay and suffer the consequences – of not just what happened there but what we have done in publicising this conflict. (quoted in Tumber and Webster 2006, p. 113)

In the years immediately following the fall of Baghdad, the levels of insurgency increased, as did the risk for local media. For example, in Fallujah, a key area of influence for the insurgents, US forces carried out several major offensives from 2004, and at times prohibited any embedded journalists. Inevitably, the events, and the allegations of illegal munitions and indiscriminate killings by the US military, made this a top story, but the lack of access for foreign reporters (and the general danger of being a foreigner in Iraq) led to opportunities for local staff and freelancers to file footage. The ethics of international news outlets providing a financial or publicity incentive for this by using this footage were widely debated in the industry at the time and have been since, as is the case for a 'duty of care' from such organisations for all local media personnel involved in reporting.

The sectarian violence in Iraq continues, but the situation further provided fertile ground for al-Qaeda and other extremist groups, which coincided with a rise in attacks on and abductions of journalists:

> [I]n the aftermath of the Daniel Pearl killing al-Qaeda-aligned and –inspired groups both inside and outside Iraq considered journalists, particularly Western journalists, legitimate targets. (Simon 2015, p. 73)

Simon quotes a CPJ report (2008) that estimated the number of journalists kidnapped in Iraq from 2003 onwards to be 57, of whom 17 were subsequently murdered. Of the journalists who responded to INSI's

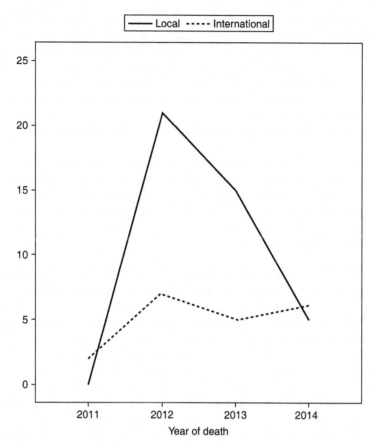

Figure 3.4 The number of local and international journalists killed in Syria (Cardiff University/INSI)

latest survey on the changing nature of risks, 79 per cent suggested that the threat of kidnapping is greater than it was ten years ago (INSI 2015).

As the instability in Iraq continued, other regions in the Middle East and across North Africa experienced their own conflicts that show similar trends. The civil war in Syria has been particularly costly for journalists (see Figure 3.4).

The deaths of Marie Colvin and photographer Remi Ochlik in February 2012 received international attention and scrutiny, as described in earlier chapters. This was followed by President Assad's ban on all international correspondents from the end of March 2012 until the Russian-American agreement on ending Syria's chemical weapons capabilities in September 2013. Syria continues to be an extremely dangerous location for all journalists, and many international news organisations are no longer operating within the country. This is not only because of the inherent dangers of a war zone, but because of the rise in the deliberate targeting of journalists.

> Early on, the government of President Bashar al-Assad barred the international press while its security forces arrested and brutalized dozens of local news gatherers. Rebel forces counterattacked – targeting journalists and news outlets believed to be pro-government. By late 2011, journalists faced yet a third front with the appearance on the battleground of non-Syrian Islamic militia groups that have attacked, abducted, and killed them. (CPJ 2014b, p. 52)

The trends outlined in Iraq are obvious here as well. Initially, the inevitable dangers of covering conflict, particularly in a civil war, and the additional risks of advanced digital and satellite technology that brings reporters close to the action but can also leave an identifiable electronic footprint that can be targeted (as in the Marie Colvin case). This is followed by the emergence of partisan media outlets and the deliberate targeting of those in the media who refuse to toe the line, both by the regime and by the rebels. Ultimately, the involvement of criminal groups, internal militia factions, and external Islamic extremists, all of whom are willing to employ kidnap and murder as a means to gain money, power, and to silence opposition or scrutiny.

Asymmetric conflicts in other regions have introduced similar dangers for journalists. The so-called 'Arab Spring' and subsequent instabilities in North Africa have claimed 14 lives in Libya and 12 in Egypt since 2011.

One of the features of these conflicts has been the shifting nature of the front lines and the ambiguous and fragmented allegiances of the combatants where various groups vie for power. Journalists have described the difficulties of covering a conflict where initially the rebels would welcome the media coverage but, as the regime makes gains, they become nervous, particularly of being filmed or photographed, and hostile towards any reporting of their activities that might personally identify them for later retribution should their rebellions fail. The death toll in Syria illustrates this more than most.

Always dangerous, the Syrian conflict began to get worse for journalists when rebels began losing ground and groups that had once helped the media move around safely started selling on reporters for profit, something largely unheard of during previous conflicts. Kevin Sutcliffe, the head of EU news programming at VICE News, says this recent development is simply opportunistic gangsterism.

'In places like Syria you are moving across territories controlled by a number of groups. This patchwork is harder to understand. Who hates who is complicated, and you can't say who controls this patch of land. It's more chaotic now.' (INSI 2015)

The influence of al-Qaeda, and latterly Islamic State (ISIS), in this region has given rise to a shocking new trend that began with the filmed execution of *Wall Street Journal* correspondent Daniel Pearl in Pakistan in 2002. He was not the first high-profile journalist to be kidnapped, and it seems that his execution may not have been part of the initial plan (Simon 2015, pp. 66–71), but it demonstrated recognition of the power of visual media and the opportunities to subvert the influence of international news outlets.

While the al-Qaeda leadership may not have made an active decision to murder Pearl, his killing did send a clear message that in the Internet era there were other ways to communicate and that traditional journalists were dispensable, useful primarily as hostages and props in elaborately staged videos designed to convey a message of terror to the world. (Simon 2015, p. 71)

The murders of Steven Sotloff and James Foley in 2014, and the seven others publicly beheaded this year (as of June 2015), show that ISIS are prepared to take extreme measures in their recruitment and propaganda efforts, and that journalists are a priority target.

Militant Islamic groups play a role in the figures for other areas of conflict. In Pakistan, pro-Taliban groups have been accused of the murders of journalists, as well as other political groups and militias in the region, and al-Shabaab insurgents have been involved in threats and murders of journalists in Somalia. The security situation there caused at least 78 journalists to flee the country between 2007 and 2012 according to CPJ, more than anywhere else in the world (CPJ 2012a).

Societies that are uncivil as a result of political or ideological conflict provide fertile ground for global extremist groups. Journalists in these regions are not seen as neutral observers but as a threat to the groups' operations and influence that must be controlled by intimidation and murder. They have also become prized assets for kidnap and public execution as a means of furthering propaganda. This global attack on the freedom of expression and information could not be illustrated more starkly than by the fact that, in the latest biannual update of *Killing the Messenger* for 2015, a prosperous, peaceful, stable, European country topped the list in terms of the numbers of journalists killed – France.

Crime, (non-)punishment and the chilling effect

More journalists are killed in countries that are not explicitly in conflict. INSI statistics show almost twice as many (1,394 against 740), and Figure 3.5 demonstrates that this has consistently been the case until last year. The statistics show that the rate of impunity (lack of any prosecution or conviction) where these deaths were deliberate remains at around 85–90 per cent.

These deaths tend to be in countries with a poor record on prosecution of the perpetrators, and where corruption and organised crime are rife.

In 2014, five alleged suspects were finally sentenced for the 2006 murder of Anna Politkovskaya, a high-profile Russian journalist known for her reporting on human rights issues. This was a case dogged with trials and retrials and with repeated accusations of bungled investigations. Even now, it is not clear whether justice has been done. Mary Dejevsky, writing in a UK newspaper, states:

> The judge, Pavel Melyokhin, was clear that this was a contract killing, with $150,000 paid by 'a person unknown'. Nor was he in any doubt about the political motivation. Politkovskaya, he said, was killed for her work 'exposing human rights violations, embezzlement and abuse of power'. (Dejevsky 2014)

Although casualty rates in Russia have declined in recent years, the country regularly features in the top ten of the most dangerous places to be a journalist, and is ninth on the CPJ's 'Impunity Index' – a list of countries where little or no official investigation into deaths of journalists exists. Media organisations and staff are commonly threatened for their reporting of human-rights abuses by authorities and security personnel, for coverage of regional disputes, and for investigations into criminal gangs.

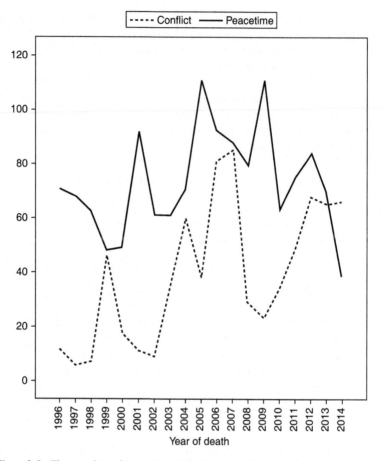

Figure 3.5   The number of journalists killed in formal 'peacetime' and in conflict between 1996 and 2014 (Cardiff University/INSI)

In India, an upward trend in journalists' deaths continues, in a complex environment of religious and political tensions, potential terrorist threats, and issues of corruption, particularly related to business practices that impact on the environment or where there are dubious working conditions. Here, the record on criminal investigations and prosecutions is slightly better, but it seems that, in the world's largest democracy, the use of deadly force to muzzle the media is still an option.

The Philippines also regularly feature as an extremely dangerous place for journalists, appearing second in Figure 3.2 that shows the top ten most deaths, and the attitude here is markedly different. While there seems to be an official will to safeguard media workers, there has been little progress. A mixture of legal inefficiency and a culture of violence as a means of silencing both media and criminal investigations places the Philippines second in CPJ's Impunity Index.

By far the worst incident has been termed the 'Maguindanao Massacre' in 2009 that claimed the lives of 32 journalists and media workers in a single afternoon (Amnesty International 2014). They were travelling with a political candidate in a convoy that was ambushed by a rival clan. The media staff, along with 26 other members of the entourage, were driven to a field, executed, and bundled into pre-dug graves.

More than a hundred suspects have been identified or arrested, released, moved between different trial locations yet there has not been a successful prosecution. There are allegations of bribery, corruption, witness intimidation, evidence tampering, and at least one individual who was prepared to testify has been murdered.

In 2014, newspaper reporter and radio host Rubylita Garcia was fatally shot in her home in front of her granddaughter by two unidentified gunmen, apparently for her investigations into corruption within a local police force. In their latest report, *Under Threat*, INSI's Philippines coordinator Red Batario suggests that, alongside the failings in the legal system, public resignation to the murder of journalists fosters this culture of impunity.

'There was no outrage among the public when a female broadcaster was shot in the head four times in broad daylight. That's an example of the blatant way that journalists are being killed.'

'The killings in Paris certainly sparked a sense of horror among journalists ... We wonder if it might make the public more sensitive to the killing of journalists in their own country.' (INSI 2015)

In other countries the culture of impunity is strengthened by systemic corruption as a result of organised crime or the influence of paramilitary groups.

Colombia's president (and former journalist) Juan Manuel Santos has recently made significant proclamations regarding tackling impunity for attacks on the press, but the effectiveness of this remains to be seen in the context of the current uneasy Pax Mafioso with the Marxist guerrilla group FARC. The country has seen an increase in stability generally as the government and the rebels have begun peace talks and an informal relationship to end decades of violence, but FARC still maintain power in certain regions of the country. Earlier this year (2015), two journalists were murdered within weeks of each other, both allegedly for their reporting of political corruption, and one in a region particularly known to be heavily influenced by FARC. The group's legacy of control over certain states means that they also have relationships with the drug cartels that will pay for freedom of movement, money that increases dominance by financing the purchase of weapons. Inevitably, these connections have implications for local journalists.

This kind of situation is particularly evident in Mexico, where a number of factors have combined to make it one of the most dangerous places in the world to be a journalist.

The long-standing, lucrative trafficking of drugs over the border into the US was severely disrupted by the security crackdown in the aftermath of September 11th. The gangs perpetrating the smuggling had developed into serious criminal organisations and now diversified their operations into kidnapping, prostitution, extortion and selling drugs within the country to maintain revenue levels.

> In essence, they morphed from trafficking organizations to criminal organizations along the lines of the mafia. And as they expanded into organized crime, the cartels were no longer satisfied with the control of a main road or border crossing. Instead, they sought to control entire territories and assert authority over key institutions ranging from municipal governments to the police and the media itself.
>
> In fact, the cartels viewed control over the media as critical and developed elaborate strategies to manage newsrooms through bribes and threats. It was during this period that journalists started dying and disappearing and massive self-censorship among the media began to take hold. The killing of two reporters from *El Diario de Ciudad Juárez* [in 2008 and 2010] ... prompted the newspaper to publish a front-page editorial asking the traffickers, 'What do you want from us?' and declaring them to be the de facto authority in the city. (Simon 2015, pp. 28–29)

Simon relates a conversation with a local journalist in Tijuana, who describes her publication as less deferential to the cartels, but also suggests that the relative decline in violence there is more related to the success of the traffickers' sophisticated tunnel system underneath the

US border (thereby re-establishing a focus on their traditional business) than to the media criticism or as a result of any crackdown by the authorities. Tijuana is a hugely popular destination for US day-trippers looking for cheap booze and cheap thrills, and therefore relative security in the city is critical for tourism revenue. In other areas of the country, including, but by no means limited to, other borders towns like Ciudad Juárez, the situation is far more dangerous.

The growth of the mafia-style cartels, the initial impact of increased border security, and an enhanced offensive against drug crime launched in 2006 by then newly elected President Felipe Calderón Hinojosa have all had a huge impact on the safety of journalists in the country.

As the cartels began to diversify their business interests, control over local authorities, police and the public became important targets. Control over, and the spread of intimidating messages via, the media was no less important. Figure 3.6 shows a huge increase in deaths after the federal and army offensive of 2006, and a wave of executions of media personnel was meant to serve as a warning not to meddle in the affairs of the cartels.

In 2010, for example, the remains of Valentin Valdés Espinosa, a local newspaper reporter, were found dumped in front of a motel that had links with the powerful Zeta cartel. He had previously written about police and military raids on the hotel, and had identified a cartel leader

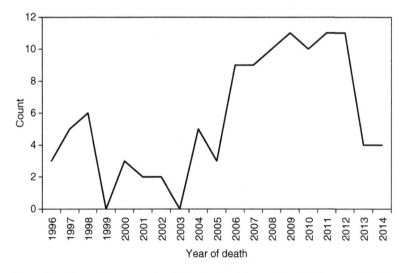

Figure 3.6 The number of journalists killed in Mexico (Cardiff University/INSI)

as one of those arrested during the operations. Local journalists deemed the location of his body significant. Valdés had been abducted the previous day, bound and tortured, and shot several times. A handwritten message near the body read 'This is going to happen to those who don't understand. The message is for everyone'.

> The newspaper did not press authorities for a thorough investigation, its editor, Sergio Cisneros, acknowledged. 'We are not going to get mixed up in it,' he told CPJ. 'I don't believe there will be results, so why push?' Cisneros said investigators did not search the newsroom or Valdés' computer. (CPJ 2010b)

This was by no means an isolated incident in terms of the graphic message this death was designed to convey. This was not 'opportunistic gangsterism' but deliberate and definitive gangsterism.

The cartels' influence began to spread to authorities involved in various states by means of the vast funds initially garnered from drug trafficking, and territorial disputes within the various gangs also became extremely violent. A report to Congress in 2010 estimated that more than 22,000 people had been killed in drug-related violence in the previous four years, 'an astonishing toll more likely associated with a conflict zone than a peace-time democracy' (CPJ 2010a).

This level of violence, combined with the cartel's influence over local authorities, the reluctance on behalf of law enforcement agencies to comment for fear that they may appear incompetent, and their network of observers and informants within the allied civilian community who alert them to any media activity, make journalism in Mexico an extremely dangerous and frustrating task.

> A reporter described it this way: 'We get a call from citizens that there's been a murder on let's say street corner X. If we call the police, they say there's nothing. The ambulance service says there's nothing. The citizens are watching the police at the scene examining the body or they see the body go into the coroner's vehicle. The coroner says they have no information. So, there's no story. There was no murder at street corner X'. (CPJ 2014b, p. 189)

This 'chilling effect' has local and international consequences.

> An organized crime cartel was never supposed to operate in metropolitan Mexico City. Middle and upper classes in the capital, where political, cultural, and intellectual power is concentrated, tend to

look down on the rest of the country. The drug war was supposed to be taking place out there in the 'provinces'.

The deep problem for Mexican journalism and for Mexicans is that while those reporters can tell CPJ that, they can't tell their readers in the rest of the country. But if they could, then the readers and policy makers might take another look at some of their assumptions about what's called the 'drug war', and what it may take to win it. (CPJ 2014b, p. 191)

A final example of this chilling effect is Brazil, the world's fourth-largest democracy. The country has seen a rapid increase in violence against journalists over the past few years. Here there is a mixture of organised crime, including drug trafficking, corruption involving local authorities and police, and a culture of impunity that is exacerbated by attacks on the judiciary and a climate of legal cases to deter or prevent publication of contentious stories. Brazil was ranked 11th on CPJ's Impunity Index in 2014.

Many of the killings take place outside of major cities, in areas without links to major news outlets, and are therefore rarely reported in the media, let alone investigated by authorities.

In Brazil, only one in 10 homicides is solved. This low rate is reflected in the impunity for crimes against journalists. In general, the police make more effort to solve crimes that receive a lot of media attention, and crimes against journalists are not always highlighted in the press. (CPJ 2012b)

In the build-up to the 2014 FIFA World Cup there was a wave of demonstrations aimed at highlighting social inequality in the country and concerns that the public cost of the tournament would not be repaid with the profits made. These gained more attention as the world's media were building up for a major sporting event, yet attacks on the media continued, including allegations of deliberate targeting by security forces to control the coverage of the protests, and by protesters annoyed at the tone of the reports.

Following 2012, the most deadly year so far for Brazil, where INSI recorded eight deaths, the government established a working group to look at the issue of violence against the media. The initial report was published in 2014.

Based on statistics provided by domestic press groups, including the Association of Brazilian Investigative Journalism (ABRAJI) and the UK-based international freedom-of-expression group Article 19, the report tallied 321 cases of murder, kidnapping, assault, death threats, arbitrary detention, and harassment. (CPJ 2014a).

There have been some successes in prosecutions, and the professed moves to formally legislate against attacks on the media are positive steps, yet this year (as of August 2015) five reporters have been killed in Brazil, including one fatally shot while presenting his radio programme live on air.

Brazil's international 'Samba' image will no doubt be highlighted as the Summer Olympics approach in 2016. The continued intimidation and murder of journalists, and the chilling effect of impunity for these attacks on the international perception of the country, cast something of a shadow on this party atmosphere.

An awareness of events and opinions elsewhere in the world, and the suppression of this through intimidation and deadly violence at a local level, impact on every citizen of a global civil society.

The resulting information deficit will have influence on a local and global scale, regardless of nationality, religious, ideological or political affiliations. Our knowledge of the world, influenced by the news media in whatever form and through whatever platform, informs our conversations with each other, our opinions of others, and how we engage with any democratic process.

Counting the cost

Compiling the statistics of these fatalities has become slightly easier, methodologically, over the years. The dramatic increase in communication and sites of information provided by the growth of the Internet have improved the detail of the casualty reports, and allowed more cross-checking of facts. This has coincided with an increased recognition of the concerns within the industry, and therefore better reporting, and the recognition that these trends urgently need to be addressed by national governments as well as global bodies, which will be discussed further in Chapters 8 and 9.

There are difficulties that persist, and perhaps have increased. A major one is how to classify who should be counted as a journalist casualty – just what is a journalist anyway?

Different agencies that compile these kinds of figures have different definitions, and therefore come to different annual totals. Fundamental to all, though, is the fact that a definition of a traditional journalist is difficult to pin down, particularly when trying to decide if that person was killed as a direct result of their work or for other reasons that may be directly or indirectly associated with it. This is not an exact science, and at INSI there are frequent debates about the inclusion or exclusion of one case or another in the annual reports.

A journalist definitely killed by a jealous husband will not make the figures. A journalist who appears to have been targeted for expressing a particular political stance, or for opposing another, is much harder to judge. Were they expressing these opinions in the capacity of an investigative social commentator? Have the results of their investigations and reporting swayed their own opinions in a particular direction? Did they become a journalist because of views that they already held and wanted to investigate further? Were they using their position as a well-known individual to express their personal views? Was their involvement a result of taking another job to supplement their meagre income?

Decisions about the motivation for the death, the likelihood of targeting, the media outlet that they were working for, and so on, are all made on a case-by-case basis.

This blurring of 'journalism' and 'activism' is one that the industry constantly struggles with, and is dependant, to an extent, on the context. Media systems operate under a variety of constraints depending on geography and political circumstances.

> Many governments – Turkey, Egypt, China, and Venezuela, to cite some examples – seem to believe 'journalists' support government policies while 'activists' oppose them. (Simon 2015, p. 158)

This was starkly illustrated in the on-going trial of Mohamed Fahmy, Baher Mohamed and, *in absentia*, Peter Greste, journalists for al-Jazeera, all arrested in Egypt on charges of spreading propaganda on behalf of the Muslim Brotherhood.

Furthermore, the system of 'embedding' is not unique to sophisticated Western militaries, and a number of cases of 'rebels with cameras' have also caused debate. In 2014 for example, INSI withdrew a case from the *Killing the Messenger* report for that year as a result of new information provided by UNESCO. The agency had initially issued a condemnation of the death of Abdullah Murtaja in Gaza who had purportedly been working for a television channel.

> On 14 November, the Director-General of UNESCO, Irina Bokova, issued an update about the statement she issued on 29 August, 2014, regarding Abdullah Murtaja, in the context of UNESCO's mandate to defend freedom of expression and press freedom.

The original statement issued on 29 August was in line with UNESCO's policy of condemning all killings of journalists. During this week, information has been brought to the attention of UNESCO that Mr Murtaja was a member of an organized armed group – an active combatant, and, therefore, not a civilian journalist. This has come to light in a video [that] was posted recently on the Internet with Abdullah Murtaja speaking as a member of an organized armed group.

UNESCO therefore withdraws the statement of 29 August.

'I deplore attempts to instrumentalize the profession of journalists by combatants,' declared Irina Bokova. 'The civilian status of journalists is critical, especially in situations of conflict, to ensure the free flow of information and ideas that are essential to the wider public and the restoration of stability and peace,' declared the Director-General. (UNESCO 2014)

This kind of situation is further complicated by the technological advances that allow frontline filming, and by the recognition that such imagery has powerful propaganda potential. Syria is a particularly complex situation in this regard, with a variety of 'news agencies' springing up that collate material from a range of sources and with a range of veracity in terms of anything like 'objective journalism'.

The Internet is filled with compelling footage of dramatic conflict scenes or emotional montages of the aftermath of tragic events designed to evoke a particular response or empathy for a particular cause. The main issue for media organisations is ascertaining whether they are genuine representations of events at that time, in that place, or whether they are stock footage from another time and place, or even deliberately staged for a specific purpose.

Even with the best of intentions, such 'journalistic' practices can be extremely damaging. In 2014 a Norwegian filmmaker uploaded a video of a 'heroic boy' who was shot while trying to save a young girl in Syria. It was viewed over eight million times on YouTube. The video was a hoax.

The video's director, Lars Klevberg, claimed he had made the film to highlight the issues being faced by young people in the vicious conflict. Journalists and others around the world condemned this as reckless and likely to have done more harm than good.

'The misery of children – and others – in Syria is very real. There is no need to fictionalise it. Fictionalising in order to draw attention to it does the exact opposite of the desired effect,' Kinda Haddad, a

Syrian-Dutch journalist, told BBC Trending. 'It introduces doubt into any story that has come out of Syria over the last few years as well as anything that will come out in future. People on both sides will use this to their advantage. And if people are unable to tell the difference between fact and fiction they will quickly lose interest in a conflict that is causing untold misery.' (BBC 2014)

This is also one reason why citizen journalists are currently not included in the *Killing the Messenger* reports. There are ways of forensically identifying the origins of footage, particularly with various digital stamps, but it isn't necessarily that easy and does take time and some level of expertise. It's also difficult to verify whether the footage comes from a genuine citizen, or whether it is some form of government, military/ militia, or organisational propaganda. There is a lot of material out there that is clearly meant to be 'activism', not simply witnessing or reporting, and classifying these filmmakers as journalists is problematic.

This is not to be elitist in any way, nor is it to underestimate the importance of some of their contributions.

Salam Abdulmunem, known as Salaam Pax, provided a fascinating insight into life in Baghdad during the 2003 war with his blog *Where is Raed?*, and his material was used extensively by mainstream media as a credible source of information that was otherwise almost impossible to get hold of.

The use of blogs, YouTube, and other social media were widely credited with bringing the world's attention to the 'Arab Spring' and the events across North Africa. In countries that are embroiled in conflicts too dangerous for conventional journalism, or where the authorities or repressive regimes make it almost impossible, these kinds of contributions can be invaluable in shining a light into very dark corners.

The second reason has more to do with the methodology of the reports. Firstly, the initial motivation was to uncover trends within the professional journalism industry that would then allow INSI to tailor specific safety advice or training packages. Secondly, the possibilities to be classified as a citizen journalist are almost limitless in a world where smart phones are everywhere. When a demonstration turns violent, and perhaps when people are killed, it is almost certain that many of the people there have a phone packed with images and video that would provide insight into the events. Anyone with a phone has the potential to be a citizen journalist. Where do you draw the line?

INSI, and many other agencies concerned with journalists' safety, do list details of prominent cases where citizen journalists have been involved, but for the reasons given above they do not feature in the specific *Killing the Messenger* reports.

This is not to say that citizen journalists, or indeed any citizens, cannot benefit from the kinds of safety advice that INSI and other agencies regularly give out.

Another issue is who they were working for at the time of their death. The distinction between freelance and staff is not as clear in some countries as it might be in others. Often. journalists will be contracted to produce a certain amount of copy for one organisation, and a certain amount for another. They will often write professionally for a newspaper, present a radio show, do a piece to camera, each for different media organisations, and will often also often blog about their stories.

One of the initial findings from the Global Inquiry was to debunk the myth that television journalists were most at risk. In fact, print journalists are more likely to be killed. Of course this is a result of several factors: the differing nature of media platforms in different countries, the technological changes to broadcast kit, changes in working practices and so on.

The most salient point is that these were people whose job it was to ask questions, to challenge authorities, and to provide context for events on a local or global scale.

With the proliferation of 'news' outlets via the Internet; of facts, lies and rumours perpetuated on social media; and a thousand other channels of information competing for our attention, it becomes even more important to have informed, investigative, competent journalists who are allowed to do their work in order to make sense of what Richard Sambrook has termed the 'information smog' (Sambrook 2015).

Writing from his prison cell while still in jail in Egypt, Peter Greste reflected on the reasons he was there.

> Sometimes it is easy to forget why we need it at all. Journalism can, at times, look pretty sordid, and few of us who work in it can claim to have never succumbed to the more base instincts of our trade. And in the wired world of the internet, with its citizen reporters and millions of sources, it is tempting to wonder why we need professional journalists at all.

> But that noise is the reason itself. Never has cleared-eyed, critical, sceptical journalism been more necessary to help make sense of a world overloaded with information.

> We should never forget that journalism is not a science. It is a human craft as vulnerable to biases and inaccuracies and flaws as any other.

And, at its worst, it can be quite destructive. But the reason we still buy newspapers, listen to the radio or switch on the evenings TV news bulletin is to find context and understanding; a sense of perspective. (Greste 2014)

Compiling these figures is difficult, perhaps not always correct, almost certainly conservative in the final tallies, but important. They help to illustrate the changing nature of risk to journalists, as well as those that remain the same, and they help to provide compelling evidence that the information deficit produced by intimidation and lethal force that silences journalists is a real threat to a global civil society.

References

Amnesty International (2014) *Philippines: Five Years on, Justice for Maguidanao Massacre Can't Wait*. Available from <https://www.amnesty.org/en/latest/news/2014/11/philippines-five-years-justice-maguindanao-massacre-can-t-wait/ (last accessed August 2015).

British Broadcasting Corporation (BBC) (2014) '#BBCTrending: Open Letter Condemns Fake "Syria hero boy" Film'. Available from <http://www.bbc.co.uk/news/blogs-trending-30087389> (last accessed August 2015).

Committee to Protect Journalists (CPJ) (2008) *Special Reports: Iraq: Journalists Abducted 2003–09*. Available from <https://cpj.org/reports/2008/04/abducted.php> (last accessed July 2015).

Committee to Protect Journalists (CPJ) (2010a) *Silence or Death in Mexico's Press*. Available from <https://cpj.org/reports/2010/09/silence-death-mexico-press-nation-crisis.php> (last accessed July 2015).

Committee to Protect Journalists (CPJ) (2010b) 'Valentin Valdés Espinosa'. Available from <https://cpj.org/killed/2010/valentin-valdes-espinosa.php> (last accessed July 2015).

Committee to Protect Journalists (CPJ) (2012a) *Attacks on the Press: Somalia*. Available from <https://cpj.org/2013/02/attacks-on-the-press-in-2012-somalia.php> (last accessed July 2015).

Committee to Protect Journalists (CPJ) (2012b) *Brazil Murders Reflect Tough Reporting, Lack of Justice*. Available from <https://cpj.org/blog/2012/12/impunity-at-heart-of-complex-backdrop-to-brazil-mu.php> (last accessed August 2015).

Committee to Protect Journalists (CPJ) (2014a) *Halftime for the Brazilian Press*. Available from <https://cpj.org/reports/2014/05/halftime-for-brazilian-press-censorship-violence-in-the-governments-hands.php> (last accessed August 2015).

Committee to Protect Journalists (CPJ) (2014b) *Attacks on the Press: Journalism on the World's Front Lines*. Hoboken, NJ: Wiley.

Dejevsky, M. (2014) 'Who Really Did Kill Russian Journalist Anna Politkovskaya?', The *Independent*, 13 June 2014. Available from <http://www.independent.co.uk/news/world/europe/who-really-did-kill-russian-journalist-anna-politkovskaya-9535772.html> (last accessed August 2015).

Greste, P. (2014) 'Messages from a Cairo Jail: Christmas Greetings, 20 December 2014'. Available from <https://www.freepetergreste.org/peter-greste-letters-from-prison-cairo-egypt/> (last accessed August 2015).

International News Safety Institute (INSI) (2003) *Dying to Tell a Story: The Iraq War and the Media: A Tribute*. Brussels: International News Safety Institute.

International News Safety Institute (INSI) (2007) *Killing The Messenger*, Available from: <http://www.newssafety.org/safety/projects/killing-the-messenger/> (last accessed August 2015).

International News Safety Institute (INSI) (2015) *Under Threat: The Findings*. Available from <http://newssafety.org/underthreat/under-threat-the-findings.html#> (last accessed July 2015).

Lewis, J., Brookes, R., Mosdell, N. and Threadgold, T. (2003) *Shoot First and Ask Questions Later: Media Coverage of the 2003 Iraq War*. Media and Culture, Vol. 7. Bern: Peter Lang.

Sambrook, R. (2015) TEDx, Cardiff: *The Information Smog*. Available from <http://tedxtalks.ted.com/video/Information-Smog-Richard-Sambro;search%3Asambrook> (last accessed August 2015).

Simon, J. (2015) *The New Censorship: Inside the Global Battle for Media Freedom*. New York: Columbia University Press.

Tumber, H. and Palmer, J. (2004) *Media at War: The Iraq Crisis*. London: Sage.

Tumber, H. and Webster, F. (2006) *Journalists Under Fire: Information War and Journalistic Practices*. London: Sage.

UNESCO (2014) 'UNESCO Director-General Statement Regarding Abdullah Murtaja'. Available from <http://www.unesco.org/new/en/media-services/single-view/news/unesco_director_general_statement_regarding_abdullah_murtaja/#.Vcy0Ofn09nG> (last accessed August 2015).

Part II
Approached in Context: History, Violence, Journalism

4

On the Violent History of the Globalised Present

Simon Cottle

We know from our work with the International News Safety Institute (INSI) as well as the annual monitoring of the Committee to Protect Journalists (CPJ) and others that journalists around the world have become increasingly targeted and killed in the course of their reporting and story investigations (INSI 2013, Clifford 2015). As underlined in Chapter 2 and statistically documented in Chapter 3, this is not only when reporting major interstate wars or intrastate civil wars, though the latter have become increasingly deadly. The despoliation of environments by unscrupulous corporations, the exploitation of precious minerals by warlords, the control of urban space and trade in drugs by criminal networks, the infliction of human rights abuses by repressive states, the exploitation of asylum-seekers and eco-refugees by traffickers, and the profiteering from humanitarian disasters by venal interests – these can all produce intimidation and violence directed at individuals and civil-society groups. And this includes journalists when seeking to report on these and other forms of social injustice and violence.

In the contemporary world, violence and threats targeting journalists emanate from different sources, in different contexts and for diverse reasons. Sometimes they are state-sanctioned or seemingly state-condoned when perpetrators are permitted to kill with impunity. At other times, the violence is outside state control in ungovernable spaces. Moreover, in an increasingly mediated and human-rights aware world, states can no longer presume to exercise a legitimate monopoly of force and violence within their territorial borders. Alongside other violent actors, they must now expect to become subject to the world's media spotlight and wider censure when perpetrating or condoning 'illegitimate' violence. For the most part, and by definition, such violence is rooted in some of the world's most unruly and uncivil places. We need to better understand this changing backdrop of societal violence if we are to arrive at a deeper understanding of the risks and dangers confronted by journalists and media workers in the world today. So too do we need to better understand how the changing historical nature of violence alongside other trajectories in human society motivate journalists to report on such issues and thereby become positioned at risk and, sometimes, in mortal danger.

The fact that the changing nature and forms of violence in the world today position many journalists and media workers in harm's way seemingly runs counter to broad socio-historical trends and accounts of the 'pacification of societal violence', the 'civilizing process' and the 'decline of war' (Elias 1994, Rifkin 2009, Pinker 2011, Goldstein 2012, Gat 2013, Gleditsch 2013), trends discussed further below. Media workers along with formerly sacralised groups such as humanitarian workers and religious leaders can now all find themselves deliberately targeted by belligerents and other uncivil actors. Civilians more generally are also becoming deliberately targeted in so-called 'new wars' and processes of ethnic cleansing (Kaldor 2007), or are put at risk through euphemistically termed 'collateral damage' – the deadly fall-out from changing forms of warfare and the 'new western way of war' (Shaw 2005). This chapter argues that the deliberate targeting of non-military personnel, including journalists, can only properly be understood and theorised when situated in the 'longue durée' of socio-historical trends. Such trends have unfolded across centuries and currently converge in today's rapidly globalising world. They include the growing global communications reach and professional dispositions of journalism to report on, and, in some cases, bear witness to, endemic violence and injustices around the world.

This chapter and the next set out to review these broader sociohistorical trends in human society and how, paradoxically, they both condition but also exacerbate the risks, intimidation and violence that now confront journalists. The increased dangers and risks confronted by today's journalists are in part accounted for by journalism's historically forged, deepening and geographically expanding commitment to report on the precarious lives of those inhabiting dangerous, violent places around the world. This 'expanding reach' and 'civic deepening' of journalism are part and parcel of contemporary globalising society, a world marked by expansive communication systems, increased interdependency *and* human insecurity. But this same world also exhibits democratising, cosmopolitanising and human-rights impulses, no less historically forged and on the move, and these characterise not only most democratic states and national civil societies in the world today but also emergent transnational civil society. The practices, philosophy and performance of journalism, we contend, are produced *within* and emanate *from* these wider, often contradictory, societal contexts and the broader contours and communicative impulses of history; they are not *separate from* or *outside* them.

This is so despite the well-documented and academically theorised institutional structures of journalism: whether the conglomeration and profit orientation of current media industries with their competitive pursuit of readers, ratings and revenue; journalism's known and documented dependency on elite sources and vulnerability to the strategic plays of power; and the traditions of journalism encoded into professional practices and the pursuit of emotionally detached and impartial reporting (Cottle 2006). Notwithstanding these and other shaping constraints and conditions, the normative aims and ambitions of many journalists today – outlooks etched into journalism's preferred self-image and actualised in its best reporting performance – are in fact also *expressive of* and *responsive to* wider and historically formed civil-society norms and expectations. This is too often overlooked and remains theoretically underdeveloped within most contemporary accounts of journalism, with the latter failing to recognise contemporary journalism's imbrication within the surrounding and shifting sociohistorical field and how in recent decades, for example, this has become increasingly empathic and sensitised to humanitarian, human-rights and human-security issues (Cottle 2009, 2013). This chapter develops on these broad historical and global claims and does so as a way of better contextualising and understanding the rise of journalist killings and intimidation in the contemporary world. It proceeds across two interlinked discussions.

Firstly, we consider accounts of the historical shifts in human violence and sensibilities towards the same, as a necessary, albeit deep, historical backdrop for discerning the contemporary dispositions of journalism; and secondly, we observe a number of different global trends exacerbating human insecurity today including the breakdown of civil society in failed and failing states, and new forms of warfare, and how these all put journalists at increased risk. In the next chapter we then follow up on these historical and global contexts and address journalism's intimate connection with civil society, its expectations and outlooks, and how this both shapes and finds expression in and through journalism's deepening and widening obligation to report on precarious lives in unruly and uncivil places. Far from contradicting the overarching claims of the longer-term historical pacification of violence and the rise of an increasingly humanitarian, human-rights and, possibly, empathic world, it is in part precisely because of these longer-term historical developments, we argue, that journalists are now increasingly at work in uncivil places and thereby positioned in harm's way.

On the history – and historiography – of violence

Some time ago, the sociologist Norbert Elias set out a persuasive case for the historical 'pacification of violence' in '*The Civilizing Process*' (1994), originally published in 1939. Observing a crucial transition in late Medieval Europe with the rise of Absolutist states in Britain, France and Germany, he theorised a profound shift in the everyday habitus, or lifestyles, norms and interpersonal behaviours of the upper class and relates this *psychogenesis* to the *sociogenesis* of state-formation. These processes would increasingly 'confine force to barracks', at least within the territorial confines of the nation state, and incrementally gave rise to feelings of moral repugnance in respect of interpersonal violence:

> The sociogenesis of absolutism indeed occupies a key position in the overall process of civilization. The civilizing of conduct and the corresponding transformation of the structure of mental and emotional life cannot be understood without tracing the process of state-formation, and within it the advancing centralization of society which first found particularly visible expression in the absolutist form of rule. (Elias 1994, p. 191)

Elias argued that the anarchic violence of the European Middle Ages became subdued and pacified with the increasing monopolisation of force by absolutist states. The violence produced by competing and warring parties within the patchwork landscape of feudalism engendered 'elimination contests' and a habitus of relatively unrestrained expressions of feelings and spontaneous outbursts of aggression. The psychological dispositions and structures of feeling of the feudal era, distributed across the different social strata, thereby became *attuned* with the prevailing social structure with its endemic rivalries and competition. This changed, however, with the historical transition to absolutist states and was driven in part through successive elimination contests, the displacement of barter by markets, and the collection of taxes allowing for the payment of standing armies and mercenaries by increasingly centralised power holders (rather than parcelling out lands to secure temporary alliances).

It was in such ways that a centralised state emerged in Europe with an increasing monopolisation of force. It was also conditioned in part by the transformations of social habitus that first became apparent in courtly etiquette based around eating, sexual behaviour and the body, social codes that gradually displaced former warrior codes based on demonstrations of strength and chivalric honour. The latter became increasingly redundant in absolutist courts where competitive military prowess was less important given the state's monopoly of force, and where royal favour and privilege thus became dependent on other forms of courtly performance and social distinction. In such ways the emergence of courtly etiquette or *courtoisie* becomes distributed into a wider habitus of *civilité* and eventually the established norms of *civilisation* in which moral repugnance at violence became generalised and pronounced (though not without periodic 'de-civilizational spurts' or reversals as Elias, an émigré from Nazi Germany, was all too personally aware).

Elias's thesis remains arresting to this day; it proposes an historically dynamic, sociologically rich and psychologically informed account of changing norms, behaviours and sensibilities to violence, and seeks to account for the moral repugnance now often felt and exhibited at public and private forms of violence in contemporary societies (Mennell and Goudsblom 1998). Unsurprisingly, perhaps, it has not escaped criticism. Before we consider some of this, it is worth underlining its continuing relevance for researching the history of violence today. A number of recent scholars, documenting how levels of violence in public and private spaces across the centuries have declined, broadly lend support to Elias's thesis.

Robert Muchembled's *A History of Violence* (2012), for example, details how a culture of essentially male violence was transformed between 1300 and 2000. 'Under pressure from the legal system', he argues, 'its status gradually changed from that of a normal collective language, which had created social ties, and helped to validate the hierarchies of power and the relations between generations and sexes in the core communities, to that of major taboo. (p. 2). Specifically, he observes:

> The principal change came around 1650, when, everywhere in Europe ravaged by interminable wars, a strong hostility developed to the sight of blood. From this time on, the Western 'factory' reshaped individual behaviour, which was habitually violent, especially among the young, by a system of norms and rules of politeness which devalued armed confrontations, codes of personal vengeance, excessive harsh hierarchical relationships and relations between the

sexes and age groups. This resulted over the centuries in a veritable transformation of the collective sensibility with regard to homicide, which culminated, during the industrial age, in its becoming a powerful taboo. (pp. 2–3)

Importantly, however, this developing sociohistorical prohibition on interpersonal violence did not completely quell the aggressive impulses of young men, given that they were 'necessary to the "just" wars of a civilization increasingly interested in conquest after the Great Discoveries' (p. 4). Pieter Spierenburg's *Violence and Punishment* (2013), significantly subtitled *'Civilising the Body Through Time'*, also documents declining homicide rates as well as the evident diminution of a range of violent practices common a few centuries ago. And the scholar Keith Krause agrees:

Violent practices that were commonplace a century or so ago (public executions, torture, lynching, etc) have today been stigmatized to the point of near extinction in the West, although there are notable exceptions. And the everyday use of violence to resolve conflicts has also been condemned; reaching even now deep into the 'private sphere', where intimate partner violence existed beyond the reach of the state. (Krause 2009, p. 348)

Krause is also explicit, however, in recognising how such Western trends may be less advanced in other parts of the contemporary world, a point of some relevance for any discussion of the globalising present and the roles and risks of journalists within this:

This is less true elsewhere, especially in parts of Africa, Asia, and the Middle East, where codes of honour and the moral economy of violence still legitimize practices such as grave desecrations, bride burning, honour killings, systematic rape, or even the choice of instruments with which to kill certain groups that are repugnant to most but acceptable to many. (Krause 2009, p. 348)

Evidently, there has been a documented and marked decline across Europe of public executions, torture and various forms of cruelty including that meted out to animals. Randall Collins brings some useful conceptual distinctions to bear on these trends. In a seminal article, 'Three Faces of Cruelty: Towards a Comparative Sociology of Violence' (1974), he observes not only the decline in 'ferocious violence' but its displacement by 'cruelty without passion', namely, modern bureaucratic means of destruction, as well as more traditional forms of 'ascetic violence' rooted in ideas of self-righteousness, honour and personal sacrifice. 'Ferocious violence', he says, is violence based on brutality and public spectacle, and he considers how '... torture and humiliation are above all forms of communication usable as threats and supports for claims of complete domination'. As we shall hear, all three forms of violence can in fact still be found in different parts of the world today, each positioning human bodies and lives, including those of journalists, at risk.

Wherever violence is enacted in the world today it would be wrong to simply assume that this is 'the antithesis of sociality', an 'expression of our animal nature' or 'the essence of evil'. According to Alan Fiske and Tage Rai, in *Virtuous Violence* (2015), 'When people hurt or kill someone, they usually do so because they feel they ought to: they feel that it is morally right or even obligatory to be violent' (p. xxii). Most violence, they suggest, 'is morally motivated by culturally informed variants of universal social-relational models', and is therefore perceived by perpetrators, if not always by victims, as virtuous; that is, as morally justified, even if not legally sanctioned (p. xxiii). This argument can be extended to the justifications of violence conducted in war atrocities, including the particularly vicious violence characterising new wars. Recent work on social-identity models further suggests that, contrary to arguments about 'the banality of evil' (the idea that people commit extreme acts of inhumanity, including genocide, because they lack awareness or control over what they are doing), people in fact commit such inhumane acts because they believe it to be right or justified (Reicher et al. 2008). Stephen Reicher and his colleagues propose a model that helps to explain how this can come about, and describe the five steps involved: (1) *identification*, the construction of an in-group: (2) *exclusion*, the definition of targets as external to the in-group; (3) *threat*, the representation of these targets as endangering in-group identity; (4) *virtue*, the championing of the in-group as (uniquely) good; and (5) *celebration*, embracing the eradication of the out-group as necessary to the defence of virtue.

In respect of war, a growing body of evidence now documents the decline in inter-state warfare and battle-related deaths across recent decades (Goldstein 2011, Gat 2013, Gleditsch 2013, SIPRI 2013). Stephen Pinker's *The Better Angels of our Nature* (2011) has probably proved the most influential of all in setting out to challenge the prevalent belief that we are living in unprecedented war-prone and violent times. He elaborates on both the decline in inter-personal, predominantly male, violence across history as well as inter-state warfare. He is explicit:

> This book is about what may be the most important thing that has ever happened to human history. Believe it or not – and I know that most people do not – violence has declined over long stretches of time, and today we may be living in the most peaceable era in our species' existence. (Pinker 2011, p. xix)

Pinker builds his thesis on the identification of six broad historical trends in human evolution and society. These comprise: (1) a general pacification process from primal anarchy/hunter-gathers to the first agriculture-based civilisations of 5,000 years ago; (2) drawing on Elias's ideas, a civilising process from the Middle Ages continuing to the present; (3) the Humanitarian Revolution identified with the Age of Reason and Enlightenment, which is closely associated with the decline of socially sanctioned violence; (4) the 'Long peace' – following the Second World War, characterised by the decline of inter-state wars; (5) the 'New Peace' evident in the decline in civil war and genocide since the end of the Cold War; and (6) a 'Rights Revolution' that, since 1948, has contributed to the growing culture of Human Rights and associated revulsion towards violence against minorities and vulnerable groups. Based on this suite of historical arguments, Pinker maintains mankind's 'better angels' of cooperation, empathy, self-control, moral sense and reason have progressively overcome mankind's 'inner demons' of predatory violence, dominance, sadism and utopian ideology. Pinker advances a bold thesis, one eloquently stated and empirically detailed, but it can also be read essentially as a non-apologia in which Western civilisation is seen as the inexorable advance of Enlightenment, moral progress around the globe. Unsurprisingly, it has often elicited vehement criticism.

John Grey, for example, challenges Pinker's happy narrative of Western moral progress, pointing to the continuing involvement of Western states in bloody proxy wars, the methodological problems of confining war violence to counting battlefield deaths, the continuing threat of human annihilation by nuclear weapons, and the involvement of Enlightenment science and rationality within state-planned and prosecuted mass atrocities across the twentieth and twenty-first centuries (Grey 2015). It is this transformation of 'ferocious violence' into 'cruelty without passion' (Collins 1974), and not the disappearance of violence per se, that characterises the bureaucratically routinised application of the means of physical punishment and human destruction by states across late modernity. This last point, a point indebted to Weberian sociology, has been developed and applied most forcefully by Zygmunt Bauman in his treatise *Modernity and the Holocaust* (1989). The Nazis regime was chillingly calculating in its end-means reasoning and its followers nothing if not bureaucratically diligent in their record keeping of the systematic processes of human annihilation. Siniša Malešević (2013), a sociologist of war, makes a similar argument in his sociological critique of the changing nature of state violence. Here, *contra* Elias and Pinker, he suggests that such changes are in fact far from historically progressive:

> [R]ather than extinguishing violence, modern social organizations transform violent action into cumulative coercive power that is periodically unleashed with devastating results. Not only that, the monopoly on the legitimate use of violence over a particular territory often successfully redirects violence from the inside toward the outside, but relying on the most advanced organizational and ideological knowledge, it also creates an unprecedented bureaucratic machine of destruction. ... It is the prevalence of moral equality and ethical universality that creates the structural conditions for the proliferation and ultimate justification of mass murder. (pp. 283–284)

Malešević is surely right to invite us to consider the changing nature of warfare and forms of historical violence before conceding that we live in increasingly pacified times of declining human destruction. However, the debate too easily becomes polarised into mutually exclusive positions of Western Enlightenment conceived as inexorable, universalising moral progress on the one side, or as the bearer of seeds of human destruction on the other (see also, Adorno and Horkheimer 1974/1944). To argue, as Malešević does above, that there is an inherent anti-humanism, a destructive impulse implicit to Enlightenment universalising tenets of moral equality and ethical universality, that permits all those on the 'outside' of such norms to be misrecognised as less than human and subject to instrumental rationality and bureaucratic state destruction, is to fundamentally misrecognise the contingencies of the political battleground as well as the multiple trajectories and reversals played out in history. It conflates the political contingencies and outcomes of force, struggle and power to an overarching philosophical determinism. This is not to suggest that Enlightenment tenets of reason and rationality cannot be distorted when deployed in the name of 'equality' or when

government jurisdiction is violently imposed on indigenous populations in the name of 'democracy' (Mann 2005, Totten and Parsons
2013). But these and other genocidal practices are neither immanent
to Enlightenment ideas or those of democracy, though both can be
cynically put to work as a legitimising rhetoric for brutal and inhumane
practices.

But Pinker is no less secure in his equally one-sided absolutism concerning Western advance and the pacification of violence, as we have
heard. These debates are instructive, nonetheless. They help us to reflect
on and hopefully secure a better fix on the nature of violence in the
contemporary world, as well as the risks experienced by journalists and
why, as we shall hear later (Chapter 6), they have become increasingly
motivated to undertake such dangerous assignments. But each of the
positions summarised above essentialises in an unfortunate way, either
beneficently or malevolently, the historical role of Enlightenment philosophy and practices in world violence today. The view of history, its
historiography, underpinning our discussion and approach to violence
here, is necessarily more politically contingent and seeks to acknowledge the multiple and complex trajectories of history. Together these
problematise ideas of a teleological convergence on a predetermined
outcome, be it world peace or world destruction. Human history is characterised by, often violent, ruptures and reversals as well as longer-term
trajectories of change and advance.

Implicit to our discussion, then, is a view of historical change and
development that challenges a widespread, academic incredulity toward
meta-narratives as well as historical presentism (of simply reading history
through the prism of the present). It is a view informed by the growing
body of scholarship on long-term processes and trends in human society (Singer 2011, Mann 2012, Mazlish 2014, Harari 2014). Our historiographical approach navigates between two significant if contrasting
bookends. The liberal philosopher Karl Popper dedicated his influential
The Poverty of Historicism (1957) to the 'memory of the countless men
and women of all creeds or nations or races who fell victim to the fascist
and communist belief in Inexorable Laws of Historical Destiny'. A few
decades later, postmodernists influenced by Jean-François Lyotard's *The
Post Modern Condition: A Report on Knowledge* (1984) also entertained
a strong suspicion of history, but now in terms of 'incredulity to all
meta-narratives.' Both had good reasons to question, from their very
different philosophical standpoints, messianic views on the inexorable
laws of history and a teleological faith in Western Enlightenment and
civilisational progress. However, both these philosophical positions

assert their claims by eclipsing the longer-term changes in the course of human society, especially those accelerating vortices from the sixteenth century onwards leading to globalisation, that continue to shape both the real world and idealist views on the same (Rifkin 2009, Mann 2012, Mazlish 2014).

A more productive historiographical standpoint for the purposes of this discussion, and we suspect more widely, invites a deeper historical appreciation of the trajectories of violence as well as the dispositions of journalism to report on it. Whilst declining, therefore, a strong teleological and mono-causal historicism, this position recognises the longer-term and multiple trajectories of world history, their complex dynamics, tumultuous ruptures and violent reversals as well as accelerating speed toward globalisation (Weber 1968, Giddens 1985, Iggers 2005, Marks 2007, Mann 2012). Western societies have assumed the position of the 'leading-edge' (Mann 2012) in state processes of violent military conquest and market expansion since the sixteenth Century (Ferguson 2003, Mann 2012, Mazlish 2014), but alongside these and often emanating from them are also 'modern' dynamics of increasing empathy and moral repugnance at violence (Rifkin 2009, Pagden 2013, Nussbaum 2014), as well as corresponding struggles for justice and civil rights (Johnston 2011, Robertson 2012), democracy (Keane 2004, 2009), humanitarianism (Wilson and Brown 2009, Simms and Trim 2011), human rights (Hunt 2007, Ishay 2008) and human security (Kaldor 2007). These changing sensibilities and struggles for change have found historical expression in reportage of human suffering, atrocity and violence across the ages (Carey 1987), and have done so in and through evolving narrative forms, changing visual media (Hunt 2007, Perlmutter 2009, Danchev 2011, Laqueur 2011, Cottle and Evans 2015) and, importantly, journalism as we know it from the seventeenth century onwards (Conboy 2004), and in its changing practices and reporting commitments to an expanding civil sphere (see Chapter 5).

To be clear, as indicated earlier, these developments are not separate from the altogether more brutal and violent processes and past struggles that helped spawn them: state formation (Tilly 1990, Elias 1994), endemic European wars (Morris 2014), slavery and colonialism (Blackburn 2011), and the early frontier 'dark side of democracy' (Mann 2005). There is no comforting teleology or cunning hand of reason gently unfolding through history (Bauman 1989, Malešević 2010). Still, these same destructive forces have simultaneously contributed to historically expanding ideas and outlooks of a more inclusive 'human circle', both spatially and morally conceived. And here the changing technologies, forms and practices of media and communications have played their part. This includes the historical emergence of journalism documenting, defining and giving narrative and visual forms to issues and identities and representations of conflict (Taylor 1995, Briggs and Burke 2002, Conboy 2004, Allan 2012) and, more recently, bearing witness to human injustices including wars and atrocity (Hunt 2007, Sambrook 2010, Laqueur 2011, Batchen et al. 2012, Cottle and Hughes 2015). Journalism not only has the capacity to alert publics and governments to violence and injustices in unruly and uncivil places (and historically changing definitions of the same), it can also variously inscribe and invite empathic, morally charged responses to those same threats, events and circumstances (Chouliaraki 2006, 2010, Cottle 2009, 2011, 2013, Taylor 1998, Thompson 1995, Tait 2011). Today, it is no longer possible to understand contemporary threats in and from uncivil places without also contextualising them within the contemporary globalising world.

Globalisation, precarity and journalists at risk

Many of today's crises and conflicts are globally endemic. They are spawned by an increasingly interdependent world of global expansion, inequality of life chances and precarious lives. Climate change and ecological degradation, transnational terrorism and Western military interventionism, financial meltdowns and international criminal networks, forced migrations and pandemics, food and water shortages, impending energy crises and humanitarian disasters, new wars and the permanent emergency of world poverty, human rights abuses and human insecurity. These are just some of the globally enmeshed crises and conflicts whose origins and outcomes cannot for the most part be adequately encompassed or explained by national frames of reference. They all have the potential to, and many already do, stunt life chances and end lives, positioning millions of people around the globe in a situation of *extremis*: that is, of precarity and frequently confronting violence. This is a context that now, and inevitably in the future, will also confront local journalists and fixers as well as international 'parachute' correspondents and other media personnel flown into some of the world's most dangerous places (Pedelty 1995, Tumber and Webster 2006, Murrell 2010, 2015, Sambrook 2010).

In today's interconnected and interdependent world, such conflicts and crises represent the dark side of a 'negatively globalized planet' where 'there cannot be local solutions to globally originated and globally invigorated problems' (Bauman 2007, pp. 25–26). Global crises cannot be regarded as exceptional or aberrant events only, erupting without rhyme or reason or dislocated from the contemporary world (dis)order (Cottle 2009, 2011). And nor can they be adequately understood as the dreadful remnants of an earlier premodern era that has somehow escaped the civilising forces of modernity (Albrow 1996, Beck 1999, Calhoun 2004, Duffield 2007). Rather, they are endemic to the contemporary global world, enmeshed within it and potentially encompassing in their ramifications and required responses. Today, global crises are publicly defined, legitimised and variously mobilised within the world's news media (Shaw 1996, Beck 2009, Cottle 2009). Here the world's journalists occupy a pivotal role in *signalling, symbolising* and dramatically and deliberatively *staging* the crises and conflicts of the contemporary globalised world (Beck 2009, Lester and Cottle 2009). And some become imperilled as they do so.

Globalisation and world risk society

Debates within the field of globalisation theory have tended to polarise between those who either emphasise multiple or mono-causalities, cultural homogeneity or heterogeneity, Western universalism or particularism, late modernity or post-modernity, and the global or the local (Harvey 1989, Giddens 1990, Robertson 1992, Appadurai 1996, Waters 2001, Held and McGrew 2003, Urry 2003, Held 2004, Ritzer 2007). So-called 'globalists', 'skeptics', and 'transformationalists' also stake out their positions on this contested field (Held and McGrew 2003). Importantly for our purposes, a number of theorists also observe how globalisation gives rise to diverse conflicts and crises, many of them spilling over into violence. David Harvey, for example, theorises globalisation and the condition of postmodernity in terms of capitalist 'crises of over accumulation' (1989, p. 327) – processes later theorised as driving globalisation and 'accumulation by dispossession' (Harvey 2003, p. 141). Manuel Castells's magnum opus on the 'network society' and the new 'space of flows' (Castells 1996), theorises how informational capitalism produces a 'fourth world' of social exclusion and 'black holes' of communication (Castells 1998, pp. 70–165), and Zygmunt Bauman addresses the systemic production and reproduction of globally 'wasted lives' (Bauman 2004). David Held and Anthony McGrew – who regard globalisation as the widening, intensifying, speeding-up and growing impact of worldwide interconnectedness – observe how this same interconnectedness generates new 'animosities and conflicts' (Held and McGrew 2003, p. 4). And John Urry's thesis of 'global complexity'

(2003) argues that 'emergent systems of information and communication are the bases for increased reflexivity' (Urry 2003, p. 139), especially in response to 'collective global disasters' (pp. 135–137). (See also Albrow 1996, p. 4.)

Perhaps most influentially of all, Anthony Giddens defined globalisation as a 'stretching process' in which there is 'an intensification of worldwide social relations that link distant localities in such a way that local happenings are shaped by events occurring many miles away and vice versa' (Giddens 1990, p. 64). This definition, as well as core concepts of 'time-space distanciation', 'action at a distance' and 'reflexivity', all speak to today's global interconnectedness as does his general theoretical statements on the globalisation of risk in the modern world and the media's indispensable role in the forward march of democracy (Giddens 1990, 1994, 2002). 'In a world based upon active communication', he suggests, 'hard power – power that comes only from the top down – loses its edge' as authoritarian regimes become undermined by their 'loss of information monopoly' in today's 'intrinsically open framework of global communications' (Giddens 2002, pp. 72–73; see also Castells 2009). In these and other influential statements about globalisation, then, theorists identify a number of conflicts and crises as endemic to and emanating from contemporary globalising society.

Ulrich Beck, more than any other social theorist, posits global threats and dangers centre stage in his theorisation of the global age, extending ideas of 'risk society' (1992) to 'world risk society' (1999), and discerning at least three different axes of world crises that he terms, respectively, 'ecological, economic and terrorist interdependency crises' (2006, p. 22). Not only does he point to the endemic nature of global crises and conflicts as defining forces of the global age, he also theorises how they may yet unleash radical impulses in a new global 'civilizational community of fate' (2006, p. 13):

> [T]he cosmopolitan outlook means that, in a world of global crises and dangers produced by civilization, the old differentiations between internal and external, national and international, us and them, lose their validity and a new cosmopolitan realism becomes essential to survival. (Beck 2006, p. 14)

World risk society is produced essentially, argues Beck, by those manmade, incalculable, uninsurable threats and catastrophes that are anticipated, but which remain invisible and therefore highly dependent on how they become defined and contested in 'knowledge' and, importantly, visualised and dramatised in the news media. Though we may want to argue, contra Beck, that not all that is important is confined to knowledge and the anticipated; that for some of us we don't so much 'live under the volcano', as daily suffer its eruption through stunted and lost lives; that 'risks', in other words, are ontologically real and devastating, as well as epistemologically constructed and media dependent. We may nonetheless want to recognise, along with Beck, the changing nature of late-modernity and the dark side of globalisation (Cottle 2011). Beck's emphasis on staging in world risk society also helps to position journalism and journalists as key protagonists and mediators of the unprecedented risks of 'world risk society.' Insofar as journalism and journalists now seek to report on the often violent manifestations of global risks and unequal interdependency crises, they themselves are put 'at risk.'

On the changing nature of contemporary warfare

As a means of securing more traction on the changing nature of globalisation and how this positions journalists in the 'eye of the storm', it is useful to explore three ways in which contemporary warfare is changing and how this variously positions not only military personnel but also civilians, humanitarian workers and journalists at increased risk. As we have already indicated, the risk and threats spawned by globalisation are diverse, often overlap, and generate different hazardous environments; so it would be misleading to suggest that it is only war correspondents who are positioned in the 'killing zone'. As our statistics demonstrate (see Chapter 3), recent trends indicate that journalists and media personnel can now be placed in the firing line in and across a range of conflict scenarios. These include, for example, human-rights abuses associated with environmental struggles conducted around corporate exploitation of natural resources, habitats and traditional ways of life; repressive states targeting civil-rights groups and pro-democracy activists; and the violence of drug cartels and international criminal networks. Nonetheless, war, as the deliberate collective expression of human violence, continues to kill many journalists and, in the post-Cold War era, its changing forms indicate why more and more journalists are becoming deliberately targeted when reporting on them.

The new Western way of war

In the 'new Western way of war', argues Martin Shaw, the physical risks of war are transferred from governments to the military, and, because of the potential political and electoral damage generated by news reports of military causalities and images of returning body bags, military risks are then effectively transferred to civilian non-combatants. Military actions prosecuted through high-altitude bombing, in contrast to boots on the ground, for example, incur far less 'risks', both physically and politically (see also Tumber and Webster 2006, Burri 2015). In other words, this concern with public perception and public reactions to media images of military casualties becomes incorporated into a complex process of risk-transference. And it is this that helps to explain the increased incidence of civilian casualties, so-called 'collateral damage', in contemporary Western wars in contrast to the deliberate targeting of non-combatants in new wars discussed next (though importantly, in both, civilians become exposed to increased deadly violence). Shaw's thesis of risk-transfer war thus recognises the enhanced importance of the news media in managing public perceptions of war as well as the added risks to the political legitimacy of states, politicians, and military when war becomes subject to global media surveillance:

> Because electorates are almost exclusively national, Western governments still think largely of national surveillance. However, even this element of surveillance is mediated through the global and the international. National publics take notice of what allied governments and publics think, as well as of broader international official and public opinion. National media are influenced by global media. National politics and media are affected by norms of international legality and by decisions and judgments in international institutions. Although governments think in terms of accountability in a national public sphere, this is never autonomous to anything like the extent to which it was in the total war era. On the contrary, governments must always recognize how integrated global media, institutions and public opinion have become. (Shaw 2005, p. 75)

The new Western way of war, with its sought deployment of overwhelming firepower coordinated through computerised surveillance and communication systems, and delivered from a safe distance with devastating 'shock and awe', seeks to avoid the political risks of losing legitimacy. In such a context, the aestheticisation of high-altitude bombing or 'computer game' imagery of electronically guided ordnance finding their targets perpetrates, to borrow a phrase from Pierre Bourdieu, a form of 'symbolic violence', imagistically dissimulating and occluding the human consequences and carnage of war and contributing to the physical disappearance (and destruction) of combatant and civilian bodies alike (Cottle 2006, pp. 155–162). The significance of global media surveillance is not exhausted however, with reference to the conditioning impacts exerted in the risk-transference of the 'new Western way of war' and its representational 'symbolic violence'.

Chris Paterson, in a detailed analysis of the US media and war reporters, observes a disturbing trend across recent years with the increased US military killings of Western as well as other journalists legitimately engaged in reporting wars and conflicts. He discerns:

> a deadly paradox which has become apparent since 9/11: that of an entrenched culture of acceptance and impunity which permits states that are nominally democratically governed, human rights oriented, and bound by democratically established national and international legal conventions, to conceal violations of human rights and rules of war, and to kill, injure and arrest those journalists who are in a position to witness and report on those violations. (Paterson 2014, p. 1)

At the time of writing *War Reporters Under Threat* (2014), Paterson notes how the US government had been directly responsible for the deaths of over 40 journalists and media workers in Serbia, Afghanistan and Iraq (see also Chapter 2). This included the deliberate bombing of Serbian Television in Belgrade in 1999, with the death of 16 media workers. In these contexts, he suggests, the term 'friendly fire' is a poor euphemism for what is more accurately and tellingly described as an evolving and hardening military culture of 'friendly threat'. Here, 'the new threat of violence and extreme forms of coercion facing journalists covering war' is 'coming from the US government and some of its closest allies and partners' (p. 2). Paterson's thesis – based on a wealth of critical commentaries, case studies and insider military, political and press statements – argues that the new modes of information war have incrementally contributed to a growing military, and, in part US-media-condoned, control of reporting in US wars:

> A Pentagon culture of increasing press hostility following the Vietnam war gave way to increasing threats to journalists in the 1980s and 1990s, then to active investigation of journalistic processes by the US military in the late 1990s, before leading into the patterns of violent attacks on installations and individuals. (Paterson 2014, p. 18)

He further suggests, 'it is not only governments but many in the media who have come to dispute the concept of military obligation of press protection' (p. 18). Three strands of US military strategy, and by extension new Western military strategy more widely, underpin this new coercive and sometimes deadly threat to journalists: (1) the broad acceptance in Western military circles of a doctrine of silencing the communications of perceived enemies and controlling 'message space' and crucially, says Paterson, this now includes not only where the conflict is taking place but where significant public opinion informing policy goals takes place; (2) the willingness of high-level US government personnel to employ deadly force against civilian journalists in the pursuit of strategic objectives, even when in defiance of international law; and (3) the evolution of a 'force protection' doctrine in the US and allied militaries which countenanced the use of disproportionate force against any perceived threat to military operations or personnel (pp. 150–151).

Paterson's book makes for disturbing reading, documenting as it does the targeting of journalists by US military (see also Knightley 2003, Miller 2003), as well as the sometimes less than robust defence of their targeted journalist colleagues, whether from the US or overseas. He accounts for this in part by a nationalistically inflected and fuzzy sense of journalist objectivity, that seemingly positions some journalists and their less than patriotic reporting within the acceptable borders of the military's killing zone ('If you're not with us, you're against us'). This study, along with the conceptualisation of the 'new Western way of war', signals the changing nature of information war in a global age and here brings its consequences for journalists and media workers, as well as non-combatants, into sharp focus. But there are at least two other forms of warfare that are changing in the context of globalisation and these too pose new threats and risks to today's journalists and media workers.

New wars and failing states

The first of these includes the human insecurity and precarity of life found in failed and failing states – by definition, unruly, uncivil places. These also pose new threats and challenges to reporters seeking to shine a torchlight on the human jeopardy and violence that afflicts such ungoverned, ungovernable spaces. Peter du Toit describes the shift from interstate warfare to the more complex, indistinct and often borderless conflicts that now can result in undisciplined violence and atrocities around the world – unruly, uncivil places that journalists seek to navigate as best they can. Such conflicts, says du Toit, are:

> happening across borders as armed movements seek to dominate territories that are not defined by traditional post-colonial boundaries. Armies loyal to the state clash with rebel forces; government-sponsored militias fight insurgents; armed ethnic and religious groups struggle for dominance and recognition; and criminal cartels engage in turf wars that engulf neighboring communities. Both regular and irregular forces ignore internationally accepted norms governing conventional warfare and civilians fall victim to organized plunder, systematic sexual abuse, and abduction into combat and servitude.
>
> Too often unarmed men, women, and children are the targets of brutal unprovoked acts and journalists find themselves reporting on events so horrific that observers describe them as atrocities. (du Toit n.d., p. 3)

The human insecurity and humanitarian catastrophes that result from new wars in failed and failing states cannot be seen as aberrations only. As Mary Kaldor has argued, their violence is endemic and results in the deliberate targeting of non-combatants, use of systematic terror, and forced expulsions ('ethnic cleansing') (Kaldor 2006, pp. 95–118, see also Ignatieff 1998). They can also be situated and theorised in a global context (Duffield 2001, SIPRI 2004, Kaldor 2006, Ploughshares 2007, Shaw 2013) where their global entanglement 'challenges the distinction between the "internal" and the "external"' (SIPRI 2004, p. 1). Global economic forces, for example, exacerbate processes of state failure and dissolution which in turn can prompt shadow economies, illicit global transactions in minerals and the plundering of natural resources by criminal and terrorist networks (Duffield 2001, 2007, Kaldor 2006, UNEP 2009). Military intervention, under the guise of humanitarian motives ('military humanism'), and humanitarian interests allied to military and state objectives ('humanitarian war'), have also come to characterise Western military force in recent decades (Macrae 2002, Rieff 2002, De Waal 2007, Duffield 2007, Weiss 2007, Barnett and Weiss 2008, Shaw 2013). In such ways, those on the receiving end of intervention become enmeshed within the surrounding regime of global power.

If new wars are characterised by extreme violence targeting non-combatants in contravention of international humanitarian law and universal human rights, those who seek to commit such acts will generally seek to do so out of sight of the world's news cameras (Rwanda, Srebrenica, Aceh, DRC, Darfur). It is for this reason, in part, that the deliberate targeting of journalists and humanitarian workers by insurgents and combatants has increased over recent years, with perpetrators seeking the cloak of invisibility for their inhumane acts, including mass atrocity. It is also worth pausing here to consider how humanitarianism as well as journalism have become caught up in these wider global power plays, further underlining the deep-seated and destructive nature of the trajectories now unfolding around the globe. Humanitarian Outcomes documents 460 aid workers deliberately subjected to violence in 2013 (155 killed, 171 seriously wounded, 134 kidnapped) (Humanitarian Outcomes 2014). The Director of Operations for the UN's Office for the Coordination of Humanitarian Affairs (OCHA), John Ging, sums up well the changed global context of human insecurity confronting humanitarians: 'More and more we're seeing parties to conflicts around the world ignore the rules of war to achieve a political end – directly targeting civilians, carrying out collective punishment, inciting ethnic violence, impeding the delivery of lifesaving humanitarian supplies to affected people and attacking humanitarian actors themselves' (Ging cited in Whiting 2014).

Asymmetric image wars

A third way in which contemporary warfare is changing involves deliberately turning the media spotlight onto the journalists (and humanitarian workers), forcing them to become both spectacle and story. And here, the perpetrators of violent atrocity far from seeking the cloak of media invisibility actively set out to court the world's media by the deliberate staging of morally repugnant acts in front of cameras. In August 2014, the Islamic State of Iraq and Al-Sham (ISIS) captured US journalist James Foley. In a chilling video he was beheaded in the desert in an orange jump suit in front of a camera, images that were subsequently posted to the world via the Internet, though quickly censored by most websites. The video was preceded by the words of a British jihadist extolling the virtues of the Islamic State and challenging both the US and Western governments and their interventionist actions. Over the following two months Steven Sotloff, another US journalist, was also paraded on video by the same group and similarly killed. British aid workers, David Haines, and then later Alan Henning, former taxi driver and volunteer aid worker, and American aid-worker Peter Kassig, followed. Video appeals by friends and families and condemnatory statements by politicians and religious leaders became part of the visual iconography surrounding these staged, choreographed, videoed killings.

In these DIY but increasingly sophisticated 'shock and awe' video productions, the iconic and symbolic become merged in an inhumane spectacle. Such inhuman acts and repugnant images are produced to shock and assault most, though clearly not all, moral sensibilities. They communicate a dreadful message to journalists and media workers, as well as foreign nationals and aid workers. This calculating 'violent symbolism' – staged, choreographed and disseminated around the world via the latest communication technologies – functions as both weapon and tactic in this asymmetric warfare (Cottle 2006). As Michael Ignatieff observes: 'Terrorists have been quick to understand that the camera has the power to frame a single atrocity and turn it into an image that sends shivers down the spine of an entire planet. This gives them a vital new weapon' (Ignatieff 2004, p. 2). This positions Western journalists and others at risk of becoming caught up in someone else's 'image wars'.

In 'image wars', violence and war are enacted and conducted in and through media and communications as well as being communicated and represented by them. To the extent that this deliberate use of media both prompts and shapes the practices of violence, as it most certainly does, this becomes an example of *mediatised conflict* (Cottle 2006, pp. 143–166). In mediatised war and conflicts, then, the involvement of media and communications becomes actively and performatively heightened, becoming implicated in the acts of violence themselves. This now places journalists and media workers alongside others in symbolic and mortal peril. Such violent, inhumane, media productions are constructed in a global context of political and religiously inspired enmity, and often for local-global audiences. They are part of asymmetric warfare. They should not simply be taken, in technologically determinist fashion, as manifestations of the latest new communication technologies, but as expressive of a dangerous global turn in world affairs where journalists as well as humanitarian workers have become perceived by some as working at the behest of Western governments and/or colluding with them. Such barbarities are not confined to distant, faraway, unruly places; they also migrate to Western heartlands whether via hijacked airliners targeting New York or militant jihadists slaughtering journalists en masse in Paris or others in major European cities.

It is in this global context that humanitarian workers as well as journalists find themselves on the receiving end of targeted violence. In such circumstances we see the deliberate production of 'violent symbolism' in contrast to the 'symbolic violence' of aestheticised and emotionally distanced war images in the new Western way of war, or the often hidden and invisible violence of new wars. But in all of them, as we have heard, journalists are now positioned at increased risk and, increasingly, in mortal peril.

Conclusion

In this chapter we have noted the seeming paradox of how it could be that in a time in world history when violence is apparently in decline, increasing numbers of journalists are placed at risk and, unacceptably, many are losing their lives. Attending to Elias's ideas about the historical 'pacification of violence' and growing 'moral repugnance' at violence as well as subsequent studies and debates on the history and historiography of violence, we began to discern how some of these unfolding and accelerating processes of history have increasingly positioned journalists in unruly and uncivil places.

The nature of contemporary globalising society, itself an outcome of multiple preceding and often accelerating historical vortices, has also been addressed where we examined the changed nature of global society and its endemic, enmeshed and increasingly encompassing crises and conflicts. These now produce not only interdependency and often exacerbate inequalities but also generate diverse threats and risks unevenly distributed around the globe. Though these are not confined to contemporary forms of warfare (given the globally enmeshed nature of today's ecological, economic and political interdependency crises), the changing nature of contemporary warfare has variously served to illuminate how and why it is that journalists are often exposed to increased risk. The 'new Western way of war', 'new wars' and 'transnational and mediatized terror' increasingly embroil civilians and non-combatants, which is disturbing enough, but they also often now put journalists at increased risk and – sometimes, deliberately – position them in harm's way.

References

Adorno, T. and Horkheimer, M. (1944/1974) *Dialectic of the Enlightenment.* London: Verso.
Albrow, M. (1996) *The Global Age: State and Society Beyond Modernity.* Cambridge: Polity Press.
Allan, S. (Ed.) (2012) *The Routledge Companion to News and Journalism.* London: Routledge.

Appadurai, A. (1996) *Modernity at Large: Cultural Dimensions of Globalization*. Minneapolis: University of Minnesota Press.

Barnett, M. and Weiss, T. (Eds) (2008) *Humanitarianism in Question: Politics, Power, Ethics*. Ithaca and London: Cornell University Press.

Batchen, G., Gidley, M., Miller, N. and Prosser, J. (Eds) (2012) *Picturing Atrocity: Photography in Crisis*. London: Reaktion Books.

Bauman, Z. (1989) *Modernity and the Holocaust*. Cambridge: Polity.

Bauman, Z. (2004) *Wasted Lives: Modernity and Its Outcasts*. Cambridge: Polity Press.

Bauman, Z. (2007) *Liquid Times*. Cambridge: Polity Press.

Beck, U. (1992) *Risk Society: Towards a New Modernity*. London: Sage.

Beck, U. (1999) *World Risk Society*. Cambridge: Polity Press.

Beck, U. (2006) *Cosmopolitan Vision*. Cambridge: Polity Press.

Beck, U. (2009) *World at Risk*. Cambridge: Polity Press.

Blackburn, R. (2011) The *American Crucible: Slavery, Emancipation and Human Rights*. London: Verso.

Briggs, A. and Burke, P. (2002) *A Social History of the Media*. Cambridge: Polity.

Burri, N. (2015) *Bravery or Bravado? The Protection of News Providers in Armed Conflict*. Brill/Nijhoff.

Calhoun, C. (2004) 'A World of Emergencies: Fear, Intervention, and the Limits of Cosmopolitan Order', *The Canadian Review of Sociology and Anthropology*, 41(4): 373–395.

Carey, P. (Ed.) (1987) *The Faber Book of Reportage*. London: Faber and Faber.

Castells, M. (1996) *The Rise of the Network Society*. Oxford: Blackwell.

Castells, M. (1998) *End of Millennium*. Oxford: Blackwell.

Castells, M. (2009) *Communication Power*. Oxford: Oxford Univesrity Press.

Chouliaraki, L. (2006) *The Spectatorship of Suffering*. London: Sage.

Chouliaraki, L. (2010) 'Ordinary Witnessing in Post-Television News: Towards a New Moral Imagination', *Critical Discourse Studies*, 7(4): 305–319.

Clifford, L. (2015) *Under Threat: The Changing State of Media Safety*. International News Safety Institute. Available from <http://www.newssafety.org/under threat/> (last accessed on 30 June 2015).

Collins, R. (1974) 'Three Faces of Cruelty: Towards a Comparative Sociology of Violence', *Theory and Society*, 1(4): 415–440.

Conboy, M. (2004) *Journalism: A Critical History*. London: Sage.

Cottle, S. (2006) *Mediatized Conflict: Developments in Media and Conflict Studies*. Maidenhead: Open University Press.

Cottle, S. (2009) *Global Crisis Reporting: Journalism in the Global Age*. Maidenhead: Open University Press.

Cottle, S. (2011) 'Taking Global Crises in the News Seriously: Notes From the Dark Side Of Globalization', *Global Media and Communication*, 7(2): 77–95.

Cottle, S. (2013) 'Journalists Witnessing Disasters: From the Calculus of Death to the Injunction to Care', *Journalism Studies*, 14(2): 232–248.

Cottle, S. and Hughes, C. (2015) '"The Responsibility to Protect" and the World's Press: Establishing a New Humanitarian Norm?', pp.76–91 in J. Hoffmann and V. Hawkins (Eds), *Communication for Peace*. Routledge.

Cottle, S. and Evans, K. (forthcoming) '"Massacre of the Innocents": On the Historical Shifts in Sensibility Toward Atrocity', in M. Brown and E. Carrabine (Eds), *The Routledge International Handbook of Visual Criminology*. London: Routledge.

Danchev, A. (2011) *On Art and War and Terror*. Edinburgh: Edinburgh Press.

De Waal, A. (2007) 'No Such Thing as Humanitarian Intervention: Why We Need to Rethink the "Responsibility to Protect" in Wartime', *Harvard International Review*. Available from <http://www.harvardir.org/articles/print. php?article=1482> (last accessed on 21 March 2009).

Duffield, M. (2001) *Global Governance and the New Wars*. London: Zed Books.

Duffield, M. (2007) *Development, Security and Unending War*. Cambridge: Polity Press.

Du Toit, P. (n.d.) *Reporting Atrocity: A Tool Box for Journalists*. Available from <https://internews.org/sites/default/files/resources/Internews_Reporting AtrocitiesToolkit_2014-11.pdf> (last accessed on 12 January 2016).

Elias, N. (1994) *The Civilizing Process*. Oxford: Blackwell.

Ferguson, N. (2003) *Empire: How Britain Made the Modern World*. London: Penguin.

Fiske, A. and Rai, T. (2015) *Virtuous Violence*. Cambridge: Cambridge University Press.

Gat, A. (2013) 'Is War Declining – and Why?', *Journal of Peace Research* 50(2): 149–157.

Giddens, A. (1985) *The Nation State and Violence*. Cambridge: Polity.

Giddens, A. (1990) *The Consequences of Modernity*. Cambridge: Polity Press.

Giddens, A. (1994) *Beyond Left and Right*. Cambridge: Polity Press.

Giddens, A. (2002) *Runaway World*. London: Profile Books.

Gleditsch, N. (2013) 'The Decline of War – The Main Issues', *International Studies Review* 15(3): 397–399.

Grey, J. (2015) 'John Grey: Steven Pinker Is Wrong about Violence and War', *The Guardian*, 13 March 2015. Available from <http://www.theguardian.com/ books/2015/mar/13/john-gray-steven-pinker-wrong-violence-war-declining> (last accesed on 13 March 15).

Goldstein, J. (2011) *Winning the War on War*. New York: Dutton, Penguin Books.

Harari, Y. (2014) *Sapiens: A Brief History*. London: Harvill Secker.

Harvey, D. (1989) *The Condition of Postmodernity*. Oxford: Blackwell.

Harvey, D. (2003) *The New Imperialism*. Oxford: Oxford University Press.

Held, D. (2004) *The Global Covenant*. Cambridge: Polity Press.

Held, D. and McGrew, A. (2003) 'The Great Globalization Debate: An Introduction', in D. Held and A. McGrew (Eds), *The Global Transformations Reader* (pp. 1–50). Cambridge: Polity Press.

Humanitarian Outcomes (2014) *Aid Worker Security Report 2014*. Humanitarian Outcomes. London: Canalot Studios.

Hunt, L. (2007) *Inventing Human Rights*. New York: W.W. Norton and Company.

Iggers, I. (2005) *Historiography in the Twentieth Century: From Scientific Objectivity to the Postmodern Challenge*. Middletown, CT: Wesleyan University Press.

Ignatieff, M. (1998) *The Warrior's Honour: Ethnic War and the Modern Conscience*. London: Chatto and Windus.

Ignatieff, M. (2004, November 20). The Terrorist as Film Director. *The Age*. (Melbourne) p. 2.

International News Safety Institute (2013) *Killing the Messenger*. Brussels: International News Safety Institute.

Ishay, M. (2008) *The History of Human Rights*. Berkeley: University of California Press.

Johnston, D. (2011) *A Brief History of Justice*. London: Wiley-Blackwell.

Kaldor, M. (2006) *New and Old Wars: Organized Violence in a Global Era.* Cambridge: Polity Press.

Kaldor, M. (2007) *Human Security.* Cambridge: Polity Press.

Keane, J. (2004) *Violence and Democracy.* Cambridge: Cambridge University Press.

Keane, J. (2009) *The Life and Death of Democracy.* London: Simon and Schuster.

Knightley, P. (2003) *The First Casualty.* London: André Deutsch.

Krause, K. (2009) 'Beyond Definition: Violence in a Global Perspective', *Global Crime*, 10(4): 337–355.

Laqueur, T. (2011) 'Mourning, Pity, and the Work of Narrative in the Making of "Humanity"', pp. 31–57 in R. Wilson and R. Brown (Eds), *Humanitarianism and Suffering.* Cambridge: Cambridge University Press.

Lester, L. and Cottle, S. (2009) 'Visualizing Climate Change: Television News and Ecological Citizenship' *International Journal of Communication*, 3: 920–936.

Lyotard, J.-F. (1984) *The Postmodern Condition: A Report on Knowledge.* Manchester: Manchester University Press.

Macrae, J. (Ed.) (2002) *The New Humanitarianism: A Review of Trends in Global Humanitarian Action.* HPG Report 11, London: Overseas Development Institute.

Malesevic, S. (2010) *The Sociology of War and Violence.* Cambridge: Cambridge University Press.

Malesevic, S. (2013) 'Forms of Brutality: Towards a Historical Sociology of Violence', *European Journal of Social Theory*, 16(3): 273–291.

Mann, M. (2005) *The Dark Side of Democracy.* Cambridge: Cambridge University Press.

Mann, M. (2012) *The Sources of Social Power. Volume 1: A History of Power from the Beginning to AD 1760.* Cambridge: Cambridge University Press.

Marks, R. (2007) *The Origins of the Modern World.* London: Roman and Littlefield.

Mazlish, B. (2014) *Reflections on the Modern and the Global.* London: Transaction.

Mennell, S. and Goudsblom, J. (Eds) (1998) *Nobert Elias: On Civilization, Power and Knowledge.* Chicago: Chicago University Press.

Miller, D. (Ed.) (2003) *Tell Me Lies: Propaganda and Media Distortion in the Attack on Iraq.* London: Pluto.

Morris, I. (2014) *War: What is it Good For?* London: Profile Books.

Muchembled, R. (2012) *A History of Violence: From the End of the Middle Ages to the Present.* London: Polity Press.

Murrell, C. (2010) 'Baghdad Bureaux: An Exploration of the Inter-connected World of Fixers and Correspondents at the BBC and CNN', *Media, War and Conflict*, 3(2): 125–137.

Murrell, C. (2015) *Foreign Correspondents and International Newsgathering: The Role of Fixers.* Routledge: New York and London.

Nussbaum, M. (2014) *Political Emotions: Why Love Matters for Justice.* London: Belknap Harvard.

Pagden, A. (2013) *The Enlightenment: And Why It Still Matters.* Oxford: Oxford University Press.

Paterson, C. (2014) *War Reporters Under Threat: The United States and Media Freedom.* London: Pluto Press.

Pedelty, M. (1995) *War Correspondents.* London: Routledge.

Popper, K. (1957/1980) *The Poverty of Historicism.* London: Routledge and Kegan Paul.

Perlmutter, D. (1999) *Visions of War.* New York: St. Martin's Griffin.

Pinker, S. (2011) *The Better Angels of Our Nature*. London: Penguin.

Ploughshares (2007) *Armed Conflict Report 2007 Summary*. Ontario: Project Ploughshares.

Reicher, S., Haslam, S. and Rath, R. (2008) 'Making a Virtue of Evil: A Five-Step Social Identity Model of Collective Hate', *Psychology Compass*, 2(3): 1313–1344.

Rieff, D. (2002) *A Bed for the Night: Humanitarianism in Crisis*. London: Vintage.

Rifkin, J. (2009) *The Empathic Civilization*. Cambridge: Polity.

Ritzer, G. (Ed.) (2007) *The Blackwell Companion to Globalization*. Oxford: Blackwell Publishing.

Robertson, G. (2012) *Crimes Against Humanity*. London: Penguin.

Robertson, R. (1992) 'Mapping the Global Condition: Globalization as the Central Concept', pp. 15–30 in M. Featherstone (Ed.), *Global Culture*. London: Sage.

Sambrook, R. (2010) *Are Foreign Correspondents Redundant?* Oxford: Reuters Institute for Journalism.

Shaw, M. (1996) *Civil Society and Media in Global Crises*. London: St Martin's Press.

Shaw, M. (2005) *The New Western Way of War: Risk-Transfer War and its Crisis in Iraq*. Cambridge: Polity.

Shaw, M. (2013) *Genocide and International Relations*. Cambridge: Cambridge University Press.

Simms, B. and Trim, D. (Eds) (2011) *Humanitarian Intervention: A History*. Cambridge: Cambridge University Press.

Singer, P. (2011) *The Expanding Circle*. Princeton, NJ: Princeton Press.

Spierenburg, M. (2013) *Violence and Punishment: Civilizing the Body Through Time*. Cambridge: Polity.

Stockholm International Peace Research Institute (SIPRI). (2004). *SIPRI Yearbook 2004: Armaments, Disarmament and International Security*. Oxford: Oxford University Press.

Stockholm International Peace Research Institute (SIPRI) (2013) *SIPRI Yearbook 2013: Armaments, Disarmament and International Security*. Oxford: Oxford University Press.

Tait, S. (2011) 'Bearing Witness, Journalism and Moral Responsibility', *Media, Culture & Society*, 33(8): 1220–1235.

Taylor, J. (1998) *Body Horror: Photojournalism, Catastrophe and War*. Manchester: Manchester University Press.

Taylor, P.M. (1995) *Munitions of the Mind: A History of Propaganda from the Ancient World to the Present Day*. Manchester: Manchester University Press.

Thompson, J. (1995) *The Media and Modernity*. Cambridge: Polity.

Tilly, C. (1990) *Coercion, Capital, and European States, AD 990–1990*. Cambridge: Blackwell.

Totten, S. and Parsons, W. (Eds) (2013) *Centuries of Genocide: Essays and Eye Witness Accounts*. London: Routledge.

Tumber, H. and Webster, F. (2006) *Journalists Under Fire: Information War and Journalistic Practices*. London: Sage.

United Nations Environmental Programme (UNEP) (2009) *From Conflict to Peacebuilding: The Role of Natural Resources and the Environment*. New York: UNEP.

Urry, J. (2003) *Global Complexity*. Cambridge: Polity Press.

Waters, M. (2001) *Globalization* (2nd edn). London: Routledge.

Weber, M. (1968) *Economy and Society.* New York: Bedminster Press.

Weiss, T. (2007) *Humanitarian Intervention.* Cambridge: Polity Press.

Whiting, A. (2014) 'Attacks on Aid Workers Worldwide Hit Worst Levels on Record'. Reuters. Available from <http://uk.reuters.com/article/2014/08/19/uk-foundation-aid-attacks-idUKKBN0GJ05820140819> (last accessed on 19 August 2014).

Wilson, R. and Brown, R. (Eds) (2009) *Humanitarianism and Suffering: The Mobilization of Empathy.* Cambridge: Cambridge University Press.

5
Journalism and the Civil Sphere

Simon Cottle

Today a number of global trends and endemic conflicts position journalists in harm's way. This includes, as we have heard across preceding
chapters, when reporting on repressive and warring states, criminal
gangs and warlords, venal corporations and transnational terrorists – all
of whom can violently disregard human rights and deliberately waste
human lives. Though globally enmeshed conflicts and crises are not
confined to the sharp-end of killing characterised in the new Western
way of war, the particularly brutal forms of ethnic and gender-based
violence associated with new wars, or new forms of mediatised transnational terror, our preceding discussion in Chapter 4 has served to
highlight how global trends increasingly position not only civilians and
non-combatants at risk, but also journalists.

Journalism and journalists navigate their way through these proliferating crises and conflicts as they can and, as we indicated in Chapter 4,
there are a number of deep-seated historical trends that compel them to
do so. This chapter now sets out to situate how journalism variously gives
expression to these wider historical trends and shifts in human sensibility, and how, in globalising times, this can serve to progressively 'expand
the human circle', incorporating others positioned in jeopardy who
deserve and now rightly demand wider recognition and world response.
As such, this is a departure from the principal theoretical frameworks
usually entertained when seeking to critically engage with contemporary journalism, its production, practices and performance – whether
political economy, the sociology of news organisations and practices,
or cultural-studies approaches to journalism's texts, representations and
dominant discourses (for reviews see Cottle 2003, 2006, Schudson 2011).

We have heard already Chris Paterson's (2014) detailed and critical
account of the workings of contemporary US journalism informed, for

example, by a political economy reading that privileges the political culture of US media, its connection to US elites as well as its underpinning economic interests in world affairs . By this means he arrives at a pessimistic account of US journalism performance when reporting on the deadly 'friendly threat' posed by its own military. Paterson's study theoretically acknowledges Herman and Chomsky's *Manufacturing Consent* (1988) with its 'propaganda model' rooted in the tradition of political economy. But he also offers insights into how the professional codes of journalism and a widespread subscription to norms of 'objectivity' become fuzzy in times of national conflict, and how this may, inadvertently, open the way to US journalism becoming complicit with or uncaring about the targeting of journalists perceived by their colleagues to be 'not on side'. These latter insights are more theoretically indebted to the established literature on the sociology of news organisation and production and how journalism culture and norms inform journalist practices.

The point here, therefore, is that available theoretical frameworks most certainly can and do help to make sense of journalism performance and practices, but their sights are often fixed on a relatively short time span, and they thereby overlook the considerably longer-term historical trajectories at play in journalism's communicative aims and professional and civil commitments. If we are to better understand the motivations of journalists and the mobilisation of journalism as a distinctive, communicative and collective enterprise, one that is capable of both reporting on and recognising the human plight of others in unruly and uncivil places, it is important to understand how journalism is also caught up in the vortices of history. And it is this, as well as the political economics of the marketplace, the sociology of news organisations and the contending discourses of propaganda and power, that helps to historically ground and better account for the assignment of journalists who knowingly place themselves in perilous conditions.

Going deeper: journalism in the vortices of history

To understand how and why journalism has increasingly sought to document, depict, report and bear witness to human injustices and violence perpetrated in unruly and uncivil places, we need to situate the emergence and development of journalism in relation to deep-seated historical antecedents and continuing influences based within civil society. This includes the growing historical recognition of distant others as not so different from ourselves. This 'expanding human circle'

(Ignatieff 1998, Rifkin 2009, Singer 2011, Nussbaum 2014) can be traced in respect of a number of underlying historical processes, some reaching far back in human society (Harai 2014). The rise of the first axial age (monotheistic, universalising) religions in the middle centuries of the first millennium BC, for example, has been seen as pivotal in helping to open up a religio-normative space for critique and social challenge:

> In the first millennium BCE, theoretic culture emerges in several places in the old world, questioning the old narratives as it recognizes them and their mimetic bases, rejecting ritual and myth as it creates new rituals and myths, and calling the old hierarchies into question in the name of ethical and spiritual universalism. The cultural effervescence of this period led to new developments in religion and ethics but also in the understanding of the natural world, the origins of science. For these reasons we call this period axial. (Bellah 2011, p. xix)

The development of monotheistic, universalising religions, in other words, opened up a religio-ethical space for criticism and critique that could, potentially, be developed through time and directed at the hierarchies of power and structures of dominance (see also Armstrong 2015). This theoretic, communicative disposition developed upon earlier forms of communication that had evolved in the Paleolithic age, adding to earlier mimetic (gestural) and later ritual modes of sociability and collective life (Bellah 2011, Bellah and Joas 2012).

The origins and formalisation of justice and law, both on and off the battlefield (Walzer 2006, Johnston 2011, Robertson 2012, Crowe 2014), have also contributed to historically evolving views on what can be perceived and experienced as fair, equitable and ethical. These views have been based on deep-seated moral values and normative expectations (Singer 2011), which is not to suggest that in their historical origins they were not principally also about vengeance and the recognition of hierarchical power (Bahrani 2008, Johnston 2011). But through time and evolving conceptions of justice, such ideas and sentiments came to fuel social critique and support projects for change (Alexander 2006).

The expansion of city states, trade and the 'gentle hand' of commerce (Gellner 1990, Mann 2012) has further served to encourage social intercourse across different communities and geographically dispersed groups, contributing to associational relationships based not on mistrust or traditional enmities but shared interests and common recognition – which is not to suggest, of course, that competitive rivalries and the marketplace cannot also underpin new forms of conflict or even war.

State formation, war and the (internal) pacification of violence from the Middle Ages to the present within the West, and in countries and cultures beyond (Giddens 1985, Elias 1994, Goldstein 2011, Pinker 2012, Morris 2014), as we have heard, have contributed to a growing sense of moral repugnance at naked, brutal violence in public spaces, and, increasingly, these have also encroached upon the private sphere.

The recent wave of moral revulsion expressed around the world to the 'barbarous' executions by the so-called Islamic State (ISIS), and advanced by prominent politicians, publics and journalists, is testimony to the contemporary hold of a generalising (though clearly not yet universal) sense of moral and emotional repugnance that perceives such violent acts as something that should have been relegated to medieval, pre-Enlightenment history.

The Enlightenment – both of science and, importantly though somewhat neglected, the philosophy of sentiments and sympathy (Rifkin 2009, Pagden 2013, Mazlish 2014) – has also left its indelible mark on Western consciousness, and through processes of colonisation, capitalist accumulation and cultural synthesis, possibly human sensibility more globally. This more empathic consciousness becomes progressively encoded within and normatively elaborated across different cultural forms and representations, as in depictions of acts of inhumanity and human suffering found in: Western art throughout its history (Hughes 2003, Danchev 2011, Brandon 2007, Cottle and Evans 2015); the rise of the novel (Hunt 2007); photography (Linfield 2010, Borer 2012 Kennedy and Patrick 2014); and film, documentary, video and journalism (Perlmutter 1999, Willis 2003, Allan 2006, 2015, Laquer 2011, Cottle 2014, Cottle and Cooper 2015, Cottle and Hughes 2015). According to Anthony Pagden (2013), the Enlightenment served to move people's thinking and practices from Thomas Hobbes's *Leviathan* and the 'war of all, against all' to the moral-sense philosophers of sentiment and sympathy, who marked a fundamental shift in social and political consciousness. It was David Hume who famously argued in *A Treatise of Human Nature* (1739), 'No quality of human nature is more remarkable than that propensity we have to sympathize with others, and to receive by communication their inclinations and sentiments however different from, or even contrary to, our own' (Book II, Part I, Section XI). This Enlightenment standpoint continues to resonate in contemporary positions of humanitarianism and ideas of cosmopolitanism today:

The shift from 'selfishness' to 'sentiment,' from the calculation of interests to the awareness that all humans were bound together by bonds of mutual recognition, became the basis on which a new conception of the social and political order of the entire world would eventually be based. For the truly enlightened person, he or she who lived according to the new specification of the laws of nature, who could be moved imaginatively by the 'fates of states, provinces, or many individuals', could not be anything other than cosmopolitan. (Pagden 2013, p. 78)

The advances of humanitarianism and, more recently, human rights have also informed contemporary Western cultures and societies and now do so normatively as well as institutionally and legally (Hunt 2007, Tilly 2007, Ishay 2008, Keane 2009, Rifkin 2009, Robertson 2012). Increased recognition of distant others as not so dissimilar to ourselves, and their perception through an increasingly empathic and compassionate lens (Rifkin 2009), suggest therefore that contemporary trends in humanitarianism and increasingly empathy-filled journalism have long historical antecedents. Moreover, these are considerably more deeply embedded within the ebb and flow of human societies than any easy idea of technological or communications determinism can accommodate (Wilson 1998). That said, the expansiveness and reach of modern communication systems can surely not be underestimated in 'bringing home', both figuratively and literally, the human plight of others from around the globe (Robertson 1992). Human beings have historically become depicted – and, for many, discerned – increasingly less as strangers and foreign, exotic and Other, and more as not so different to ourselves, and, in such terms, can therefore become seen as deserving of both our recognition and, sometimes, response (Ignatieff 1998, Chouliaraki 2006, 2010, Cohen 2006, Orgad 2012, Cottle and Cooper 2015). Michael Ignatieff puts it well when considering broadcasting:

Through its news broadcasts and spectaculars like 'Live Aid,' television has become the privileged medium through which moral relations between strangers are mediated in the modern world. ... television has contributed to the breakdown of the barriers of citizenship, religion, race, and geography that once divided our moral space into those we were responsible for and those who were beyond our ken. (Ignatieff 1998, pp. 11–12)

But Ignatieff is also reluctant to posit a simple media causality accounting for the increased recognition of, and possible sense of obligation to, others in faraway places. The expanding human circle has also to be premised, he suggests, on an underpinning civil society predisposed to recognise and to care:

> [T]elevision images cannot assert anything; they can only instantiate something. Images of human suffering do not assert their own meaning; they can only instantiate a moral claim if those who watch understand themselves to be potentially under obligation to those they see. (Ignatieff 1998, pp. 11–12)

In a world of exponentially increasing global communications, a number of authors have begun to discern the progressive possibilities associated with such communication flows, and how this affects relations of power:

> Today, many of the good ideas of globalisation are taking root. Computers and digital media store unlimited quantities of images and texts, insuring that a ready stock of cultural information is always available. As part of the process, the world's political, economic, military, religious, and cultural elite must be able to stand up to the disinfecting sunlight of transparency and the discerning court of global public opinion. Acts of cultural intolerance, oppression, and abuse are becoming increasingly plain for everyone to see and repudiate. (Lull 2007, p. 149)

Such views on the power of contemporary media or, more precisely, the power of progressive forces rooted in democratising and transnationalising civil society to inform and mobilise such communication flows are now on the academic agenda (see, for example, Thompson 1995, McNair 2006, 2015, Silverstone 2007, Cottle 2011, Lule 2012) and, in large measure, it is the practices and performance of contemporary journalism around the world that has helped put them there.

Journalism and the politics of recognition

Journalism, it can be said, along with other media such as photography (Sontag 1979, 2003, Linfield 2010) and video and film, as well as citizen journalism (Torchin 2012, Allan 2013, Thorsen and Allan 2014), have all entered increasingly into the politics of recognition. That is to say, journalism has helped to grant identities to images in the wider force field of politics where not only material redistribution of goods and services but also the collective pursuit of identity recognition by the wider culture and society become essential for group well-being and collective advance. Journalism has even proved on occasion capable of taking the position of the 'Other', recognising differences and championing social causes based on perceived injustices and the hurt suffered by denigrated and marginalised social groups (Cottle 2004, 2006, pp. 167–184). This, again, is not to suggest that journalism has not in the past or continues in the present to contribute to those very processes of Othering that some journalists now feel obligated to question, doing so through crafted, experiential and humanly sympathetic forms of reporting and analysis. But it *is* to say that journalism can and sometimes does perform roles and responsibilities that, inevitably, are both expressive and constitutive of wider and changing civil society.

Journalism also contributes to what John Keane distinguishes as today's 'monitory democracy', namely, an evolving, communications-based form of democratic practice that can be differentiated from earlier historical waves of 'assembly' and later 'representative' democracy (Keane 2009). Monitory democracy, he argues:

> is a 'post-Westminster' form of democracy in which power-monitoring and power-controlling devices have begun to extend sideways and downwards through the whole political order. They penetrate the corridors of government and occupy the nooks and crannies of civil society, and in so doing they greatly complicate, and sometimes wrong-foot, the lives of politicians, parties, legislatures and governments. (Keane 2009, p. xxvii)

In today's 'message-saturated democracies', Keane suggests, people are encouraged to be suspicious of unaccountable power and 'citizens are tempted to think for themselves', and 'to see the world in different ways' and 'sharpen their overall sense that prevailing power relationships are not natural', they are 'contingent' (Keane 2009, p. 747). Keane positions his major disquisition on the remarkable advances of democracy around the world and the growth of 'monitory democracy' post-1945 in large part on media and communications and, specifically, todays 'communicative abundance'. It is this, in combination with 'monitoring' human-rights organisations and an expansive culture of humanitarianism now institutionalised in the established and growing field of non-governmental organisations and international frameworks of law, that prompts journalism and journalists to recognise not only an expanding human circle of former others but also their own responsibility to report. And this in a period when, for the first time in human history, the UN falteringly moves towards the enactment of principles of the 'responsibility to protect', requiring signatory states since 2005 to honour their commitment to protect civilian populations from the four atrocity crimes: war crimes, crimes against humanity, ethnic cleansing, and genocide (Evans 2008).

Again, it is important to be clear. Symbolic annihilation, demeaning stereotypes and outright denigration certainly continue to be found in some forms of journalism and are encoded into their representations of minorities and victim groups (Cottle 2000, Thompson 2007). And where this is so, this undermines group claims for public recognition and social acceptance or, worse, creates a climate in which deep-seated fears, enmities and hatreds can flourish (Taylor 1994, Benhabib 2002, Frazer and Honneth 2003). In such ways, the 'expanding human circle' is fractured and stunted in its historical trajectory of increased interdependency and widening circumference of recognition. Nonetheless, there is evidence enough to suggest that mainstream media and journalism can and sometimes do produce public representations that give identity to image, voice to the voiceless, and that these play an important part in the symbolic rehabilitation and recognition of former Others – whether, for example, racialised minorities, asylum seekers, aboriginal people or the victims of famine, war and atrocity (Bell 1998, Cottle 2004, 2006, 2009, 2013, 2014, Matheson and Allan 2009, Berglez 2013). These more progressive forms of mainstream journalism, too often over-looked in the critical default positions of much research, play a performative part in today's politics of recognition and they do so through journalism's powerful communicative modes of display and deliberation, both affective and analytic, expressive and expository, image-based and ideational (Cottle 2004, Cottle and Rai 2006, Fink and Schudson 2014).

Journalism bearing witness

Current scholarship on mediated bearing witness also helps to focus claims about journalism's mobilisation and motivations in respect of reporting on the plight of others in unruly and uncivil places, as well as the generalising disposition to recognise victims and survivors of war, disasters and catastrophes as deserving or, rightly, demanding, recognition and response. Scholars have usefully drawn attention to the historical etymology of 'bearing witness' with its origins in law, theology and atrocity – origins that endow current ideas of witnessing with 'extraordinary moral and cultural force' (Peters 2011, p. 708). Ideas of bearing witness clearly have evolved historically, but in the field of modern journalism and international reporting they have also become powerfully associated with the reporting of some of the major conflicts and human disasters across the twentieth century (Taylor 1998, Leith 2004, Sambrook 2010, Tait 2011).

Bearing witness and its media enactment are clearly important dimensions of the work of journalists in crisis and conflict reporting, and may even contribute to the 'democratization of responsibility' (Thompson 1995: 263), though it can thereby also put them at increased risk if this same reporting can subsequently be put to work as evidence when prosecuting perpetrators through the International Criminal Court (ICC) in The Hague. Recent research based on the accounts and reporting performance of disaster correspondents, for example, finds a deep ambivalence in the contemporary journalism field (Cottle 2013). This alternates, sometimes uneasily, between an institutionalised indifference encoded in the professional journalist's 'calculus of death' where national interests, cultural proximity and total death figures generate increased news value of some disasters around the globe, but not others, on the one hand; and an 'injunction to care' on the other, where the latter is performatively crafted and enacted in and through news narrative and potent visuals that deliberately encourage audiences to vicariously see, hear, touch, smell, feel, know and understand, and then, possibly, react or even respond (Cottle 2013).

Journalism and the civil sphere

A particularly persuasive theoretical lens for better appreciating the contribution of journalism within civil societies and its contribution to 'the civil sphere' and expanding human circle, we think, is provided by Jeffrey Alexander in his magnum opus of the same name (2006). This offers an unusual and penetrating optic on how justice and democracy can be sustained in complex societies and how solidarity becomes enacted in and through the 'civil sphere'. It also helps to open up a new way of seeing journalism:

> The premise of Civil Sphere is that societies are not governed by power alone and not fuelled only by the pursuit of self-interest. Feelings for others matter, and they are structured by the boundaries of solidarity. How solidarity is structured, how far it extends, what it's composed of – these are the critical issues for every social order, and especially for orders that aim at the good life. Solidarity is possible because people are oriented not only to the here and now but to the

ideal, to the transcendent, to what they hope will be the everlasting. (Alexander 2006, p. 3)

In contradistinction to Jürgen Habermas's public sphere theory, with its emphasis upon public-opinion formation though information exchange and rational deliberation, Alexander grants processes of symbolic recognition, collective identity and affect their cultural and political due. It is how people feel and understand, and how, invariably, they do so on a basis of shared sentiments of justice, fairness and what is right, he argues, that warrant increased recognition in communication processes allied to political struggles for change. This informs people's desire and capacity to realise the 'good society' for themselves and, importantly, for others. The civil sphere overlaps with other spheres – politics and economy – and like them takes place in and through various institutions but, importantly, it also exerts its own relative autonomy.

Alexander's argument is based on three competing conceptualisations of civil society. *Civil Society I* is identified with the liberal and communitarian tradition of political thought. This includes ideas from the late seventeenth century – and in particular the post-Hobbesian ideas of John Locke and James Harrington, followed by the Scottish moralists Adam Ferguson and Adam Smith, as well as Rousseau's *Social Contract*, Hegel's *Philosophy of Right* and de Tocqueville's *Democracy in America*. Such ideas, argues Alexander, have focused on civil society in terms of the plurality of institutions outside the state, voluntary associations and individualist behaviour in the marketplace, and all conceived with an ethical and moral force. *Civil Society II*, in contrast, is principally associated with the encompassing critique of both liberal and communitarian ideas of civil society and is most forcefully articulated in the writings of Marx. Here, market capitalism colonises 'civil society', which becomes simply a legitimating mantle for social relations organised in egotistical and competitive terms and producing inequality and class conflict. This critique has contributed, he suggests, to the theoretical displacement and under-recognition of the earlier normative, ethical basis of civil society as well as the possibility of a civil sphere organised not entirely by egotistical, sectional and instrumental interests. It is on this basis that he differentiates his third view of *Civil Society III*, in the following terms:

> We need to understand civil society as a sphere that can be analytically independent, empirically differentiated and morally more universalistic vis-à-vis the state and market and for other social spheres as well. ... I would like to suggest that civil society should be conceived

as a solidary sphere, in which a certain kind of universalizing community comes to be culturally defined and to some degree institutionally enforced. To the degree that this solidary community exists, it is exhibited and sustained by public opinion, deep cultural codes, distinctive organizations – legal, journalistic and associational – and such historically specific interactional practices as civility, criticism, and mutual respect. Such a civil community can never exist as such; it can only be sustained to one degree or another. It is always limited by, and interpenetrated with, the boundary relations of other, non-civil spheres. (p. 31)

Alexander's proposed view of the civil sphere provides, then, a positive, appreciative view on how civil society can reinforce and repair a sense of solidarity through its appeal to and invocation of shared outlooks and normative horizons. This, says Alexander, necessarily invokes deep-seated cultural binaries, whether those of justice/injustice, liberty/ domination, equality/hierarchy or democracy/totalitarianism. Social movements are obliged to rhetorically and imagistically cloak themselves in the legitimising values, sentiments and symbols rooted in the normative outlooks and moral horizons of the civil sphere, he suggests; it is how they secure wider acceptance for their moral claims to recognition as well as political calls for change. In such fields of contention, both the discharge of moral pollution and moral approbation can play a potent cultural role in the realisation or thwarting of political goals. There is no automatic or progressive outcome. As Alexander is careful to note: 'The discourse of civil society can be as repressive as liberating, legitimating not only inclusion but exclusion' (2006, p. 4).

Through its harnessing of deep-seated cultural beliefs and values, journalism can grant the civil sphere a form of power that can be mobilised in the furtherance of projects for change – whether the American civil rights movement, the struggle for women's rights, the deposition of a corrupt US president, enhanced governmental responsibility for disasters and other 'mediatized public crises' or the Egyptian revolution in the 'Arab Spring' (Alexander and Jacobs 1998, Alexander 2006, 2011, Alexander and Giesen 2012). Journalism, as we have heard, potentially and sometimes actually does perform an important part in instantiating these and other collective projects for change, and it can do so through its enactment of the civil sphere.

This formulation of the civil sphere, rooted as it is in the 'strong program of cultural sociology' and neo-Durkheimian thought (Alexander 2007) has not gone unchallenged. Critics have pointed to its failure to take proper cognisance of the structural position of the contemporary mass media and its determination by the forces of political economy including corporate ownership, market competition and advertiser pressures as well as subservience to profit-maximisation and the demands of consumer culture (Popp 2015).

From this theoretical vantage point, mass media, and journalism is no exception, are apt to be conceived as 'cultural industries' rather than organs of the 'civil sphere', as producers of entertainment and propaganda (Herman and Chomsky 1988), not as constitutive of benevolent solidarities. The theory of the civil sphere has also been criticised for its failure to fully engage with the strategic and instrumental action of powerful sources in the representation of public issues, whether theorised in terms of elite indexing (Hallin 1986, Bennett 1990, Bennett et al. 2007), field theory (Bourdieu 1993) or Gramscian ideas of hegemony (Nerone 2015, Nord 2015). Elite performances displaying civic virtue within the media furthermore can sometimes be disingenuous public performances, cynically designed to deceive and manipulate while holding on to the reigns of power.

Though Alexander's social-theoretical approach can certainly be read as a little neglectful of the established traditions and theories of media and journalism scholarship, it furnishes nonetheless its own empirical and theoretical warrants for its more appreciative view of the civil sphere and journalism's performance and potential within this (Bedingfield 2015, Forde 2015). It productively reminds us of how journalism can prove central in the public elaboration and enactments of modern society's myriad contentions and power plays, and it certainly grants considerably more weight to the symbolic, dramaturgical and affective dimensions of communication than Jürgen Habermas's influential but overly rationalistic conceptualisation of the public sphere (Habermas 1974, 1996). Furthermore, it encourages us to see and to take seriously journalism's potential and performance in the reaffirmation of widely held cultural beliefs and values, and how these can become mobilised for the repair of the social fabric when torn by collective injustices. Journalists, we are reminded, can and actually do sometimes perform a vital role in shining light on some of the darkest crevices of inhumanity.

Alexander's conceptualisation of the civil sphere, then, provides an eloquent and we think necessary intervention into a field of scholarship whose default position is too often only to see journalism and journalists through a critical prism of professional deficiencies, representational distortions, marketplace determinations and dominant cultural codes and discourses. It has tremendous relevance for helping us to think through the roles and commitments of journalists reporting from unruly, uncivil places. It could, however, be more firmly positioned on a stronger historical foundation in respect of those longer-term societal trajectories already alluded to, trajectories that inform the contemporary civil sphere – individualism, democracy, empathy, humanitarianism, human rights, and globalised threats and human insecurity. The reliance upon universal cultural binaries as the motivating and mobilising force of progressive social change may also read as a little historically thin, and short-circuits how such binaries have themselves become historically forged and constituted.

Today, as we have heard above, it is crucial to recognise the increasingly global reach of an expansive 'civil sphere' that reflexively extends beyond the normative boundaries of a particular nation state or homogenised view of society (Lull 2007, Cottle and Lester 2011). As with debates about the 'postnational' and emergence of a 'transnational public sphere' (Frazer 2007), so too do we need to entertain the prospect of an emergent and potentially deepening 'civil sphere' premised on historically fermented and forged outlooks and moral horizons. This now includes ideas and sensibilities of humanitarianism, human rights, human security and an increasingly ecological recognition of today's global 'civilizational community of fate' (Beck 2006: 7). Together, then, two further ways are indicated in which ideas of the civil sphere and its enactment within contemporary journalism can be deepened and expanded if we are to better appreciate the contemporary roles and professionally enacted responsibilities of journalism and journalists when reporting on uncivil and unruly places.

Ideas of the civil sphere need to be premised on a deeper sense of the multiple, complex and sometimes contradictory trajectories of human society unfolding into the present as well as the incursions of the global into national daily life, of how the crises and conflicts of globalisation increasingly enmesh and threaten us all, demanding solidarities of recognition and response. It is in these two fundamental respects of the historical and the global that we are able to better understand the global crises and challenges that now confront journalists when reporting from unruly and dangerous places; and understand also why, historically, journalists are now increasingly prepared to put themselves in precarious and life-threatening places around the globe.

Towards understanding journalists in peril

We have sought to better contextualise and understand why it is that more and more journalists are confronting perilous reporting assignments today, and why so many are losing their lives or becoming subject to threats and intimidation around the globe (Clifford 2015). These are disturbing trends documented and discussed throughout this book, and in this chapter as well as in Chapter 5 we have converged on this simple, disturbing question seeking to provide contextualisation and explanation.

In this discussion we have sought to situate the constitutive nature of contemporary journalism within the considerably longer-term historical trends in the evolution of human society, and have granted communications an expressive role in respect of these wider shifts in sensibility and struggles for change. Here, the centrality of journalism to the enactment of the 'civil sphere', after Alexander (2006), was noted, and this was nudged in respect of its theorisation of the civil sphere so as to grant greater attention to (1) its depth historical antecedents, and (2) its extension beyond national parameters to incorporate today's globalised world of risks and threats. Only from this twin vantage point of history and the global are we in a better position to discern not only the changing nature of violence and precarity in the contemporary world, but also the increased propensity of journalism and journalists to report this world and which thereby positions many in perilous conditions and some in mortal jeopardy.

To bring this discussion to a close it is useful to think a little more about current world trajectories and their significance for a depth-historical approach to journalism's contemporary practices and reporting commitments within the globalising present. And here the thoughts of four theorists, each of whom has informed the discussion above, have something important to say in respect of questions of globalisation, empathy, democracy and world risk society. The historian Bruce Mazlish invites us to revisit the ideas of Nobert Elias and consider their relevance from the vantage point of today's globalised world. He asks:

> Can Norbert Elias's seminal work on the civilizing process be usefully applied in regard to globalization? As he argued, violence brought larger and larger social and political units into existence, and these units enforced peace and civility among their population. Will the final unity be that of a globalized humanity? If so, would this be the result of a cataclysmic conflict threatening to end all of civilization? Or can international institutions and mechanisms be established to bring about this final unity, a globalized humanity? (Mazlish 2014, pp. 85–86)

Jeremy Rifkin, in parallel terms, also poses the fundamental dilemma of contemporary world society and does so in terms of the race to global empathic consciousness premised on the expanding human circle and world communications – processes that can be traced across millennia. He observes:

> The irony is that just as we are beginning to glimpse the prospect of global empathic consciousness we find ourselves close to our own extinction. We rushed to universalize empathy in the last half of the twentieth century. In the aftermath of the Holocaust in World War II, humanity said 'never again.' We extended empathy to large numbers of our fellow human beings previously considered to be less than human – including women, homosexuals, the disabled, people of colour, and ethnic and religious minorities – and encoded our sensitivity in the form of social rights and policies, human rights laws, and now even statutes to protect animals. We are in the long end game of including 'the other,' 'the alien', 'the unrecognized.' (Rifkin 2009, pp. 25–26)

Notwithstanding these considerable advances in the politics of recognition, Rifkin is also acutely aware that 'traditional xenophobic biases and prejudices continue to be the norm' and the 'early light of global empathic consciousness is dimmed by the growing recognition that it may come too late to address the spectre of climate change and the possible extinction of the human species' (Rifkin 2009, p. 26).

John Keane, for his part, reflects on the history of democracy, including its contemporary democratic deepening under conditions of communicative abundance and the flourishing of civil-society networks, and invites us to consider:

> Will the world witness a flourishing cross-border journalism and culture of public debate, even the expansion of a global civil society – the growth of worldwide networks of journalists, experts, elected and unelected representatives and politically unaffiliated activists skilled at articulating local injustices, taming markets, educating public opinion, mounting actions when necessary, acting as a general watchdog of democratic life on a global scale? (Keane 2009, p. 869)

And finally, we must return to the powerful social-theoretical gaze of Ulrich Beck who regards World Risk Society as the culmination of the forces of late modernity, premised not only on the rapacious industrialism of 'first modernity' and the production of consumer 'goods', but also the decidedly more risk-laden, potentially catastrophic, production of ecological 'bads' by 'second modernity'. The risks of manufactured uncertainty, as well as terroristic manufactured insecurities, argues Beck, pose a fundamental question to our 'civilizational community of fate'. Will World Society be able to recognise itself within these processes of 'enforced enlightenment'? Only then will it be able to commit to the forms of transnational cooperation required for catastrophe to be averted. The endemic problems of global interdependency, he says, will increasingly make themselves apparent in the race for planetary survival, and here a new cosmopolitan realism becomes essential for survival (Beck 2006).

These, then, are fundamental questions for our time, concerning: globalisation and the pacification of violence; the race to global consciousness and empathic recognition of humanity as a whole; communicative democracy and democratic deepening around the world; and the profound risks and potentially catastrophic threats posed by the dark side of globalisation. They have yet to be widely recognised and addressed. Together, they point to some of the most profound challenges confronting humanity and its planetary environment, processes that can all too easily spill over into enmity and violence as much as cooperation and cosmopolitanism. Resource depletion, unsustainable environments, world population movements and contemporary geopolitical inequalities, to name but a few, are all set to continue to produce unruly and uncivil places in the future. And here new forms of conflict and violence will exacerbate the precarity of life for many on the planet.

Under such conditions of global precarity, journalism and journalists will no doubt feel obligated to report on and from such hazardous environments and killing zones, and they will do so in the conext of the historical trajectories already alluded to. When reporting on deadly conflicts and crises spawned by our globalised and economically riven planet, so too are journalists positioned to help constitute a 'civil sphere', premised on evolving ideas of justice, human rights, human security and normative ideas about how human society could and should be. It is in this globalised context of precarity, human insecurity and violent conflicts that growing numbers of journalists will feel themselves historically compelled to report on the plight of others around the world. Many will thereby also become subject to those same forces of threat and destruction that they seek to expose to wider world attention. It is incumbent upon us all, we think, to try and minimise such threats and dangers wherever and however we can (see Chapters 8 and 9). Journalism's constitutive role in the civil sphere and its potential in alerting threats to people's life chances, and indeed the very possibility of life itself, will prove crucial in the years ahead. The responsibility to report, as much as the fledgling responsibility to protect, applies not only to journalists but all of us who would inhabit the civil sphere of human society.

References

Alexander, J. (2006) *The Civil Sphere*. Oxford: Oxford University Press.
Alexander, J. (2007) *The Meanings of Social Life: A Cultural Sociology*. Oxford: Oxford University Press.
Alexander, J. (2011) *Performative Revolution in Egypt: An Essay in Cultural Power*. London: Bloomsbury.
Alexander, J. and Giesen, B. (Eds) (2006) *Social Performance: Symbolic Action, Cultural Pragmatics, and Ritual*. Cambridge: Cambridge University Press.
Alexander, J.C. and Jacobs, R.N. (1998) 'Mass Communication, Ritual and Civil Society', in T. Liebes and J. Curran (Eds), *Media, Ritual and Identity* (pp. 23–41). London: Routledge.
Allan, S. (2006) *Online News*. Maidenhead: Open University Press.
Allan, S. (2013) *Citizen Witnessing*. Cambridge: Polity.
Allan, S. (2015) 'Visualizing Human Rights: The Video Advocacy of WITNESS', pp. 197–210 in S. Cottle and G. Cooper (Eds), *Humanitarianism, Communication and Change*. New York: Peter Lang.
Armstrong, K. (2015) *Fields of Blood: Religion and the History of Violence*. New York: Anchor Books.
Bahrani, Z. (2008) *Rituals of War: The Body and Violence in Mesopotamia*. New York: Zone Books.
Beck, U. (2006) *Cosmopolitan Vision*. Cambridge: Polity Press.
Bedingfield, S. (2015) 'Culture, Power, and Political Change: Skeptics and the Civil Sphere', *Journal of Communication Inquiry*, 39(2): 158–189.
Bell, M. (1998) 'The Journalism of Attachment', pp.15–22 in M. Kieran (Ed.), *Media Ethics*. London: Routledge.
Bellah, R. (2011) *Religion in Human Evolution*. London: Harvard University Press.
Bellah, R. and Joas, H. (Eds) (2012) *The Axial Age and Its Consequences*. London: Harvard University.
Berglez, P. (2013) *Global Journalism*. New York: Peter Lang.
Benhabib, S. (2002) *The Claims of Culture*. Princeton, NJ: Princeton University Press.
Bennett, L. (1990) 'Toward a Theory of Press State Relations in the United States', *Journal of Communication*, 40(2): 103–127.
Bennett, L., Lawrence, R. and Livingston, S. (2007) *When the Press Fails: Political Power and the News Media from Iraq to Katrina*. Chicago, IL: The University of Chicago Press.
Borer, A. (Ed.) (2012) *Media, Mobilization and Human Rights: Mediating Suffering*. London: Zed Books.
Bourdieu, P. (1993) *The Field of Cultural Production*. Cambridge: Polity Press.
Brandon, L. (2007) *Art and War*. London: I.B. Taurus.
Chouliaraki, L. (2006) *The Spectatorship of Suffering*. London: Sage.

Chouliaraki, L. (2010) 'Ordinary Witnessing in Post-Television News: Towards a New Moral Imagination', *Critical Discourse Studies*, 7(4): 305–319.
Clifford, L. (2015) *Under Threat: The Changing State of Media Safety*. International News Safety Institute. Available from <http://www.newssafety.org/under threat/> (last accessed on 30 June 2015).
Cohen, S. (2006) *States of Denial: Knowing about Atrocities and Suffering*. Cambridge: Polity.
Cottle, S. (2000) *Ethnic Miniorities and the Media: Changing Cultural Boundaries*. Houndsmills: Open University Press.
Cottle, S. (Ed.) (2003) *Media Organisation*. London: Sage.
Cottle, S. (2004) *The Racist Murder of Stephen Lawrence*. New York: Praeger.
Cottle, S. (2006) *Mediatized Conflict: Developments in Media and Conflict Studies*. Maidenhead: Open University Press.
Cottle, S. (2009) *Global Crisis Reporting: Journalism in the Global Age*. Maidenhead: Open University Press.
Cottle, S. (2011) 'Taking Global Crises in the News Seriously: Notes From the Dark Side Of Globalization', *Global Media and Communication*, 7(2): 77–95.
Cottle, S. (2013) 'Journalists Witnessing Disasters: From the Calculus of Death to the Injunction to Care', *Journalism Studies*, 14(2): 232–248.
Cottle, S. (2014) 'Rethinking Media and Disasters in a Global Age: What's Changed and Why it Matters', *Media, War & Conflict*, 7(1): 3–22.
Cottle, S. and Rai, M. (2006) 'Between Display and Deliberation: Analyzing TV News as Communicative Architecture', *Media, Culture & Society*, 28(2): 163–189.
Cottle, S. and Lester, L. (Eds) (2011) *Transnational Protests and the Media*. New York: Peter Lang.
Cottle, S. and Cooper, G. (Eds) (2015) *Humanitarianism, Communications, and Change*. New York: Peter Lang.
Cottle, S. and Hughes, C. (2015) '"The Responsibility to Protect" and the World's Press: Establishing a New Humanitarian Norm?', pp.76–91 in J. Hoffmann and V. Hawkins (Eds), *Communication for Peace*. Routledge.
Cottle, S. and Evans, K. (forthcoming)'"Massacre of The Innocents": On the Historical Shifts in Sensibility Toward Atrocity', in M. Brown and E. Carrabine (Eds), *The Routledge International Handbook of Visual Criminology*. London: Routledge.
Crowe, D. (2014) *War Crimes, Genocide, and Justice*. New York: Palgrave.
Danchev, A. (2011) *On Art and War and Terror*. Edinburgh: Edinburgh Press.
Elias, N. (1994) *The Civilizing Process*. Oxford: Blackwell.
Evans, G. (2008) *The Responsibility to Report: Ending Mass Atrocity Crimes*. Washington DC: Brookings Institute.
Fink, K. and Schudson, M. (2014) 'The Rise of Contextual Journalism, 1950s–2000s', *Journalism*, 15(1): 3–20.
Forde, K. (2015) 'Communication and the Civil Sphere: Discovering Civil Society in Journalism Studies', *Journal of Communication Inquiry*, 39(2): 113–124.
Frazer, N. (2007) 'Transnationalizing the Public Sphere: On the Legitimacy and Efficacy of Public Opinion in a Post-Westphalian World', European Institiute for Progressive Cultural Change. Available from <http://eipcp.net/transversal/ 0605/fraser/en> (last accessed on 1 July 2015).
Frazer, N. and Honneth, A. (2003) *Redistribution or Recognition?* London: Verso.
Gellner, E. (1990) *Plough, Sword and Book*. Cambridge: Cambridge University Press.

Giddens, A. (1985) *The Nation-State and Violence*. Cambridge: Polity.

Goldstein, J. (2011) *Winning the War on War*. New York: Dutton, Penguin Books.

Habermas, J. (1974) 'The Public Sphere', *New German Critique*, 3(Autumn): 49–59.

Habermas, J. (1996) *Between Facts and Norms*. Cambridge: Polity Press.

Hallin, D. (1986) *The 'Uncensored War?': The Media and Vietnam*. New York: Oxford University Press.

Harai, Y.N. (2014) *Sapiens: A Brief History of Humankind*. London: Harvill Secker.

Herman, E. and Chomsky, N. (1988) *Manufacturing Consent: The Political Economy of the Mass Media*. London: Vintage.

Hughes, R. (2003) *Goya*. New York: Knopf.

Hunt, L. (2007) *Inventing Human Rights*. New York: W.W. Norton and Company.

Ignatieff, M. (1998) *The Warrior's Honour: Ethnic War and the Modern Conscience*. London: Chatto and Windus.

Ishay, M. (2008) *The History of Human Rights*. Berkeley, CA: University of California Press.

Johnston, D. (2011) *A Brief History of Justice*. London: Wiley-Blackwell.

Keane, J. (2009) *The Life and Death of Democracy*. London: Simon & Schuster.

Kennedy, L. and Patrick, C. (2014) *The Violence of the Image: Photography and International Conflict*. London: I.B. Tauris.

Laquer, T. (2011) 'Mourning, Pity, and the Work of Narrative in the Making of "Humanity"', pp. 31–57 in R. Wilson and R. Brown (Eds), *Humanitarianism and Suffering*. Cambridge: Cambridge University Press.

Leith, D. (2004) *Bearing Witness: The Lives of War Correspondents and Photojournalists*. Milsons Point, NSW: Random House.

Linfield, S. (2010) *The Cruel Radiance: Photography and Political Violence*. Chicago, IL: Chicago University Press.

Lule, J. (2012) *Globalization and Media*. New York: Rowman and Littlefield.

Lull, J. (2007) *Culture-On-Demand: Communication in a Crisis World*. Oxford: Blackwell Publishing.

McNair, B. (2006) *Cultural Chaos: Journalism, News and Power in a Globalised World*. London: Routledge.

McNair, B. (2015) *Communication and Political Crisis: Media and Governance in a Globalized Public Sphere*. New York: Peter Lang.

Mann, M. (2012) *The Sources of Social Power. Volume 1: A History of Power from the Beginning to AD 1760*. Cambridge: Cambridge University Press.

Matheson, D. and Allan, S. (2009) *Digital War Reporting*. Cambridge: Polity.

Mazlish, B. (2014) *Reflections on the Modern and the Global*. London: Transaction.

Morris, I. (2014) *War: What Is It Good For?* London: Profile Books.

Nerone, J. (2015) 'Music of the Spheres', *Journal of Communication Inquiry*, 39(2): 170–186.

Nord, P. (2015) 'Interest Groups, Political Communication, and Jeffrey Alexander's Sociology of Power', *Journal of Communication Inquiry*, 39(2): 125–138.

Nussbaum, M. (2014) *Political Emotions: Why Love Matters for Justice*. London: Belknap Harvard.

Orgad, S. (2012) *Media Representation and the Global Imagination*. Cambridge: Polity.

Pagden, A. (2013) *The Enlightenment: And Why It Still Matters*. Oxford: Oxford University Press.

Paterson, C. (2014) *War Reporters Under Threat: The United States and Media Freedom.* London: Pluto Press.

Popp, R. (2015) 'Solidarity, Media and the Limits of Postcapitalist Theory', *Journal of Communication Inquiry,* 39(2): 139–157.

Perlmutter, D. (1999) *Visions of War.* New York: St. Martin's Griffin.

Peters, J. (2011) 'An Afterword: Torchlight Red on Sweaty Faces', pp.42–48 in *Media Witnessing* P. Frosh and A. Pinchevski (Eds), Basingstoke: Palgrave.

Pinker, S. (2012) *The Better Angels of Our Nature.* London: Penguin.

Rifkin, J. (2009) *The Empathic Civilization.* Cambridge: Polity.

Robertson, R. (1992) *Globalization: Social Theory and Global Culture.* London: Sage.

Robertson, G. (2012) *Crimes Against Humanity.* London: Penguin.

Sambrook, R. (2010) *Are Foreign Correspondents Redundant?* Oxford: Reuters Institute for Journalism.

Schudson, M. (2011) *The Sociology of News.* New York: W.W. Norton & Company.

Singer, P. (2011) *The Expanding Circle.* Princeton, NJ: Princeton University Press.

Silverstone, R. (2007) *Media and Morality: On the Rise of the Mediaopolis.* Cambridge: Polity.

Sontag, S. (1979) *On Photography.* Harmondsworth: Penguin.

Sontag, S. (2003) *Regarding the Pain of Others.* New York: Farrar, Straus and Giroux.

Tait, S. (2011). 'Bearing Witness, Journalism and Moral Responsibility', *Media, Culture & Society,* 33(8): 1220–1235.

Taylor, C. (1994) 'The Politics of Recognition', in A. Gutman (Ed.), *Multiculturalism: Examining the Politics of Recognition* (pp. 25–74). Princeton, NJ: Princeton University Press.

Taylor, J. (1998) *Body Horror: Photojournalism, Catastrophe and War.* Manchester: Manchester University Press.

Thompson, A. (2007) *The Media and the Rwanda Genocide.* London: Pluto.

Thompson, J. (1995) *The Media and Modernity.* Cambridge: Polity.

Tilly, C. (2007) *Democracy.* Cambridge: Cambridge University Press.

Torchin, L. (2012) *Creating the Witness: Documenting Genocide on Film, Video and the Internet.* Minneapolis, MN: University of Minnesota Press.

Thorsen, E. and Allan, S. (Eds) (2014) *Citizen Journalism: Global Perspectives, Volume II.* London: Peter Lang.

Walzer, M. (2006) *Just and Unjust Wars.* New York: Basic Books.

Willis, J. (2003) *The Human Journalist: Reporters, Perspectives, and Emotions.* Westport: Praeger Publishers.

Wilson, B. (1998) *Media, Technology and Society: A History from the Telegraph to the Internet.* London: Routledge.

Part III
'We Are the Front Line': Journalist Voices

6
Reporting from Unruly, Uncivil Places: Journalist Voices from the Front Line

Simon Cottle

Across the preceding chapters we have sought to highlight and then contextualise in historical and global contexts the dangers and risks now being experienced by journalists when going about their professional practice of reporting news in and from some of the most dangerous places in the world. We have also provided hard empirical evidence about these increased dangers, and the various patterns and trends that characterise them. This chapter and the next deliberately seek to go behind some of these statistical trends and give prominence to the voices, views and experiences of the journalists themselves, in their own words. Through these first-hand testimonies and accounts, often recounted at length, we learn of the dangers and risks that now confront journalists, and how they seek to keep themselves safe.

We consider how the field of journalism reporting in and from dangerous places can be experienced and responded to by different groups of journalists. This includes senior and experienced editors and correspondents as well as relatively new entrants to the journalism field, men and women, full-time staffers and stringers and freelancers. Some work for well-resourced national and international newspapers and press agencies, others for national and international broadcasters. Most are news journalists, but our sample of interviewees also includes a photojournalist and independent documentary-maker. Amongst our interviewees are prominent, well-known correspondents associated with major international news organisations such as the BBC, Al-Jazeera and *The Times*, who regularly fly into some of the world's hotspots and crisis situations, and others are local journalists routinely reporting on the difficulties and dangers that daily confront them and their fellow citizens within their own localities and countries, whether Pakistan, Brazil or Afghanistan. We are indebted to all our interviewees whose details are listed with their permission at the end of this chapter, not only for their frank and sometimes forthright views but also for their enduring commitment to this work which regularly places themselves in harm's way – work that according to many of them, as we shall hear, is deemed essential for the enactment and/or reinvigoration of a democratically informed civil sphere. And this is so, notwithstanding that some have lost colleagues and/or themselves suffered injury or experienced not only the hardships of reporting deprivation, of being away from home, family and loved ones, but also threats, intimidation and violence.

More specifically, this chapter first delves into the motivations for carrying out this dangerous reporting. Next we consider how journalists increasingly seek to inscribe an empathetic 'injunction to care' in their reporting and through personalised forms of storytelling before considering the changing nature of risks and dangers that now confront them in today's globalising world. Three detailed case studies in the professional calculus of risk and the determinacy of events follow. Each demonstrates the impossibility of completely eradicating risks when reporting from deadly places despite following procedures designed to keep them safe. This is then followed by a more detailed and nuanced consideration of some of the demographic and other variables that differentially position journalists and correspondents at risk in the world today. Here we find that risks are unevenly distributed and responded to differently in respect of age, gender, medium and physical locations as well as by well-resourced international news organisations and well-paid professionals, who fly into different situations, often at short notice, to file their reports and then fly home again, as well as by those locally based, everyday journalists, who work day in and day out in difficult and dangerous settings and experience continuous risks on the ground. All these discussion are then followed up in Chapter 7, where we go on to examine the views and perspectives of these same journalists on the changing practices and policies designed to keep them and their colleagues safe, or at least safer, given the impossibility of mitigating entirely all risks and dangers. The following chapter also considers journalists' views on the changing nature of communication technologies and how this variously, and sometimes complexly, enters into the field of dangerous reporting and risk management.

Why do they do it?

Our sample of journalists, as with journalists more generally, are openly reflexive about their own motivations for reporting from dangerous places and, given the possible detrimental if not disastrous outcomes of such decisions on them, their friends and families, this is perhaps not so surprising. The existential threat of reporting from dangerous places sharpens minds and, evidently from the numbers of published war correspondent and journalist memoirs, proves to be a source of fascination for the rest of us who engage in less dramatic, more mundane forms of employment and everyday life. Journalists can nonetheless exhibit a wide range of responses when invited to reflect on why they should volunteer to place themselves in harm's way. As we shall hear, their thinking can express the extent to which they are personally or intimately connected to the countries, places and peoples being reported on. And so too does their professional stance to dangerous reporting often register differing journalistic epistemologies that characterise particular news organisations and their place within the wider news ecology. These can range from institutional claims to impartiality and the journalist's professional responsibility to faithfully report and inform wider publics, to positions of engaged advocacy and the journalist's felt mission to influence wider society, even helping steer it toward increased social justice and democracy – especially when reporting failing and corrupt states and criminally threatened civil societies. And more nuanced positions and epistemological reporting stances can also be heard in-between these polar positivistic–political views. Most journalists spoken to in fact acknowledge a complex of motivations and recognise how these change across biographical time and life circumstances. Anthony Lloyd, foreign correspondent for the *The Times*, for example, reflects as follows:

> Some of what motivated me at the beginning is still there and some of it has changed. I think at the beginning, 21 years ago, I was curious about journalism and I thought that reporting mattered but I was also much more narcissistic which is fine as a young man. And now why do I keep coming back? For less narcissistic reasons and some quite simple and domestic reasons too. It's a job that I've held for 21 years and I think this is actually a very good time in my life for me to be a journalist. I've had two decades of experience. I'm still physically fit and active and healthy so I can still live in the field.
> The well of experience of two decades I think is one that serves me well for what I'm doing at the moment and I still find journalism fascinating. I still love my job and I believe more so than ever that journalism does matter. ... I find it's like an extension of an education. I'm always learning things and learning new things is cool. (Anthony Lloyd, Foreign Correspondent, *The Times*)

Lindsey Hilsum, International Editor for Channel 4 News, also recognises a mix of motivations including the matter-of-factness of the job and the privileged ringside view of momentous, albeit often dreadful, historical events. She begins by alluding to the death of *Sunday Times* correspondent Marie Colvin, who was killed in 2012, alongside French photographer Remi Ochlikin, by a Syrian shell in Homs:

> I think what Marie said on that day when she decided to go into Syria and we didn't, she just said, 'anyway it's what we do' and I noticed that Lynsey Addario, the photographer who's just written a book about her experiences in war zones, she's entitled it *It's What I do*.[1] So I think that on a day-to-day level this is my job, this is what I do. So you're not actually thinking in any kind of deep and meaningful way most of the time about your motivation, it's your job and that's what you do.
>
> But beyond that, I have a big thing about seeing where history is happening. I'm very interested in being there. It's like what I was saying about Crimea. For me if I look back at the end of the year and I think wow, these were the big events of the year and I was there, that's amazing. So that's a very personal motivation. (Lindsey Hilsum, International Editor, Channel 4 News)

Hilsum is also clear that she doesn't want to be seen as an advocate or anything less than impartial as a journalist. Her motivation, nonetheless, is fuelled by a general humanitarian concern to bring to the world's attention the personal consequences of war and elite political decision-making:

> I have a motivation and I think most of us do to expose suffering in war and to show what's actually happening, because I think that there is, particularly with young people who play computer games about war, they have a particularly asinine view of the subject which is that it's just to do with call of duty and charging around killing people on a computer screen and then they get up again. So I feel a strong compulsion to explain in a very sober way and show in a very sober way, that it is not like that and that you should take these things seriously and they're not a game.
>
> Also given the interventions from Western countries, from Europe and America, I think we have a responsibility to show the impact, whether for good or bad, of those interventions and in cases lack of intervention. That is our job, to show what's really happening out there. Now that doesn't translate easily into saying what should be

done. I'm not a 'something should be done(ish)' journalist because quite often I don't know what should be done and also sometimes I've got it wrong.

So I'm much more about a pure information thing, that things are happening and Western policy has an impact and it's to do with making sure that people know. So there is also an element of saying that they – whoever they may be, government or whatever – should never be able to say we didn't know. You did know because we told you. (Lindsey Hilsum, International Editor, Channel 4 News)

As we can hear, Hilsum's commitment to a general humanitarian reporting stance – showing the victims and the consequences of war – in fact expresses an historically formed and deepening commitment to empathic humanitarianism, a normative horizon and a generally shared reporting baseline, albeit one that manages to overlook its historical relativism (see Chapters 4 and 5). Jeremy Bowen, BBC Middle East Editor, in a similar way, wants to clearly distance his reporting stance from overt partisanship while nonetheless bringing home something of the human costs of conflict at the same time as editorially offering contextualisation and analysis:

It's a mission, yes. It's important to find out what's going on and tell the stories. Give people an idea of what it's like to be there. ... If you don't think it has a purpose, really there are easier ways to earn more money. These days in the Middle East, there's so much hazard, it's difficult but you have to feel that it's an important thing to do. ... To get to a place where no-one has been or not many people have been, like the rebel-held suburbs of Damascus, I've done them a few times. I think essentially to give people, our viewers, the listeners, an idea of what it's like to be there – what it's like to be involved in the war, what it's like to be the people who are the humans in the report and to give them a wider understanding of why it's happened. ... In TV you need a good picture story and as long as you can write a script that will apply it to the wider issues and therefore provide some context and background, then if you get that, a combination of words that make sense, pictures that make sense, if you can knit it all together, it's a very powerful medium, you can reach a lot of people, explain a lot. (Jeremy Bowen, BBC Middle East Editor)

Interestingly, journalists who are more closely acquainted by birth or possibly by commitment to a particular country and its people are more inclined to emphasise the developmental and interventionist nature of journalism in not only reporting on, but also contributing to and shaping society, and doing so in ways that are informed by a deep concern for social justice and human rights. Owais Aslam Ali of the Pakistan Press Council, for example, is explicit about this, and takes the opportunity to underline the importance of human-rights reporting in the wider context of his country:

> Of course one of the basic responsibilities of the media is to point out violations of human rights. We have to show the truth that is there – abuse of powers and all those things are very much a part of the responsibilities of journalists. ... If you look at the nature of problems, the human-rights problems that occur in Pakistan, not all are related to militancy and not all will put you in harm's way. We have terrible poverty, children are treated really badly, they are not educated, health conditions are atrocious, there is harassment of women – there's a whole range of things that human rights would cover and journalists cover them. (Owais Aslam Ali, Pakistan Press Foundation)

He also goes on to identify the core problem confronting journalists in Pakistan, which is informed by the wider recognition of human rights and a sense of responsibility to report on human-rights abuses. This can position journalists in danger:

> The areas that can get you into a problem, that can threaten are a relatively small part of journalism. If you are covering militancy, that is where you can get into trouble and those are the most courageous journalists that are there. And even there, most of the time, you are warned to back off. But those journalists who are courageous, they feel the responsibility, and they'll say it's important enough that I cannot back off. (Owais Aslam Ali, Pakistan Press Foundation)

Similarly Marcelo Moreira, Senior Editor, TV Globo, based in Brazil, grants increased prominence to human-rights and social-justice issues when reflecting on his own journalistic motivations and those of his colleagues, and sees these as integral to the responsibilities of journalism in his country:

> Well, I think all journalists that work in Brazil have to have in mind the importance of their work, that when they are reporting they are

letting society know what is going wrong. So when we do a story that is dangerous, when it is decided to go on a dangerous assignment, we must be aware of the importance of the work we do. So when we are reporting against corruption, and Brazil has a lot of problems of corruption, it's important that we do that because we don't want this to continue anymore. If it weren't for the work of journalists, society wouldn't know and would not be capable of doing something to stop this. And this is the same when we report stories of violence. (Marcelo Moreira, Senior Editor, TV Globo)

Moreira goes on to underline how such problems are not best understood as confined within the borders of a particular country but are, in fact, entangled in a much more complex web of regional and international social relations and networks, a point underlined more theoretically in Chapter 4 (see also Cottle 2009, Berglez 2013):

Brazil is a country in South America that is a neighbour to Colombia that is a neighbour to Bolivia, that's a neighbour to Peru – three big countries that produce cocaine. And we are in the route – and even in the North of Brazil there are big fields that have plantations of marijuana. So although we are not a major drugs producer we are a very big country that consumes drugs and we are also on the route for these drugs to go to Africa and from Africa to Europe, and this is our big route. For the United States these drugs go via Mexico but for drugs that go to Europe, most of them pass by Brazil, through us and onto Africa and then to Europe. So we must discuss this. We must discuss what's the best policy in order to stop the violence that this industry produces. So our role is to be the ears, voice and eyes of society. When we decide to go on a story like that, it's because we are playing an important role. (Marcelo Moreira, Senior Editor, TV Globo)

Again, endemic problems of social injustice and inequality are singled out and deemed to be priorities in the normative mission of Brazilian and wider journalism:

Drugs are a problem that we have to cover but we have different problems that aren't specifically dangerous stories. In Brazil, we still have poverty, we still have problems with education, we still have problems with our health system and most of them happen also because we have corruption, because we have money that could be

spent on education, on health, or on improved means of transporta-
tion. But this money is going into the pockets of corrupt people. This
is the big story we have to cover all the time here in Brazil. ... This is
maybe the most challenging times we are facing now working in the
media. This is the story that will be told in the future. We are leading
this story as the story is growing, and I think this is helping to make
a better society, and I'm not talking only about Brazil, but society in
general a better place for us to live. (Marcelo Moreira, Senior Editor,
TV Globo)

And some journalists in today's complex, globalised world not only
identify with a particular country or group, but also see their journalistic mission in terms that explicitly give expression to overlapping
identities of difference and belonging. Idil Osman, an independent
journalist and documentary-maker, explains from her personal biographical vantage point:

It's a moral obligation more than anything else. As a citizen I feel
that I'm responsible to the different societies I belong to. I got into
journalism for exactly that reason; to have, however small, some
level of impact and to contribute to the development and the betterment of those societies that I'm part of. ... Having grown up with
the different identities of being British by culture, being Somali by
origin, being Muslim by faith, I feel responsible towards all of those
societies and I don't think that one needs to be neglected at the
expense of the other, especially when there's such a need. You know,
places like Somalia, there is such a complicated dynamic of conflict
and identities and that's not always easy to decipher. I think it's
important to have a voice there that can make some sense to the different people that are watching. And that's where I feel I can play a
role. (Idil Osman, independent journalist, documentary-maker)

An African correspondent working for Al Jazeera also sees his personal
background and deep understanding of Africa as a key component part
of his motivation to report from the continent. He once again voices
contemporary journalism's wider humanitarian disposition in his
reporting stance:

There is the danger of dwelling on the big actors rather than looking
at the victims of their actions, the victims of the conflict who sometimes are driven to some of the worst levels of desperation – refugees

in their own land who are displaced. Yesterday they were living in air-conditioned homes, today they're living in hovels or tents in the middle of a refugee camp and there may be snow or flood waters surrounding them. So people get pushed to their lowest point. I believe that somebody, somewhere should be taking the risk to tell their stories, to bring stories of those people to our living rooms so that their suffering is not in vain. And this is one of the things that I believe pushes me to do that.

Also I think it is maybe my background, coming from a region that has been marginalised by successive Kenyan governments where conflict has been the order of the day. Maybe growing up in this very volatile part of Kenya makes me go the extra mile and want to tell the stories of people who are right now in equally dangerous places, because again it's very easy for many people to say you can't go because of security, and it's very few who would say I have to go, there's a story that needs to be told here. So that's what keeps me going – to tell the stories of those people hidden behind those powers, those conflicting parties who almost always enjoy the limelight and deny those people the right to be heard. (Mohammed Adow, Foreign Correspondent, Al Jazeera)

It is not necessarily the case, of course, that only those who come from a particular country can understand its human suffering, nature and causes, and give vent to this in their reporting. Sometimes, the gruelling experience of being a foreign correspondent can itself sensitise reporting practices to the plight of those who are being reported on and lead to enhanced or deeper empathic reporting, especially when reporting on those who have endured similar violence:

I find it rather easy to empathise with my fellow human beings and usually I'm drawn back because I feel empathy, and that's what used to draw me back to Syria. No, I don't feel that thick-skinned about it. Particularly having being dragged around, tied up, beaten and shot, I think I feel a bit more empathy to other people who have had the same experience rather than removed from it. (Anthony Lloyd, Foreign Correspondent, *The Times*)

As we have heard, then, journalists can and do entertain an array of perspectives on why journalism as an institution and why they as individuals engage in reporting from dangerous places. As we have also heard, some of these views reveal differing journalist stances on the extent to which they feel journalism can or should become actively involved in the stories they're reporting on. With some explicitly seeking to hold the line, providing information, impartial comment and contextualisation only, and others interpreting the journalist's mission in terms of advocating for the responsibility of journalism in the betterment of society through the fight against corruption and exposure of social injustices. These different views and reporting stances have long been identified and discussed in the academic literature and of course by journalists themselves (Bell 1998, Willis 2003, Cottle 2013). Where most would probably agree, however, is in respect of the increasingly prevalent and now widely shared commitment to report on the human costs and consequences of violence, war and human rights abuses – a trend that has deep historical antecedents (Chapters 4 and 5).

Journalists and the injunction to care

Reporters working for global and mainstream news outlets, such as the BBC, Channel 4 News and Al-Jazeera, as we have heard above, all converge in their general humanitarian commitment to expose the human consequences and suffering caused by conflicts, disasters and wars. They do so, moreover, as we shall explore presently, by crafting personalised stories that graphically and emotionally 'bring home' the plight of ordinary people suffering at the sharp end of endemic conflicts and deliberate violence. And here we find a more universally accepted, albeit in fact historically forged, empathic recognition of the plight of others that now increasingly informs much journalistic discourse and storytelling (see Chapter 5). Even the most stalwart defenders of the BBC as a bastion of detached professionalism, impartial reporting and proclaimed objectivity can, in the context of human suffering, it seems, become potential vehicles for the deliberate construction and dissemination of powerful, dramatic and emotion-filled reports (see also Cottle 2013). Consider, for example, the following three statements, which are all oriented to providing compelling stories based on personalised narratives and/or first-hand accounts:

> I think it's very important to empathise. I think I can do that and I think it's important to empathise because you have to give people an idea of what it's like to be that person in the story that day, or what it's like to be in that place and if you don't have a sense of empathy, you can't do that. I mean you can do a piece but I don't think it'll be as good. As well as that, because of my job as editor, I have to weave

in the analysis as well into the context, into the bigger picture. So I quite like that challenge. (Jeremy Bowen, BBC Middle East Editor)

Victims: I mean they're people that are behind the lines and trying to keep life together, which are usually the women and trying to educate their children, protect them and feed and shelter them. They are every bit as heroic, if not more, as the people fighting; so I think it's important to tell those stories. (Christina Lamb, Foreign Correspondent, *The Sunday Times*)

We at Al-Jazeera say, hear the human stories which are there and cover the stories of the desperate, the people who are really feeling the pinch and the people who are feeling the effects of the activities of those big actors. So look for characters – you always look for people who will characterise the story you're going to tell, and we will tell the stories through their eyes. And when it's political, when it's the bigger picture, we always look for a way to tell it through the eyes of normal human beings. (Mohammed Adow, Foreign Correspondent, Al Jazeera)

As we can hear above, journalists working for some of the world's most prominent news organisations now generally recognise the value of personalised stories, and embed these within their crafted narratives and, often, emotion-filled accounts of human suffering. This should not be dismissed as mere 'sensationalism', though it may often produce journalism that deliberately seeks to engage all the senses (touch, sight, smell, hearing, taste) through visible means and/or the proxy of words (Cottle 2013). But, unlike some forms of tabloid journalism that also exploit the same means of storytelling, personal narratives and their affect can be deployed here to help tell the 'bigger story', registering its import, but also providing impetus for its broader background, contextualisation or even explanation. Lindsey Hilsum provides a lengthy, and we think arresting, account of how this form of personalised narrative can help underpin the 'bigger story' – an account that also, incidentally, begins to give the lie to journalism's institutional claims to be simple observation:

I think that the most compelling stories often are of individuals and the stories of individuals tell you a lot about the bigger picture and your job as a journalist is to extrapolate and to take the individual story and show what it means. Obviously I do television and that's completely different from print in the sense that you're also looking for things which are visual, and so people need to see on the screen what's going on.

If I take an example of maybe one of the most compelling stories I ever did. I can't remember if it was one day or two days after the Americans arrived in Baghdad in 2003. We just went out looking to see what was going on and we came across a place in Baghdad where the Americans had taken up positions in one of Saddam's old palaces and were shooting quite wildly into the street. There was a street in front and they didn't want anybody driving along that street but instead of going out and putting up a notice in Arabic saying do not drive along this street, they just shot anybody who tried to come along and we were there and we watched this happening.

And then we heard crying and our fixer, a very brave fixer, Mohammed Fatnan,[2] went across the road to see what was going on and came back with a small child in his arms and her name was Zahra and she was five years old and the Americans had shot her in the head because they'd shot a car which was driving towards the street and she happened to be in it. So the story that day was about Zahra who, thanks to the bravery of our fixer, Mohamed, her life was saved because he carried her across the street to where the Americans were and then they did call in the Medivac helicopter and so on.

And then there were a lot of things that happened that day; in fact, we saw six people being killed that day. But the individual story of that little girl told you the story of the Americans' unpreparedness for taking and holding Baghdad, the nervousness they had, their inability to deal with the civilian population. I mean it told you so many things which would presage the disaster which was to come of the American occupation in Iraq, and it was a story of a little girl. So, in a sense, that's a perfect example of how you're looking for both and how the story of one person tells you so much more. (Lindsey Hilsum, International Editor, Channel 4 News; see also her report 'Zahra: Story of Child Shot in Iraq', Channel 4 News.com – updated on 22 March 2008)

In such ways, as we have heard, journalists are often doing more than describing and 'reporting', when they are reporting from dangerous places; through their crafted prose, dramatic visuals and personalised and often affective storytelling, they are in fact, through their journalist practice, inviting readers to engage, empathetically as well as cognitively and analytically. And it is by such means that their commitment to the stories and people they are reporting on becomes evident and inscribed inside their professional reporting practices. And this is the case notwithstanding protestations to the contrary based on a reluctance to be seen as a moral champion or in any way as an exceptional witness:

> American journalists come out the whole time with the phrase, 'honour to bear witness'. I sort of understand what they're getting at but I don't feel that pious in my devotion to this profession. I feel quite good humoured and relaxed about it. I think journalism does matter. It's important that there are journalists and it's very important that there are journalists covering wars. It's part of the free flows of information, a very important part of the democratic process and I believe and understand that. However, if it wasn't me doing it, then someone else would do it. (Anthony Lloyd, Foreign Correspondent, *The Times*)

Journalists positioned in different parts of the world and working for different news organisations can and do proclaim their commitments to reporting from dangerous places differently, as we have heard; though most, as has also been suggested above, now agree on a normative baseline of recognising and even empathetically reporting on human suffering and the denial of basic human rights. This has arguably become deeply embedded into contemporary journalism thinking and practice when reporting on and especially when reporting inside or from dangerous places in the world today. Such is the historical infusion of ideas and sentiments of 'widening the human circle' and the historical impetus of humanitarianism, individualism, democracy and empathy that now coalesce inside the prevailing normative horizons of much of globalised society. This same globalised world also spawns, however, increased dangers and new threats as we have begun to hear above (and as was elaborated in Chapter 4). We next consider, therefore, how journalists understand these new dangers and how exactly they position them at increased risk.

Changing risks in a globalising world

Journalists working in some of the world's most difficult and dangerous places are, of course, generally aware of the risks that confront them and their colleagues. It goes with the territory. As the late Marie Colvin observed in the context of war reporting:

> Simply: there's no way to cover war properly without risk. Covering a war means going into places torn by chaos, destruction, death and

pain, and trying to bear witness to that. I care about the experience
of those most directly affected by war, those asked to fight and those
who are just trying to survive.

Going to these places, finding out what is happening, is the only
way to get to the truth. (Colvin 2012)

And today, increasing numbers of journalists, it seems, both staffers and
freelancers, are prepared to risk their lives by reporting from such dangerous places. Stuart Hughes, BBC World Affairs Producer, usefully sets
out what he and many of his colleagues see as some of the main shifts
that have occurred in recent years and which, indirectly, position more
journalists at risk than in the past. He first draws attention to declining
costs and the proliferation of news outlets and freelancers:

> Setting up and running a 24-hour news channel is a lot easier now
> probably, and a lot cheaper than it was when I first did foreign news.
> If you went to Jerusalem in 1999 or 2000, for example, it would be
> the main American networks, the BBC, CNN, Sky and so on but
> they were all the big players. Whereas now, of course, there are more
> news outlets, more news channels worldwide – some of whom have
> the resources to send people to these places, some of them don't.
> But filling in the gap there's a lot more freelancers. I come across a
> lot more freelancers than I did before. There tended to always be a
> lot of freelance photographers. Even if you go back before I started
> working in foreign news, to Bosnia, there were lots of freelance pho-
> tographers. But now we're seeing a lot more freelance – particularly
> videographers, cameramen and camera reporters, video journalists –
> than were there when I first started out. So I think the main thing
> we're seeing is numbers. I think that's partly as a result of more
> news organisations setting up. (Stuart Hughes, Producer, BBC World
> Affairs)

He also identifies the declining individual costs of entry to the journalism field and the changing nature of journalist careers as feeding
into the increased numbers of inexperienced journalists now working in dangerous places. In these ways they thereby become exposed
to increased risks, and this within an increasingly crowded field of
competing news outlets:

> Also the barriers to entry are a lot lower. Again if you go back 10–15
> years, if you wanted to set up as a freelance video journalist, it cost

a lot of money to buy a camera and then you had to have a way of feeding in material. Now, as you know, you can do it on your iPhone at the very least. Certainly it's a lot cheaper to set yourself up as a freelance and a lot of people are taking the opportunity to do that. So that's the main thing that I've seen in terms of numbers.

I guess on the safety side, foreign news tended to be somewhere that you graduated towards after having worked for some time as a journalist. It wasn't something you stepped into straight away and again, partly because of the expense, you needed the backing very often of a large news organisation. Of course a lot of that has gone now. So on the safety side, I think I'm probably seeing younger and potentially more inexperienced journalists in the sort of places that I wouldn't have seen them 10/15 years ago. ... So the number of outlets and the amount of demand is increasing all the time, and that has safety implications, it has resources implications, it affects all of the parts of the work that we're doing. (Stuart Hughes, Producer, BBC World Affairs)

It is not only structural and institutional changes in the contemporary news media field and the historically shifting social composition of its journalists, however, which increasingly position journalists at increased risk. As all our interviewees are acutely aware, an ominous political change in some parts of the world now deliberately targets journalists and puts them at peril:

I know journalism and war go slightly in cycles and trends, but in the past journalists who got killed or wounded more often than not it was just because they were on the front line and it was nothing particularly personal. They got hit by shrapnel or shot by a sniper who couldn't actually see they were journalists. It wasn't so much deliberate targeting or if it was deliberate targeting, it was fairly isolated. Now you've got major players in conflicts who interpret journalists as not only legitimate targets but *very* desirable targets. That's changed and it's made it a lot more dangerous ... I certainly see a change in the Islamic State in that they are a group which revels in violence, and violence is part of their message. Usually in war you get atrocities and war crimes but usually more the side that perpetrates those crimes goes to some lengths to actually mask them. Now we've got the Islamic State which is far from trying to mask its crimes; it tries to broadcast them, exult in its war crimes. (Anthony Lloyd, Foreign Correspondent, *The Times*)

Christina Lamb, foreign correspondent for *The Sunday Times*, agrees:

> Well now I think is much more dangerous than when I started out. When I started out covering war, if anything happened to you as a journalist, it was really because you did something silly. Now it's a much more dangerous job because we're targets. When I was going in and out of Afghanistan, both sides respected journalists, as we are supposed to be under the Geneva Convention, as not partisan and objective observers so nobody was trying to kill us. If you got killed it was because you were caught up in a dangerous situation, but now people want to kill journalists, we are the front line in fact. We're in more danger probably than the military. It's sad to say killing a soldier now in some of these countries does not get you a headline but killing a journalist does. (Christina Lamb, Foreign Correspondent, *The Sunday Times*)

As we discussed in Chapter 4, the changing tactics involved in mediatised war have become based on the deliberate construction of violent symbolism, and literally embodied in the dissemination of images choreographed and designed to instil fear and dread. This has positioned journalists, as well as humanitarian workers and others working in such places of fundamentalist-inspired hatred, on the front line of image wars. Here Lindsey Hilsum offers some useful historical perspective on the communications shift that has taken place across recent decades, while also identifying new wars and the increased accessibility afforded by today's communications environment as indirectly positioning journalists at increased risk:

> Well, obviously there's different kinds of danger but I think that in the early days, for example, in the late eighties when I was reporting from South Sudan, Uganda and so on when there were conflicts there, the people one was reporting on, whether they were governments or warlords or whatever were much more naïve about the role of journalists. There was no satellite TV, there was not much communication from outside so they weren't really aware. They didn't completely see what we did.
>
> Whereas later on, every two-bit commander has satellite TV so they know how they are portrayed and they understand much more what we are doing, which is trying to expose atrocities, the human-rights abuse, and so on. So it hasn't made them less accessible. In many ways they're more accessible because they really want to get

their propaganda across, but it has made them much more conscious of the damage we can do to their cause and how we can expose them. So I think that that has made journalists more of a target than they used to be. I think that that's one big change. (Lindsey Hilsum, International Editor, Channel 4 News)

Jeremy Bowen offers a similar perspective on today's changing communication environment:

> More dangerous for the reasons that people want to get into the 24/7 news cycle. People are more aware of the media. The media is more visible. There's more of it around. I think there are many more people covering stories so that can mean, statistically, there's probably more deaths or more injuries or more kidnappings. I think in general, as I said earlier, it's a media-saturated world and the media is just way, way more important in terms of influencing debate I think than it was. It's incredibly powerful, and that's why people want to affect it and to win the media battle and to do that, sometimes journalists are getting in their way.
>
> There are times when journalists are just in the wrong place at the wrong time and get hurt, or worse, but sometimes they're targeted. It obviously happens in dictatorial countries to local journalists or even less dictatorial countries with local journalists, and sometimes more directly with foreign correspondents. (Jeremy Bowen, BBC Middle East Editor)

These are insightful observations and ones that run against the grain of a prevalent view that sees the increased surveillance capacity of today's communication ecology as in and of itself likely to inhibit violence directed at journalists and other non-combatants. Hilsum is also clear that there is an unfortunate tendency in the West and on behalf of the main news outlets to concentrate on the risks and dangers confronted by Western correspondents only, neglecting the increased number but lower profile of indigenous journalists working day in, and day out in some of the most extreme, uncivil places, characterised by endemic, often targeted, violence:

> I think there is a danger of overestimating or concentrating on the foreign journalists covering conflicts like Syria rather than looking at Mexican journalists covering the drug wars and so on because I think that you'll probably always find that the Mexican journalists

covering the drug wars and Philippines organised crime and so on, that the numbers are much higher. But we pay less attention to them because we are less interested in journalists from those countries, which is wrong.

But I think that Syria obviously has been a particularly deadly conflict and I think that there's a number of reasons for that. I think that it's partly because of the use of indiscriminate weapons by the Assad forces, which means that the number of civilians killed is very high as well, and obviously more recently because of the kidnaps and murders by Islamic State. So you have these two particularly vicious antagonists who make no exceptions for journalists and who, certainly on the ISIS side, have targeted journalists. (Lindsey Hilsum, International Editor, Channel 4 News)

Journalists are in no doubt of the chilling effect that the image wars conducted by Islamic State and others have had upon their own reporting and that of colleagues. Jeremy Bowen is explicit that he wouldn't want to go anywhere near Al-Raqqa in Syria, for example, and for perfectly understandable reasons:

Because the Islamic State are there. I wouldn't go anywhere where I thought that there was a strong risk of kidnap. Some parts of danger I can deal with, like potentially being shot or being in a violent situation or shelling. I've been in those situations and I can cope, but I think being in a place where you might get kidnapped and decapitated is just beyond terrifying. (Jeremy Bowen, BBC Middle East Editor)

Stuart Hughes, BBC World Affairs producer, also comments on the chilling effect of ISIS and other violence around the world deliberately perpetrated against journalists:

My rule of thumb is I wouldn't go to anywhere where I might end up in an orange jumpsuit. That is a whole level of trauma that I really wouldn't want to put myself through. I would hesitate to go anywhere where journalists are actively being targeted and either taken hostage or killed. So anywhere where there is a strong Islamic State presence at the moment, forget it, I'm not interested. Again that gets into the question of the nature of risk is changing for the news industry. It's a relatively new thing that journalists are actively being targeted because they're journalists and anywhere in that situation I would hesitate to go.

Equally, there are probably stories in Mexico for the same reason that I wouldn't want to cover. I wouldn't want to cover a drug gang that really does not want journalists around, because I just think the threat level is too high. This evening I'm going for dinner at the Frontline Club in London; on the wall there's photographs of all of our colleagues who have been killed in conflict and I'm very aware and thankful for the sacrifice that they make but I don't want my photograph to be on that wall. And that's the truth and I'm very aware of that now. I hope I've got a pretty good life. I've got a good job, I've got a wonderful family, I want my son to see me grow up. I don't want to be a photograph on the wall of the Frontline Club. (Stuart Hughes, BBC World Affairs Producer)

So far we have heard of the changing nature of the news industry – proliferating news outlets and platforms, increased numbers of journalists reporting from dangerous places, including relatively inexperienced freelancers, and the increased targeting of journalists in an increasingly media-saturated and media-aware world. These all contribute to the increased numbers of journalists now being killed and maimed around the world. Before we move to explore with the help of our interviewees how perceptions and practices of risk-reporting are conditioned by different factors and stances to risk, it is worth pausing perhaps to remind ourselves of how unforeseen circumstances and unpredictable contingencies can all too easily result in maiming and loss of life when reporting from volatile and conflicted parts of the world. In these circumstances, the journalist's calculus of risk can all too easily, and unpredictably, be rendered redundant.

Three case studies in the calculus of risk – and the determinacy of events

Circumstances on the ground can often exert their own determinacy, sometimes with dreadful outcomes and irrespective of the many different ways in which policies, plans and practices have been designed and even followed with the aim of keeping journalists safe.

Here we offer three extended accounts volunteered by our interviewees that provide insights into the contingencies and dangers of reporting from the ground. The first by Stuart Hughes, BBC World Affairs producer, painfully reminds us of how even the best laid plans and security-conscious risk assessments can be thwarted. He recounts the events that preceded a fatal incident when he stepped on a landmine in 2003 in Iraq, resulting in part of his leg being amputated, and which tragically killed his film cameraman, Kāveh Golestān Taghavi Shirazi (8 July 1950–2 April 2003):

> I was in Northern Iraq, I remember it like my birthday and I think the one thing I was struck by afterwards when I thought about it was how quickly a very normal situation can become life-threatening. It was a very normal day. I'd been in Northern Iraq for two months covering the Iraq War. The front lines were shifting – as I say, we were in Northern Iraq and the front lines between Kurdistan and the part of Iraq controlled by Saddam Hussein were shifting quite quickly. So an area that up until the previous night had been controlled by Saddam Hussein's forces had suddenly shifted, the troops had retreated.
>
> So we drove up to the nearest town. We spoke to a local Peshmerga commander who was in charge of that area, to get a sense of what was going on there. He said that there had been quite a lot of mortar shelling, incoming mortar fire up until the day or so before but that the mortar fire had died down. So he gave us one of his soldiers to escort us up to a trench, a front-line position, a defensive position that had been abandoned. We drove up there. There was me, Jim Muir the correspondent, Kāveh Golestān the cameraman, the soldier that we'd been assigned, and our translator/fixer. So we drove up to the trench with the intention of filming it.
>
> As I say, a very normal day – something that we'd been doing for the previous two months, nothing unusual about it. No incoming mortar fire, no shooting, nothing. I stepped out of the vehicle. Immediately stepped on a landmine. I knew that I'd been hit. Hit the ground, looked down, could see that my leg was pretty badly injured. Didn't know at that stage it was going to be amputated but I knew that it was pretty badly injured. The hostile-environment training kicked in so I did all the things that I'd been trained to do, to try and make sure that I wasn't going to bleed out.
>
> While all of this was going on in the chaos of the seconds that followed, Kāveh, our cameraman, thought that we were coming under mortar fire. He ran out of the vehicle thinking that the vehicle was being targeted and he stepped on one landmine and then fell onto a second. I didn't know any of this at the time because I couldn't see, he was some distance away. Jim Muir recovered his body, brought it back into the vehicle. While this was going on, I climbed into the back of the vehicle and we realised that the area was very heavily mined. Jim put Kāveh's body on the back seat of the car and then reversed the vehicle out of the area because, of course, we didn't

know how many landmines there were, how densely mined it was. So he reversed the vehicle out the way that we'd come in until he was out of the mined area, turned the vehicle around.

We drove to the nearest place of help, there was a very basic first-aid station run by an NGO that was nearby just a couple of miles away. So went there initially and they gave me fairly basic first aid. While this was going on, Jim was able to get a call into our guys in London and the guys in London started putting the emergency system in place, finding out where the nearest proper hospital was, getting in touch with our colleagues from ABC, the American network who were embedded with US Special Forces, and it was initially the medics from the US Special Forces who treated me. Then when I was stable, I was able to be flown initially to Cyprus to the British Air Force base in Cyprus. I was there for a couple of days while they stabilised me and then flown back to the UK four days after the accident, where they operated and amputated the leg.

I knew broadly about explosives and I knew about the risks of landmines. I kind of knew that they were a risk. I guess I didn't know as much as I know now but I was aware that they were a potential threat. I was aware that some booby traps and mines aren't marked. But the one thing that we're always told is to take notice of local knowledge and given that we had a local soldier with us, no soldier is going to put their own life at risk for a car full of journalists and the fact that the soldier had directed us to this area and assured us that the area was safe made us think he knows the area better than we do, so probably it's going to be okay.

Obviously, the minefield wasn't marked. There were no signs there and no indications that it was mined. So I think we were unlucky. It was one of those situations where, even with the training, there was nothing to suggest that there was something there. If I'd seen a great big skull and crossbones, we wouldn't have gone near the place in the first place, but there was nothing to indicate that there was anything there. (Stuart Hughes, BBC World Affairs Producer)

Christina Lamb, foreign correspondent for *The Sunday Times*, also insightfully recounts the circumstances and confusion that are so often characteristic of fast-moving wars and conflicts, and how this nearly cost her life in an incident in Iraq in 2003 that also led to the death of ITN correspondent Terry Lloyd (1952–2003) as a result of US military actions:

During the war in Iraq in 2003 I was in the South and went into Basra from Kuwait at the beginning of the war. The war started, the bombing started in the early hours of Friday I think, and Saturday early morning I drove into southern Iraq and my newspaper comes on a Sunday so Saturday was our deadline, and I was driving with a colleague towards Basra. ... I was supposed to be covering Basra, so I started driving towards Basra and I was not embedded, I was just in a car with a colleague, and we didn't see any soldiers or anything and I thought this was a bit odd.

We got to the outskirts of Basra where there's a series of bridges and we came to the first bridge and I called my office and said, 'We are on the edge of Basra and there's no sign of any fighting or soldiers' and they said to me, 'We are reading from Reuters some copy saying that US jets are bombing the bridges of Basra, pounding bridges' and I said, 'Nothing's pounding anything, I'm at the bridges'. Now I'd only just joined *The Sunday Times* then from another newspaper a couple of months earlier and my Foreign Editor said to me, 'are you sure you're on the right road?' and I was cross because there are only three roads, and I said, 'That copy is propaganda, there's nothing pounding anything'. In fact it was the MoD telling Reuters that this was happening, so I said, 'I'm going to turn back, there's something that doesn't feel right.'

There's no signs of troops, there was nothing happening, so we turned back and on the way we saw the car of a television company, people with 'TV' on the front of their cars and it was from ITN, a British TV company, and it was somebody I knew, Terry Lloyd, and they stopped briefly and I said to them, 'I don't think ... there's nothing going on and it doesn't feel right to me' and I couldn't explain why it didn't feel right, just you develop a sense after years of doing this.

They carried on and we went back to where the roads split and there were a group of British Military Police there and they said to me, 'What on earth were you doing going up there, you were way ahead of the front line', and I said, 'Well, we didn't know that' and they said that it was incredibly dangerous. They got a message saying that a vehicle had been attacked and it was these television people that we had seen and Terry Lloyd was killed, so I think I was right to come back. I cannot explain why I felt it was wrong, and my newspaper had certainly thought I was making the wrong decision coming back. They didn't want me to do it, they wanted me to carry on into Basra, so that shows the importance of trusting somebody's instincts on the ground. (Christina Lamb, Foreign Correspondent, *The Sunday Times*)

As we can hear, the fog of war can easily create confusion and lead journalists astray, positioning them in the firing line. In such circumstances, to place ones faith in a 'sixth sense' or felt 'instinct' to keep safe, especially when set alongside counter journalistic traits to 'go the extra mile' and 'get the story' can, to say the least, sound highly precarious, with some journalists – as we have already heard – prepared to push themselves further than their colleagues and paying with their lives.

A third account, from a freelance/independent film-maker, illustrates how even someone familiar with her own country, Somalia, can find herself in harm's way. And here, in retrospect, she reflects on what could possibly have been done to mitigate the worst effects of this and similar encounters:

It was the wrong time, the wrong place on both occasions, but I think I also was a bit silly in the sense that I should have taken precautions, because I wanted to do some filming.

The first time I was kidnapped was in a neighbourhood in one of the northern districts of Mogadishu. There's an IDP (internally displaced persons) camp there, and the IDP camp was there for several years but the demographics were changing. So whereas before you had a lot of people that were affected by the drought, for example, a lot of those people had found a way to resettle themselves. They'd been able to go back to their regions, and now it was being flooded with local people.

That's something I wanted to look into. You had local residents that a lot of the time they are businessmen, businesswomen, they're running maybe the local kiosk but they also have a shelter in the IDP camp, so that means they can claim double money. This was something that was orchestrated, it was quite organised, and there was a connection between the camp leaders, there was a connection with the central government, there was a connection with the NGOs involved, and that was something I really wanted to look into because I thought something is really iffy here.

What I should have done is I should have scouted that local territory before I put myself there, and that's the bit that I didn't do. I went there all guns blazing with my cameraman and I wanted to shoot the place and just speak to the people. Before I could actually go to the camp the local clansman that would be consider themselves to be the 'controllers', the agents that patrol the local neighbourhood, call it policeman, that's what they were calling themselves, they came up to us whilst we were wandering in the neighbourhood and one of them said, 'what are you doing here, why are you here without our permission, you should have come through us first.' And I replied, 'why do I need permission to shoot?', so I'm talking as a Somali, I was saying, 'you were born here right?' and he said, 'yes' and I'm saying, 'I'm born here too, how do you have more rights over me?' I think that was a bit unnecessary. I should have diffused the situation. The fact I said that also triggered the other two guys to be really forward, and these guys were going to respond with violence.

This is the thing, it's a learning curve because a lot of the things I know now I didn't know then; so the fact that people speak through violence is something that I was aware of in theory but it hadn't manifested in my job, so I just went with the notion that I could just speak with these people and talk sense into them. That's not the case and that quickly became a reality. The two guys I was with started speaking on my behalf and saying, 'you can't stop us from filming' and the three armed local clansmen just started beating them and taking our stuff. They quickly called for backup. Luckily they didn't touch our car but they took all of our stuff and then they dragged us to their 'office', so it is these things that can trigger these types of kidnapping. (Idil Osman, freelance/independent journalist/documentary-maker)

As we have heard in the three accounts above, quickly changing circumstances and unforeseen contingencies can never be entirely predicted or controlled for; some risks are and will always remain inherent to dangerous situations. Even so, it is incumbent upon us all to try and minimise them to keep journalists if not safe, then safer than they might otherwise have been. The following drills down further into some of the disparities and differences evident between different journalists and how this informs their reporting practices when reporting in and from unruly and uncivil places around the world.

Disparities and differences in the calculus of risk

Here we address some of the disparities and differences of risk-reporting and how these are variously conditioned in respect of demographics of age and gender, as well as by medium and, importantly, by disparities of resources and reporting stances in respect of the calculus of risk at local/national and international/global journalist levels. Earlier, we heard about the structural changes in the news media marketplace and how these have indirectly positioned more journalists, and freelancers especially, at risk. Younger journalists seeking to establish their credibility and names within a competitive news industry are also particularly at risk. As well as being less experienced in calibrating the risks involved, they may also often be less inhibited about doing so since they have fewer family ties to worry about. Jeremy Bowen usefully reflects on how determinations of age have influenced his reporting career over the years, first as a young man and then as a more experienced and established correspondent:

When I started, I was quite anxious to take on difficult stories that other people didn't want to do because I was very ambitious and I saw it as a way to raise my head above the crowd, and it worked actually because you get the glory, that's the thing. You do dangerous stuff and you do it well, you get the glory. If it goes badly, there are some very serious consequences.

The general process of maturity. There's a point comes in your life when you don't feel indestructible anymore. I felt indestructible to start with and you get moments, friends and colleagues getting hurt, my colleague Abed Takoush getting killed when I was with him in 2011,[3] that was very traumatic obviously, and for a couple of years after that, I decided not to do any dangerous stuff. I still feel differently. I don't really like doing it very much anymore but I do do it. In the nineties and the late eighties when I started, I really liked it. I liked the challenge. I didn't feel scared but since I've had kids, since Abed was killed, many other friends of mine have been killed, I don't really welcome dangerous situations in the way that once I did, I absolutely don't. (Jeremy Bowen, BBC Middle East Editor)

Stuart Hughes develops the point further, identifying the mythical status of the war reporter (see Pedelty 1995) – now often celebrated in films and cultivated in notable memoirs – as holding a dangerous allure for the aspiring, young journalist:

There is a sense that the only way I can be a good journalist is to be a foreign correspondent or to be 'a war correspondent. There is this mystique around this idea of the war correspondent and I always say to students what stories do you actually want to tell? What are you interested in? Why do you want to go to wherever it may be? What story do you want to tell? And sometimes they don't know, they just feel that they should. It's like a rite of passage for a young journalist. It's like I need to do a war. It's like something you need to do, it's like you do your gap year, you do your journalist training and then you do a war and then you can say I've done a war, I'm a proper journalist. It's kind of like a stamp you have to have in your passport. (Stuart Hughes, BBC World Affairs Producer)

Christina Lamb also worries about the young, aspiring journalists:

I worry about young people going like I did when I was 21, but then it was a very different world. Now young people going and trying to make their name in some of these places, which are incredibly dangerous, is scary and I think newspapers and media outlets should be very careful about using some of these people.

Now because there are a lot more social media outlets and things like VICE, which does very good work, but maybe they have not got quite the same safety standards that the established media have, and maybe just using people who are actually taking enormous risks, and maybe even encouraging them to do that instead of counselling them to be careful. That worries me. (Christina Lamb, Foreign Correspondent, *The Sunday Times*)

Considerations of age also overlap with those of gender, as we have heard above in respect of older male correspondents and their family responsibilities; a factor, however, that too often only seems to surface publicly in the discussion of female correspondents who are mothers (see, for example, Porter 2011):

Being a mother, you are responsible for somebody else, so you think much more carefully about things that you do. When I started I was 21, and it never occurred to me anything would happen. I don't remember even thinking about it, and actually in Kandahar when the Russians where there, I was in a trench where we were trapped for two days by a Russian tank and lots of the people we were with were killed, and it never occurred to me. I don't remember really being scared. Obviously, as you get older, you realise things more and if you're a parent you look at things differently. Is it really worth going somewhere; what are you going to get? (Christina Lamb, Foreign Correspondent, *The Sunday Times*)

Recently public debate has also sometimes focused on the particular risks of sexual assault and violence directed at women journalists reporting in conflict situations. This was given added impetus following the sexual attack in Egypt on Lara Logan of CBS News, when reporting on the 'Arab Spring'. She said 'men in the crowd had raped me with their hands'. There were attacks also on the Egyptian journalist Mona Eltahawy, and a France 3 TV reporter Caroline Sinz by Egyptian security forces in 2011. More recently, a female photojournalist was gang-raped in July 2013 (see Sreberny 2014).

Lindsey Hilsum, however, offers a note of caution. She makes the point that current concerns about the increased risks encountered by women correspondents in conflict and war reporting may be exaggerated, and worries about how this could unintentionally limit the opportunities of female correspondents in the future:

> There's a fashion for saying that female journalists are at great risk of rape and sexual assault, and I have never seen any empirical research that shows me whether female journalists, particularly foreign correspondents, are at more risk … I have a lot of concern about an over-emphasis on particular dangers for women war correspondents or foreign correspondents that will just end up in making editors more nervous about sending women out to cover conflict. And I think that we haven't spent all this time as feminists screaming and shouting to get to do the same stuff as the men do in order for people to tell us now that we're delicate flowers and at terrible risk and so we shouldn't go. (Lindsey Hilsum, International Editor, Channel 4 News)

Clearly, there is a tension here between differing points of view, though both seek to ensure the safety and well-being of women journalists, and it is one that reliable research can help to clarify in respect of the empirical evidence documenting assaults, both sexual(ised) and other, on female (and male) journalists, and in which parts of the world this occurs.

Journalists are also aware of the different reporting practices associated with different news mediums, whether press, TV or social media, and how these can indirectly exacerbate or reduce the exposure to risks and violence, though this can also play out differently in different situations. Lindsey Hilsum reflects on the differences between TV and newspapers in the following ways:

> When one is in television you're quite often under very severe time constraints and so one of the differences with, for example, Marie Colvin, who was an example of the bravest person who went in

furthest and stayed longest, and that was partly because of her nature as a person and it was partly because she worked for a Sunday newspaper. So we would be together and she would go and disappear for five days because she had five days to go off and do her reporting which often meant she ended up in some very dodgy situations. Whereas I had to come back the same day to the hotel to cut a package and do a live. You're in quite different situations there.

On the other hand, doing the TV is more dangerous, particularly for the camera person, because you are so obvious, you stick out. Whereas Marie would just slip in with a group of guerrillas or whoever and you wouldn't really notice her because she's just one person and a notebook. So in those senses, even though she would be exposing herself to much greater danger because she always did, she was less conspicuous. So the nature of the work she did – and this is true for all print journalists – is slightly less dangerous. (Lindsey Hilsum, International Editor, Channel 4 News)

Christina Lamb also reflects on considerations of medium, but again notes how different reporting assignments can also be at work, exacerbating or possibly reducing the risks that cannot simply be seen as endemic to particular mediums:

Certainly one of the reasons I work for a weekly paper is because I want to have more time to develop the story and have more space to write it, so that's why I work for *The Sunday Times*, and also I write books because that enables me to explain things more, so I use lots of the stories I find that I can't fit into newspapers, so that's why I do that. I'm not sure that it makes it more or less dangerous. I mean certainly knowing a lot about a place makes you more of a threat and, therefore, you might be seen as dangerous to that regime, or those people, that you're talking about. So Pakistan, for example, you can go there and very safely report if you're just touching the edges of what happens; if you're going there and writing in-depth stories and really going there for a while and know a lot, then you are a threat to people and some journalists are, therefore, more at risk. (Christina Lamb, Foreign Correspondent, *The Sunday Times*)

Similar complexity also surfaces when considering the different risks confronting local/national and international journalists. While it is undoubtedly the case, as our statistics clearly demonstrate (see Chapter 3), that locally and nationally based journalists comprise the bulk of all journalist killings, attacks and serious threats, the changing nature of today's conflicts can also position local and international journalists at changing levels of more or less risk. Mohamed Adow explains, for example, how this occurred in Somalia:

> In the past it used to be foreign journalists that used to be targeted in Somalia and if you look at the statistics on journalists in Somalia, between 1990 and 2006, you will find that most of them were foreign journalists who were targeted. But after the 2006 invasion of Somalia by Ethiopia and the knocking out of power of the Islamic Courts Union, who had brought some semblance of law and order to Mogadishu for about six months, I'd say the situation changed. And that's around the time Al-Shabaab came into the political state, whereas before they were hiding under the Islamic Courts Union as their defence, as their military wing. After the Ethiopian invasion and the removal of the Islamic Courts Union, Al-Shabaab came out in its true colours and started carrying out attacks in their name. And that is when the tables got turned on local journalists. Possibly 2011/12, there where 17 journalists killed in just a single year and from then on, it was just a bloodbath for (local) journalists. Journalists were getting targeted for saying the least harmful thing about Al-Shabaab or any of the groups that are operating in Somalia. It became almost legitimate to kill journalists. I would say today journalists are taking all kinds of measures, including arming themselves, to continue doing their job. (Mohammed Adow, Foreign Correspondent, Al Jazeera)

Lindsey Hilsum also points to the changing fortunes of local and international reporters when reflecting on her experiences in Africa and, in particular, the duopoly of risks when international journalists are working with local fixers:

> It's an interesting thing because situations change. There are occasions when we are safer and occasions when they are safer. There are certainly situations I can remember – this is quite a while back – in Democratic Republic of Congo, 1997 maybe. There were a lot of foreign correspondents there, including black South Africans, and the black South Africans went out and took pictures and were safer than we were because they were black and so they sort of fitted in, whereas white people going out were an immediate target of mobs. So that was an advantage, it was an advantage to be black in that situation.

There are many other situations where it's an advantage to be white because people say oh, they're a foreigner and we should be nice to them and all that kind of thing.

So it's different in different places, but I think the most important thing is in any situation when you're working with local fixers or stringers is that you are going to leave and they are going to stay, and that is the most important thing – that if you're reporting on people who are not going to like your reporting when it comes out, you may be long gone and so you're fine but the local fixer or stringer is still there, and that is the thing to be most aware of.

I think that's one of the difficult things because quite often they really want to expose something and they may not be as aware of the danger to themselves as you are. So they say no, it's really important we have to expose the corruption of this Minister or whatever it is, this is a really, really important thing – they can be very idealistic and you're saying yes, but are you sure you're going to be safe afterwards? And that is one of *the* most difficult things I think to deal with because you want to get the story but you absolutely don't want somebody else who you've been working with to suffer for it afterwards. (Lindsey Hilsum, International Editor, Channel 4 News)

Such accounts serve to remind us of the dynamic and changing nature of conflicts and how this can introduce further levels of complexity in terms of the professional calculus of risk, and who is most at risk; tendencies that may be occluded in generalising claims about which group of journalists experiences the most dangers (see also Murrell 2010, 2015). Owais Asiam Ali of the Pakistani Press Foundation, also points to a further complexity in the relationship that sometimes obtains between international news organisations and local journalists:

Most of the media organisations, they have a correspondent who will be based in the capital city and maybe they will be the ones that are in capital cities or in Karachi, they will be given security training, they will have insurance, they will have rights.

But then they don't ask where are you getting your news from? You cannot cover this conflict which is taking place in Baluchistan and in FATA sitting in Islamabad or Karachi. So these correspondents in turn ask local correspondents in these conflict areas to send them the news. The international organisations do not own those correspondents who are in fact providing the news to them, and they are on their own basically. International organisations should treat all journalists the same, as far as the safety and life of their journalists is concerned. (Owais Asiam Ali, Pakistani Press Foundation and Pakistani Press International news agency)

Western journalists for the most part profess themselves to be equally concerned about the risks and dangers encountered by local journalists, or stringers, and the fixers and translators and others working on assignments for them. Kathleen Carroll, Senior Vice President and Executive Editor of Associated Press, is clear:

> Anybody who goes into a dangerous situation for us is treated exactly the same. We even make sure that we have equipment for drivers and fixers that we might need to hire on the spot. We make no distinction if we're using someone who is not a full time employee. We still make sure that they're someone we know or that we've trained them or they have the training, they have insurance, we make sure they have the equipment. ... We don't subscribe to the idea that you draw down in a dangerous place staffers for whom you're responsible and then hire people with some kind of lesser relationship. People who are on our team are on our team from beginning to end. (Kathleen Carroll, Senior Vice President and Executive Editor, Associated Press)

Different professional and organisational initiatives and policies now deliberately seek to recognise and forefront the inequalities of risk-reporting unfairly borne by different groups of journalists:

> The Frontline Club in London has been doing a lot of work trying to set up a fixers' fund, because obviously we do rely on these people and they should be properly paid for what they do and properly provided for their service. They should have the same kinds of protection too ... That's what I was saying, in Pakistan I don't use fixers because I think they are more at risk than we are, but in other places we are more at risk, Westerners are a target. (Christina Lamb, Foreign Correspondent, *The Sunday Times*)

Though such professed concerns are sincerely made, the differences informing actual reporting practices on the ground sometimes undermine such good intentions, as we shall hear in the next chapter when we explore further organisational processes and professional practices designed and deployed to keep everyone as safe as possible.

Conclusion

Our discussion so far, to recap, has identified a number of differences and commonalities evident across the dangerous reporting field. Journalists and their news organisations can be motivated by differing views and values, and informed by differing news epistemologies that impact on their reporting practices and modes of storytelling. However, all generally recognise victims of war and other social injustices and take it upon themselves to provide sometimes graphic and emotion-filled reports that aim to 'bring home' something of the human suffering involved – reporting that is often informed by a journalistic 'injunction to care' (Cottle 2013). It is this that often positions them in the eye of the storm and in hazardous, dangerous conditions. Moreover, in a globalising world in which journalists alongside other 'representatives' of Western society and interests have become deliberately targeted, this encounter with danger and risks has shifted in ominous ways.

We have also heard how demographics of age and gender, as well as journalist standing and status, whether local or national, or international and peripatetic, impacts on the field of risk-reporting; and how the inherent dangers of reporting from unruly and uncivil places can never be fully mitigated. Such are the unforeseen circumstances and contingencies of risk that often unpredictably position journalists in immanent as well as imminent danger. To what extent and how journalism seeks to manage and accommodate risks and dangers and in ways that seek to minimise their possible harm now forms the focal point of discussion in the following chapter.

Notes

1. Interviews were conducted for the purposes of this book by Dr Susana Sampaio-Dias, either by phone or via Skype, between April and July 2015, and then professionally transcribed. The authors gratefully thank Susana for all her help and insightful comments during the course of this research. We are also extremely grateful to all our respondents below for their views, accounts and testimonies. These, we feel, offer deep insights into the nature of their work, why they do it, the dilemmas and difficulties confronted, and

how risk and danger can, to some degree, be predicted and minimised, but never entirely controlled and contained when reporting from the world's unruly, uncivil places. We acknowledge and sincerely thank the following: Owais Aslam Ali – Secretary General, Pakistani Press Foundation, and Chairman, Pakistani Press International (news agency); Stuart Hughes – Producer, BBC World Affairs; Anthony Lloyd – Foreign Correspondent, *The Times*; Lindsey Hilsum – International Editor, Channel 4 News; Kathleen Carroll, Senior Vice President and Executive Editor, Associated Press; Jeremy Bowen – BBC Middle East Editor; Marcelo Moreira – Senior Editor, TV Globo, Rio de Janeiro, President of Abraji – Brazilian Association for Investigative Reporting, INSI Member; Idil Osman – freelance/independent journalist, documentary-maker; Christina Lamb – Foreign Correspondent, *The Sunday Times*; Shah Marai – photojournalist, Agence France Press – Afghanistan; Mohammed Adow – Foreign Correspondent, Al Jazeera; Irfan Ashraf, Pakistani freelance journalist who collaborates with Dawn News, Press TV and the *New York Times*, also Professor of Journalism at the University of Peshawar.

2. Mohammed Fatnan, who saved the little girl who formed the focal point of the Channel 4 news story, subsequently continued to offer help to her and her family. He worked for Channel 4 news with Lindsey Hilsum as an Iranian fixer and translator. He was later kidnapped in Iraq and disappeared, presumed killed, one week before he was due to be married.

3. Abed Takkoush died on 23 May when the car in which he had been transporting a BBC news crew was hit by an artillery shell fired from an Israeli tank.

References

Bell, M. (1998) 'The Journalism of Attachment', in M. Kieran (Ed.), *Media Ethics*. London: Routledge.

Berglez, P. (2013) *Global Journalism*. New York: Peter Lang.

Colvin, M. (2012) *On the Front Line: The Collected Journalism of Marie Colvin*. London: Harper Press.

Cottle, S. (2009) *Global Crisis Reporting: Journalism in the Global Age*. Maidenhead: Open University Press.

Cottle, S. (2013) 'Journalists Witnessing Disasters: From the Calculus of Death to the Injunction to Care', *Journalism Studies*, 14(2): 232–248.

Murrell, C. (2010) 'Baghdad Bureaux: An Exploration of the Inter-connected World of Fixers and Correspondents at the BBC and CNN', *Media, War and Conflict*, 3(2): 125–137.

Murrell, C. (2015) *Foreign Correspondents and International Newsgathering: The Role of Fixers*. New York and London: Routledge.

Pedelty, M. (1995) *War Correspondents*. London: Routledge.

Porter, R. (2011) 'Is It Selfish to Be a Mum on the Frontline? Her Son's First Words Were "Bye, Bye" and He Saw Her Blown Up on TV, But This Woman War Reporter Has No Regrets', *Mail Online*, 2 September 2011. Available from <http://www.dailymail.co.uk/femail/article-2032400/Is-selfish-mum-frontline-Christina-Lamb-regrets.html#ixzz3iVkfbXrN> (last accessed on DATE).

Sreberny, A. (2014) 'Violence Against Women Journalists', in E.V. Montiel (Ed.), *Media and Gender: A Scholarly Alliance for the Global Alliance on Media and Gender*, pp. 35–39. Paris: United Nations Educational, Scientific and Cultural Organisation/International Association for Media and Communication Researchers. Available from: www.unesco.org/new/fileadmin/MULTIMEDIA/ HQ/CI/CI/pdf/publications/gamag_research_agenda_sreberny.pdf> (last accessed on 7 August 2015).

Willis, J. (2003) *The Human Journalist: Reporters, Perspectives, and Emotions*. Westport, CT: Praeger Publishers.

7
Keeping Safe(r) in Unruly, Uncivil Places: Journalist Voices in a Changing Communications Environment

Simon Cottle

This chapter follows on from Chapter 6 in forefronting the views, accounts and experiences of our representative sample of journalists, and moving beyond the previous discussion of motivations, demographics and different responses to risk-reporting, whether in respect of age, gender, medium, or staffers and freelancers, nationally based or internationally peripatetic journalists. Here, we consider the processes directly involved in dangerous assignments and how these variously impact journalists' decision-making and their professional practices. Sometimes these deliberately strive to keep them safer but sometimes they can also inadvertently contribute to heightened exposure to risks.

Firstly, we consider the logistics and planning that inform from the outset dangerous reporting assignments, and how experienced journalists on the ground as well as senior decision-makers back in the news office regard these efforts to keep journalists safe. Then, we explore further the practices of journalists in the field, how these have evolved to become more safety-conscious over recent years, and why and how it is that some journalists differentially enact them or even choose to ignore some of them. Finally, we revisit today's rapidly changing communications environment and consider in what ways it may either contribute to journalists' safety or in fact expose them to more dangers. We begin, then, by hearing accounts of the practicalities and pragmatics of story assignment and how this enters into and shapes the nature of dangerous reporting.

Practicalities of dangerous reporting

To begin, a senior newspaper correspondent describes in some detail how he typically gets involved in story assignments, and how – at least as far as he is concerned – story assignments should no longer be made on a snap judgement following world events but require careful and collective deliberations:

> It's teamwork. It's quite a developed relationship I have with *The Times* after working for them for so long. I've worked with them consistently for 21 years … I'm actually only on their books for six months a year which is a time limit which is good for both parties, because as I'm covering war so much of the time, I would burn out if I was doing it for more than a certain amount of time each year. Not necessarily just being in wars but just involving oneself in the whole research procedures, the violence and all the rest is quite a negative experience after a while.
>
> So what usually happens is occasionally I'll get a call from my foreign editor saying we're interested in this particular area of the world or perhaps this country or this emerging story in this country, can you examine ways of going there or how you would cover it? Or probably more often, probably more than two-thirds of the time, it's me submitting a couple of ideas to *The Times* and saying this looks interesting. Waiting to hear back from my Foreign Editor – yes, it does sound interesting, can you present a plan to go there?
>
> So then I present my plan and what's changed now is I also have to budget for it and present a costing's list of approximately how much the whole thing's going to cost and break that down too. Then there'll be a couple more further decision points along the way before I either get the green light to go or the paper decide against it. More often than not, they go for it. So it's quite holistic and balanced. I'd be horrified if they said, can you get on a plane tomorrow to fly somewhere, which I hadn't even thought about that morning. It has happened in the past but it doesn't happen so much now.
>
> I feel much more aware of it than I used to. When I'm drawing up a budget list, I try and give them the tightest budget I can so they agree to the assignment. I set out what I need to do effectively but there's no frills on my budgeting because I'm aware that it's one of their considerations in agreeing to an assignment or not. I feel there is pressure to achieve more in a shorter space of time than there was. I definitely feel that. (Anthony Lloyd, Foreign Correspondent, *The Times*)

Similarly, a broadcaster reflects on processes of story assignment as a collective process and one that now has become increasingly conditioned by available resources and budget:

And I think because of the constraints, both in terms of money and resources, if you're going to take yourself off for a week, people in London want to know you're going to get a story out of it. In the days before mobile phones and 24-hour news, correspondents could take themselves off for a fortnight and nobody would hear from them and they might come up with a story and they might not, but that was the luck of the draw. Now the conversations we have quite regularly are what's the story?

I'm sitting in London, say for the sake of argument I wanted to go to Tikrit tomorrow. The first thing any News Editor would say to me is what's the story? Well, I don't actually really know what the story is. I won't know until I get there. Well, is that the best use of our money and is that the best use of our time, and there's a plane crash happening and there's Ukraine happening and there's this and there's that. And you'll go in and you're not quite sure what you're going to get out of it. (Stuart Hughes, Producer, BBC World Affairs)

Evidently budget inevitably impacts what resources are available and this is something that all news organisations, big and small, now explicitly contend with:

Every news organisation is facing financial constraints and the question that any news editor would ask if you went to them with a story is how newsworthy is it? Are you going to be able to get it on air? I think what we find more difficult nowadays is I think a lot of the best reporting isn't planned. You turn up somewhere and you meet a family or you meet a person or you see a situation that you couldn't have predicted and the story just happens, you get lucky. (Stuart Hughes, Producer, BBC World Affairs)

Lindsey Hilsum at Channel 4 also points to the collective nature of the decision-making involved and how a degree of deference within this process can be extended to experienced correspondents working on the ground, who are evaluating close-up the risks and dangers involved:

The decision on when to go somewhere and whether it's too dangerous or not tends to be a collaborative decision in the situation I'm in now, where I'm an employee. So there tends to be a discussion. Sometimes quite often it's very hard to make those judgements and you make a judgement that it's safe enough and you get in there and it's a bit dodgy and then you make a decision whether to stay or go, and most of those decisions have to be made on the ground.

One of the good things about Channel 4 News is that they trust us to make those decisions on the ground, and you're making decisions as a team because I tend to be working with a camera person, a producer, a local fixer and sometimes a security person as well. So you're making a collective decision and within a team, there's always differences about the person who wants to go a bit further and the person who doesn't want to go so far and all of that kind of stuff. You kind of iron that out as you go along. (Lindsey Hilsum, International Editor, Channel 4 News)

Hilsum then recounts how exactly this conversation took place with colleagues working for other news organisations and Maria Colvin, just before the latter was killed in Homs:

In February 2012 four of us had dinner in Beirut. That was me, Neil MacFarquhar from the *New York Times*, Jim Muir of the BBC and Marie Colvin of the *Sunday Times* and we discussed going over the border into Syria with the rebels, being smuggled in and reporting from Homs and three of us, Jim, Neil and myself said that was beyond our danger threshold and Marie said, 'anyway it's what we do.' Marie went and the rest of us didn't and three of us are alive and one of us isn't. ... I think that you always feel the responsibility to push it as much as you can within the bounds of what your team is willing to do and wants to do, and within the bounds of whether you think it's worth it. You have to believe that you're going to get a really good story. There's no point in exposing yourself to danger for no good reason. So it's kind of hard. (Lindsey Hilsum, International Editor, Channel 4 News)

Such an account exposes the inherent risks of such deliberations no matter how well informed they are or the amount of collective experience informing the final decision. Some correspondents, evidently, are prepared to go further than their colleagues, and even those close to the ground, or sometimes perhaps because they are so close to it, may not always occupy the best vantage point from which to make a clear risk-assessment and safety-informed decision:

In fact my colleague Marie who was killed she had been in Homs, filed a story, left to safety and then went back the following week;

maybe somebody should have said to her, it's too dangerous to go back, you've already done an amazing story, you don't need to go back again. So I differ with some people that say you should leave it up to the correspondent on the ground, like I said, sometimes you're too caught up. (Christina Lamb, Foreign Correspondent, *Sunday Times*)

Sadly, it also seems to be the case that news organisations sometimes only respond vigorously in seeking to implement safety-aware procedures and offer or enhance their hazardous-environment training following the shock of losing one of their colleagues:

Since Marie died, that made the company reassess how we do things so we now have to do risk assessment forms, which we didn't used to have to do, and a couple of times I've filled in forms and they've come back and said, no, that's too dangerous. But then I've kind of argued, actually I know lots of people in this place or it's not ... because what I do you can't fill in ... Like Afghanistan, for example, might look dangerous on a form but I've been going there for years so I know the people and the area so I'm not going to be stopped from going there. ... Before my colleague was killed, yes certainly we were highly encouraged to go to places. It was always said to us, you are the correspondent on the ground so it's your decision, which actually I don't think it is. I mean in theory it's the right thing, the person on the ground knows what the situation is, but in practice sometimes if you're on the ground and you're really caught up in a story, you might not be making a rational decision about what you're doing. (Christina Lamb, Foreign Correspondent, *Sunday Times*)

BBC World Affairs producer Stuart Hughes also discerns an industry shift in terms of taking journalism safety more seriously than in the past, and this in part prompted by earlier journalist causalities. He usefully explains at length:

And what I'm glad to see is that people are discussing now the ethical dimensions and the moral dimensions of news gathering, the fact that you can't just send somebody with no experience or training out to somewhere dangerous and if they get injured or killed, you can just forget about them – they're not our problem. There is a duty of care there and I think that is something that's really encouraging to see. I've had conversations with some of the most commercial parts of the news industry, like news agencies, AFP and Reuters and so on. People that perhaps you might think would only be thinking in commercial terms but now they're starting to think in moral terms and in terms of duty of care.

And that's a discussion that I haven't heard up until recently and that gives me encouragement that some of these things will become part and parcel. If you think back 35 years when people first started talking about physical safety courses, there was some resistance to it – either very experienced correspondents saying I don't need an armoured car or I don't need body armour or whatever it might be. And then, unfortunately, some journalists got killed and they got killed but perhaps if they'd been wearing a flak jacket or driving in an armoured car, they wouldn't have been.

And that shifted the debate and now physical, hostile-environments training is very commonplace, and I think what's happening now is we're seeing the next evolution, if you like, in the safety debate. The big news organisations and the staff journalists have always had more money and more luxury so we adopted some of this stuff earlier on. Whereas I think now because of the changes in the news industry and the economics of the news industry, now the freelancers are being incorporated in that debate. It's taken a long time but I think it's long overdue but it's encouraging. (Stuart Hughes, Producer, BBC World Affairs)

Though the increased recognition of journalism safety and a moral obligation to extend Western news-industry concerns and responsibilities to local journalists, stringers, fixers and freelancers can only be welcomed, the situation for local journalists constantly working in difficult circumstances continues to pose different challenges, especially when freelancing and/or working for under-resourced and understaffed news organisations. Not all major news organisations have yet mustered the capacity of the BBC to offer local fixers and stringers the same degree of support and training that their own journalists receive:

I feel awful because most of the fixers that we use are people we use quite frequently and they're very good people. I just wish they could get some of the benefits that we get, including hostile environment training and I think that's the most important because their lives are worth no less than ours. There is the possibility of them being in harm's way.

So what will we say if our local eyes and ears have been shot in the head and it's because they didn't have the knowhow that we've developed and that might have led to us getting out of harm's way?

It's a tricky issue. I've had instances where I've spoken to managers in order to take some of these journalists on hostile environment training, which they have yielded to once or twice but again it's an issue of resources at the end of the day. (Mohammed Adow, Foreign Correspondent, Al Jazeera)

And here a local photojournalist freelancing for Agence France Press, based in Afghanistan, provides insights into his very different working conditions and consequent increased exposure to dangers:

> In Afghanistan if you compare it with other countries, and I have been in other countries, I know when they are working it's very different. Here it's like we are working for 24 hours. If I'm in the office, if I'm at home I have to cover. For example, if something happened at midnight, I have to go and cover that; if it's a blast, if it's an attack on some place. It's not only me; it is like this for all the journalists working here. It is not easy sometimes. For example if there is a blast and you go in the night time to get a good picture, a strong picture, if you are five or ten minutes late the security will have blocked the roads, so you cannot then get to see what's going on at the site. (Shah Marai, Photojournalist, Agence France Press, Afghanistan)

The photojournalist in Afghanistan is not only seemingly on call all hours of the day and night but is also expected to secure the very best pictures, arriving at the scene of a bomb explosion, for example, before security forces have secured the area and exposing himself to the possibility of a second bomb blast. All the journalists we have spoken to, however, and this includes those working as local journalists in some of the most difficult circumstances, are adamant that their editors have not, and do not, put pressure on them to accept story assignments that the journalists may feel are too dangerous:

> When we went to cover the news in Kunduz, my boss said if you are feeling okay then you can go, otherwise don't go. So it's just up to me. For me I know what to do, but my company has never placed pressure on me and said you have to go. So first of all, they are thinking if the security is not good and you are feeling that something could happen to you, then don't go. Kunduz: the office said when there is a news story but you feel it is too dangerous, don't *you* become the news. (Shah Marai, Photojournalist Agence France Press, Afghanistan)

Marcelo Moreira, senior editor of TV Globo, reiterates the point and describes the editorial processes and aversion to unnecessary risks involved:

> When we understand that we have to report a story, because it's reporting for society, and if to get that story our people will be placed in danger because there is never 100 per cent safety, then we try to deploy the group with a big plan, the best plan that we can have, and we try to have them back as soon as possible with the story.
>
> So planning is very important. Training is very important and most of all, understanding the importance of this story. If the story really needs to be told, we go after it. Some, though not all of the cases that we have here of reporter or cameraman casualties are because the individuals went without planning. The story that they could bring back, the shots taken, aren't worth a life. So we don't need to lose anybody's life only for a spectacular image or shot. (Marcelo Moreira, Senior Editor, TV Globo)

The BBC, as one of biggest news organisations in the world, currently employing over 2,000 journalists and supporting 50 foreign news bureaux, is generally recognised as an industry leader in respect of its efforts to incorporate extensive training and safety procedures aimed at journalists deployed in hostile environments. Stuart Hughes describes the efforts the organisation currently goes to in trying to ensure the safety of its direct employees and others associated with its news reporting around the world:

> At the BBC we have a pretty well established and a pretty standard protocol that we're expected to follow. There was a time maybe some years ago where it wasn't followed completely to the letter, where people could go out to a hostile environment course if their training wasn't quite up to date, but in recent years that has been tightened up pretty considerably. So, as you probably know, we have our own in-house high-risk team who are responsible for policing the risk side of things.
>
> So the basic procedure is that before anybody goes on a hostile environment deployment, they've got to do initially a five day residential hostile environments and first aid training course, provided by one of our training providers which covers everything from pre-deployment preparation through to filling in risk assessment forms, to a lot of role play scenarios dealing with checkpoints, dealing with

ambushes, hostage taking, very practical things like checking a vehicle is safe before you hire it in case there's anything there that needs to be looked at.

And the part of the course that I know that most people find useful is the first-aid part, practical first aid training – fairly simple but potentially life-saving, as I know from my own experience. And the courses have been altered in recent years to include the psychological side and the psychological first aid, if you like, which I think is important as well.

So everybody goes through that. That has to be refreshed every three years – I'm about to do my refresher next month – and if you're not up to date with your training, you can't go to a hostile environment. And whenever anybody is about to go out there, our high risk team check that they're up to date with their training and if you're not up to date, there's no, yes you can do this one but you'd better sort it out. Now we're at a position where if you're more than three months out of date with your training, you don't go – end of story. There is a bit of paperwork that we do, a risk assessment which is quite practically based for hostile environment courses. It's things like blood groups, next of kin, proof of life details – making sure that those are all filed in the event that they're needed. (Stuart Hughes, Producer, BBC World Affairs)

Safety training and procedures – though not always so well resourced or advanced as those found at the BBC – are now also found across most established Western and many other news organisations. Importantly and revealingly, however, the journalists themselves do not always universally embrace the procedures and policies designed to keep them safer, especially when deemed to run against the grain of their journalist mission and/or traditional reporting practices. Some, for example, are concerned that an institutionalised culture of risk-aversion can have a detrimental impact on journalist reporting from dangerous places, whilst also appreciating the continuing organisational efforts and support offered to journalists when things go wrong:

> I can only speak really from *The Times'* point of view and there's been a complete revolution in safety of journalists and all the rest of it. Ten/fifteen years ago no one ever asked really where I was going or what I was doing or anything, whereas now I have to ring in the whole time and this, that and the other and it's all discussed and thought and looked at and weighed up before I go. As I saw when

I was kidnapped and shot, there's quite a big machine will roll in to try and pick you back up, as long as you can escape back over the border, and I was very well treated by *The Times*. I should have been well treated, and I was well treated.(Anthony Lloyd, Foreign Correspondent, *The Times*)

But Anthony Lloyd also goes on to observe what he sees as a danger from the profession's overcompensation of risk:

At the point that the profession thinks we can lose no journalist ever in wars, then they're going to stop sending journalists to wars. As I said, war is governed by the dynamic of chaos and you can't just go to war and see other people getting killed and wounded without ever being at risk of that happening to you as well as a journalist, and it's a very difficult understanding for particularly the corporate side of news organisations to take on board.

And there is a danger that if they over-egg it too much, you're actually going to start restricting journalists in their movements so much they might actually as well not bother going out on assignment. We're not at that point yet and I don't think ... well, I hope we won't get to it, but I see more of a threat from overcompensation in trying to protect journalists than I do in negligence in trying to protect journalists. (Anthony Lloyd, Foreign Correspondent, *The Times*)

Christina Lamb also voices a note of scepticism in her reflections on journalism safety training, and does so based on her first-hand experience of reporting from dangerous places and her reliance on her intuitive sense of when something is not quite right, signalling heightened precaution. She explains:

I have been on these hostile environment courses but not many. The first one I did was in 2003 just before the war in Iraq, which frankly we were sent on because they wouldn't insure us otherwise, and then I went on one last year, so I've only ever done two. First aid is useful but the rest of it – I've been a war correspondent for 28 years and in a week's course or a few days' course, I'm not really likely to learn that much I think.

What I learnt on the ground, like I said to you, some of it you can't explain, you sense it sometimes, the road isn't quite right, and you sense if people are looking at you in a certain way or if something is happening. For example when we were ambushed in this village in Afghanistan, no children came in the village which is really strange because the kids always come and ask for sweets. So that was a signal immediately that something was odd, we weren't offered tea by the village. So a lot of it you need to know their society to know some of the things to look out for. (Christina Lamb, Foreign Correspondent, *The Sunday Times*)

Similarly long-standing journalist Lindsey Hilsum also provides a slightly sceptical eye, though also recognising the good intentions and perhaps need for journalist safety training:

We have quite a system now where you fill in a risk assessment form before you go which, to some extent, is just bureaucracy and box ticking and very irritating for people like me. On the other hand, it does make you think through what are the risks before you go. Is there a risk of kidnap? Is there a risk of being shot? Is there a risk of being arrested? Is there a risk of street crime? All of those kinds of things and you just try and think all that stuff through and we have quite a formal system for that and then you go off and do it.

But you can't know what's going to happen, so a lot of stuff is to do with judgements that you make on the ground. I have a bad feeling about that street so we're just not going to go there, and you also have to be guided by local people. Last week there was quite a lot of filming on the streets that I wanted to do in Benghazi and the fixer didn't want to do it, not because we were going to get shot but because we were going to get arrested by some idiot on a checkpoint who would waste our day. So all those kind of judgements you're making as you go along. (Lindsey Hilsum, International Editor, Channel 4 News)

Evidently there is a lingering, professional reluctance to fully embrace safety and hostile-environment training when it is perceived to inhibit journalist autonomy or override the journalist's proclaimed 'sixth sense' – whether based on intuition and experience or local knowledge assimilated from extensive time in the field.

A similar tension also surfaces in consideration of safety and reporting practices when in the field, as we shall hear a little later. But first, here's a BBC spokesperson describing in overview some of the practices now carried out in the field and designed to try and keep BBC reporters out of harm's way:

And once we're out there, depending on the nature of the environment, if it's very high risk or if it's particularly challenging like a natural disaster, we will often have our own high-risk advisor with us who will be taking care of logistics and also providing a professional military background very often to try and keep us safe. And then we'll all be responsible for playing our part in safety. So for me, the most important things are making sure that I've got identification and blood group close at hand if it's needed. It'll be making sure that I've got proper communications equipment, whether that be a satellite phone or whatever. If necessary, having a plan to check in with a designated person at the BBC regularly to reassure them that everything's okay.

There are occasions where we will have tracking devices attached to vehicles, GPS trackers so that if a vehicle does go astray that there is the chance that it can be tracked. And things like knowing where the nearest hospital is, knowing the blood groups of my colleagues, having the next of kin details for my colleagues and that sort of thing.

So fairly standard stuff but I think it's probably formalised a lot more than it used to be, and the hope is that if anybody does find themselves in any kind of difficulty, whether it's a physical difficulty or an abduction situation, that there is a system in place whereby we know about it pretty quickly. The other thing I should probably add is that the BBC provides pretty comprehensive hostile environments insurance. So, for example, when I was injured in Iraq, I was insured for medical evacuation. So if somebody does find themselves in a severe physical situation, then they're insured to get them back home. (Stuart Hughes, Producer, BBC World Affairs)

With regard to the wearing of body armour, journalists recount how the decision to wear this or not can often be more complex than perhaps initially thought. Most journalists do not wear this heavy, uncomfortable equipment unless exposed to an unfolding violent situation. Bomb attacks, unexpected shootings, and stray bullets, of course, do not always announce their imminence in advance. Body armour is nonetheless provided for journalists by news organisations, and this is generally extended to local fixers and translators by major international news organisations:

I've got a big case with flak jacket, helmet. I don't wear them all the time. I wear them as rarely as possible because they're heavy. Gas mask, you name it, first aid kits. No, I don't wear them the whole time at all. I wear them when it's really strictly necessary but I'd rather not wear them, no, it's too heavy and it's not always necessary. It's not always necessary that you need them but you should have them close at hand just in case. ... We always bring flak jackets for fixers and translators, and helmets and we wouldn't take them out without that stuff, and they have to sign a form which means they get covered by BBC insurance. The BBC's not bad about things like that and we try and look after people. (Jeremy Bowen, BBC Middle East Editor)

No, I don't wear body armour. I wear it when the situation merits it. We have hostile-environments courses and you have a refresher course every two or three years, I can't remember which, and yes, if I'm going to a hot war zone, we all take body armour but you only wear it when you're in a situation where bullets are flying, you don't wear it all the time. (Lindsey Hilsum, International Editor, Channel 4)

Some particular circumstances also militate against the wearing of body armour:

And then in terms of gear, I don't always take a flak jacket. I usually do but it depends. In the old days of crossing Syria on foot, you look like an idiot in a flak jacket and a helmet and everybody's going to be staring at you and thinking who's that weird Westerner wearing all that kit, perhaps we should take that kit off him because we need it for ourselves? So you wouldn't, you'd just go in a shirt and baggy trousers with a pack on your back. But generally in a war situation I would take a flak jacket, probably a helmet too. (Anthony Lloyd, Foreign Correspondent, *The Times*)

In some non-Western countries the availability of body armour as well as the preparedness to wear it can also be patchy. Owais Ali explains this in respect of two key factors at work simultaneously:

The situation is quite bad in Pakistan for the safety of journalists. Two problems – first of all, safety jackets and things are quite expensive so nobody wants to spend the money and they should. ... The second problem is that even if where there are a few available, journalists that have them, when working for foreign organisations, say, they don't wear them. So the awareness is not there anyway.

For example, last month there was a big demonstration against Charlie Hebdo cartoons in Pakistan and in Karachi they were going to the consulate. The photographer for AFP, he got shot, he survived but he was hit in the chest and it was later found that he had a bulletproof jacket in his car but he chose not to wear it. So the awareness of safety should be a part of your everyday activities, to be aware of security. That has not yet started and that's why it's very important to raise the awareness and to give them skills – safety and security training. ... He thought it won't happen to me. We are a very fatalistic people. (Owais Aslam Ali, Pakistan Press Foundation)

Idil Osman, freelance journalist, goes further and points to the increased risks that can actually follow from wearing body armour, and especially if seeking to be unobtrusive and meet local people on their own terms. Referring to her assignments in Somalia, she explains why she doesn't wear any security body armour as follows:

No, because you tend to stand out much more because of that. Lots of people they don't expect you if you put yourself in that position, because by wearing these jackets and these helmets and things like that you're already giving them the idea that you don't trust them, that you feel they are putting your life in danger, so when you approach with that persona, with that character, they're already put off, and on the extreme side of that you'll have people that think, okay well this person is protecting themselves, they obviously have reasons to protect themselves, so they'll hunt you down. Many people have been killed because of that. This is a territory where life is worth less than a bag of chips so you really have to play by their rules. (Idil Osman, freelance journalist and documentary-maker)

Interestingly, she goes on to say how wearing local clothes rather than heavy armour can in fact help to keep you safer in unruly places such as Somalia:

I try to dress like the locals; I'll buy clothes from the local shops. I don't go there with a suitcase, I literally just go there with the bare minimum I need for the journey itself, but when I go to Mogadishu I'll buy clothes from there, so I'll dress like them, I'll speak only Somali, and I'll sit down with them on their level, so if we're going to somewhere like the market I won't sit on a chair because most of them are sitting on the floor. It's just little things like that, you know you sit down with them on the floor, you talk to them and they'll come to you. That's how you protect yourself really just by immersing yourself with them and so you're not a threat then. Once you put yourself outside of them and you're coming in from the outside that's when you're likely to have more of a threat. (Idil Osman, freelance journalist and documentary-maker)

A key part of keeping safe in hostile environments is the employment of fixers or translators, people with expert local knowledge who are part of or close to the local and wider community. They therefore know the risks and dangers more than anyone as conflict situations and their key protagonists move through space and time:

> The key thing is the fixer. Particularly now I suppose my average assignment's much shorter in length than it used to be. By choice my average assignment would be three weeks – you need to work out where you are and what the context of the story is from the ground and then you've got ten days really good work and then you tail off a bit in the last few days. That's shorter now, it's probably like ten days to two weeks each assignment; again because of cost concerns.
>   So basically the way I work it is that you get the best fixer you can and you throw whatever cash you need at it for a short time to get the job done and then leave. I think it starts becoming a false economy if you try and stretch things out without putting the right cash into it because it only means you end up not with the best fixer and all the rest of it and it just doesn't work. So if I'm going in for a short space of time, I get the best fixer that I can and pay for the best fixer I can, do the job, go home. So much of it is dependent on the fixer. (Anthony Lloyd, Foreign Correspondent, *The Times*)

As we have heard, news organisations and their professional journalists are generally concerned about and protective towards their fixers and translators, though the risks they encounter are likely to be longstanding in comparison and they cannot always be kept out of harm's way (see also Murrell 2010, 2015):

> I'm on my own and I try to look for a translator maybe within that locality. First of all, it helps because that person comes from that locality and secondly, you only have one more head to worry about in terms of security. But when there are four of you, it's just too many people and if you're all foreigners in that part of town, you can attract attention. The bigger the group the more attention. So I like going into hostile environments with the least of people – the cameraman and myself, and that's all. Many instances, we have

left the producer or the fixer behind. (Mohammed Adow, Foreign Correspondent, Al Jazeera)

So far, we have heard how today's journalists are increasingly expected to undergo hazardous-environment training and must conform to a number of bureaucratic procedures designed to ensure risk assessments are conducted and that decisions about dangerous assignments are informed by collective processes of deliberation, though the view of the experienced reporter on the ground is often likely to be afforded a degree of deference and sometimes greater weight within such processes. We have also heard of the differing views and responses towards news-industry policies and practices designed and deployed to keep journalists safe(r) in potentially dangerous reporting situations. These are variously recognised and implemented as was illustrated most graphically perhaps by the varying availability of, and personal decisions made about, whether to wear body armour. As previously discussed, local and national journalists working for relatively under-resourced news organisations and reporting in sometimes extreme situations of prevailing violence, as well as young or relatively inexperienced freelancers setting out on their own, do not enjoy the same degree of benign bureaucratic monitoring or experienced senior decision-making input, and they are thereby placed at increased risk. Local fixers and translators, though increasingly recognised as part of the news organisation's news team and therefore deserving of the same protections, both physical and financial, nonetheless often occupy very different positions of risk, with both themselves and their families potentially exposed to threats and intimidation long after the Western news producers have filed their stories and moved on to the next in a different country or region.

Communications change and its impacts on risk reporting

We live in a world in which communication flows circumnavigate the Earth, sometimes in almost real time, and they do so through an increasingly complex media ecology plied by global-local, mainstream-alternative news organisations and all variously making use of extensive telephony, eye-in-the-sky satellite systems and close-up and personal social media that together can bear witness to some of the world's worst conflicts and atrocities. Mainstream journalists, political and military elites as well as citizen journalists, activists, ordinary soldiers, torturers and terrorists all have access to today's increasingly crowded media ecology and its interlinking news communications environment. We invited our representative sample of journalists to reflect on how this changing communications environment impacted the field of risk reporting, and whether for good or ill. The following provides an overview of their collective and different responses and offers, we think, a series of important insights into how communications change is now deeply at work within the field of risk and dangerous reporting:

I think there are both opportunities and challenges but I'm one of the last of the dinosaurs there. Basically if a breaking news event occurs in a country where I am, if I'm out in the field somewhere reporting on some different story, I may be unaware of that other event and the person who writes it for *The Times Online* will probably be someone in Britain looking at the wires. If I'm aware of the event and it's happening where I am then I can do that but it may not happen that way. So I still work in the way that I've largely always done, whereby I sort of do my stuff and then file at the end of the day for the paper the next day. So the paper, if it's a good story I've got, will Tweet it and all the rest of it. I don't Tweet it but other people will.

Now what that means is that the platform of people who are aware of my story is much, much bigger and much, much more quickly than it used to be. Now on the one hand that's a good thing because more people get to read the story and on the other hand, that can be a bad thing because more people might be pissed off about the story in the country with the war in which I'm working, which will bring added risk to me. (Anthony Lloyd, Foreign Correspondent, *The Times*)

Interestingly, this same newspaper correspondent also points to the increasing difficulties of remaining fairly low-profile or anonymous when reporting, simply because of the growing tendency for everyone wanting to take their picture of you, preferably in selfie-mode and standing next to them:

On a separate level not related to the paper but everyone wants to take one's picture ... Today I was working with some Kurdish bomb disposal guys and they all wanted me to take their picture and they wanted to take their picture with me and they wanted to take my picture and all the rest of it. Who knows where that's going to end up? It's probably going to end up on some Kurdish Peshmerga Facebook site, which could really not do me a lot of favours when I'm working with people who don't like the Kurdish Peshmerga. It's hard to control and it's not all good. I like low profile. I hate people taking my picture and putting it on Facebook or other sites. So technology brings advantage and disadvantage I'd say. (Anthony Lloyd, Foreign Correspondent, *The Times*)

Kathleen Carroll of Associated Press is in no doubt of the dramatically increased risks that new and extensively accessible technologies now afford to combatants, and how this positions journalists at increased risk because they are no longer as indispensable as they may once have been when monopolising news communications:

> Well, almost everything is dangerous now because the actors, whether they are criminal elements or governments or combatants in a traditional conflict, no longer need an independent press to get their message out. Journalists used to be welcome because people felt like at least if a journalist is with me, they'll tell my story; and they can do that now themselves.
>
> The rise of social media has made it possible for them to be their own storytellers and they prefer that because they prefer to tell their story from their own point of view rather than having someone who might be critical, or at least someone who'll put another side in the story as well. So every place now is more dangerous because journalists generally are unwelcome. (Kathleen Carroll, Senior Vice President and Executive Editor, Associated Press)

She also observes, however, some of the more beneficent ways in which new technologies can assist journalists and help to keep them safe(r) when reporting dangerous situations:

> That you have an ability now to track people. You can use technology as a safety device and people can be in touch more easily, and that can be because there's more cellphone footprint in more parts of the world than there was ten years ago and you don't necessarily have to use sat phones which sometimes are more easily traced by the bad guys who might be looking for you.
>
> Technology is lighter, for the most part. You don't necessarily always have to have a big kit of heavy video camera gear. You don't have to travel with a satellite dish and all those things that can draw attention to you and slow you down and require fuel and things like that.

So generally I think it's a little bit safer and sometimes even when you can't get a sat phone or a cellphone signal out, you can find an internet café somewhere where you might be able to send texts and things. So you generally can be more in touch and that's generally a safety issue, and the lighter equipment makes things a little bit easier as well, you're less easily identified. So on the whole, I would say technology has made things a bit better. (Kathleen Carroll, Senior Vice President and Executive Editor, Associated Press)

Stuart Hughes, from a broadcasting perspective, also sees both advantages and possible, increased risks following the introduction of new, lightweight, easily portable communications technologies. He ruminates on the possible psychology at work with these new technologies, and how this can indirectly inform risk-reporting behaviours:

Now with your mobile phone, you can broadcast live from anywhere. You can file video from anywhere and I think that's fantastic. It means that you're not travelling like an Egyptian caravan on camels across the desert with hundreds of kilos of kit.

And that's good and potentially makes you safer. It means that you can get in and out of places more quickly. It means that you are potentially less of a target because the cameras are smaller and that's all good and of course, you can get the stories out. Think back to the Falklands War in 1982 when the tapes were being shipped back from the Falkland Islands on a ship. Now as long as you've got a little satellite briefcase gadget you can send them from anywhere. So potentially that does create an opportunity for being safer.

Conversely, does that mean that in some people's mind they think that they're less of a target because they're less conspicuous, because they're not carrying big cameras. Does that encourage people to take risks that they wouldn't take otherwise, to go a bit further, to stay a bit too long, to be a bit too casual? I don't know the answer to that. I think there's pluses and minuses. Maybe if you're in a particularly challenging situation, if you've got a lot of kit, maybe you think we know that we're a target so we'll just quickly do what we need to do and get out. Whereas if you're just there with a little camera, maybe your sense of risk or your awareness of you being a target, you get a little bit complacent. So there are pluses and minuses. (Stuart Hughes, Producer, BBC World Affairs)

A younger, independent journalist and documentary-maker offers a different perspective in terms of how social media, particularly, can enhance her work, informing her thinking and continuing to build networks of interest based on her earlier and current media reporting and productions:

> For me I see it as an opportunity that has increased my capacity really. Some of the things I need to do, for example, is to poll local opinions; now just on my Facebook alone I have 20,000 followers, I have close to 5,000 friends, and all of these people, the majority of them are people that used to listen to me on Voice of America, folks that are on the ground in Somalia, all over the world, partly the Somali Diaspora. So if I wanted to do polling before I went off and did some shooting, for example, I could easily just put a question on my Facebook page and say, 'hey guys could you help me out?' and I would get enough people to respond without having to move. This is how social media, I think, has helped me.
>
> Similarly if I want to find out what the prevailing opinions are on a specific issue before I take a certain approach in my story development, the script I'm writing, then I'll put that out on Twitter, I'll put it out on Facebook, and ask people, 'hey what do you think of this?' and people start generating their opinions.
>
> For me I think it's a helpful tool from the journalist practitioner perspective, so from a practice perspective it's quite helpful, but it can be dangerous in the sense that it's an ungoverned space, so when you have people living and residing in ungoverned territories engaging with an ungoverned space online anything can happen, and that's why I think problematic issues can arise. (Idil Osman, freelance journalist and documentary maker)

In such ways, journalists weigh up both the advantages and disadvantages of today's rapidly changing communications environments and their associated technologies. As we can see, they both recognise the increased risks afforded by universalising accessibility and the capacity for independent communications within conflict situations and how this devalues the former use-value of journalists to combatants and the 'bad guys' to get 'their message across'. But we have heard too of how the portability of new, lightweight technologies as well as their surveillance capacity considerably enhances the speed of communications and manoeuvrability of journalists on the ground, though how exactly this plays into the psychology of risk assessment and reporting behaviours has yet to be seriously explored – and needs to be. And we have also heard how social media and online communications can sensitise and inform reporting and media productions before, during and after the production of such reports, building constituencies of interest but also, potentially, recreating conflicts in such virtual environments and facilitating hatreds and threats.

The dark side of the Internet and digital surveillance, we also found, have yet to fully register with most of the journalists consulted, with some only vaguely aware of how to secure their communications during the production processes of news reporting and involving possibly vulnerable sources. Stuart Hughes describes the situation at the BBC in respect of digital surveillance and its associated risks, and provides what we suspect is a widely shared view on the situation that currently obtains within major news organisations more generally, a view that suggests more will have to be done in the future to try and ensure both the safety of journalists and their sources in a context of anticipated malevolent digital surveillance:

It's something we're starting to think about more seriously. I would say that we – we being the BBC and I can't speak for the BBC but I think most journalists who work for large news organisations are aware that we're probably further behind in the data security side of things than a lot of the hacker technology community. I've certainly learned a lot from what's going on outside and I often describe the BBC as being like one of these big cargo ships. If you decide you want to turn around, it takes a very long time for this big ship to turn around. ... I think we're aware of things like geolocation, the dangers that that can pose. I think we're aware of some of the operational security in terms of giving away information about where we are through Tweets and that kind of stuff. I think we've probably still got a way to go on some of the more advanced stuff in terms of hacking and so on. I think up until now probably most news organisations have been quite lucky in that all of the hacking that has taken place has been just nuisance. Nuisance hacking like the Syrian Electronic Army tries to hack the BBC Twitter account. It's annoying but it doesn't put anybody's life at risk.

But I think those kind of issues, especially because so much of our communications now are digital and because we're used to having connectivity and because we're used to having Gmail and being able to Tweet and being able to send Facebook messages, I think there's a danger that we lose sight of the potential for that to be used maliciously and I think that's probably going to be an area that the BBC as a whole looks at more and more. (Stuart Hughes, Producer, BBC World Affairs)

Conclusions

This chapter has sought, with the help of our journalist practitioners, to get closer to the world of reporting in hazardous environments, and to better appreciate the processes and practices involved, whether organisationally and at the outset of the assignment decision-making or professionally and expediently when working in the field. We have heard experienced and less experienced journalists' views and accounts on some of the policies and procedures designed to keep them safe(r), and how and why it is that these are not always strictly adhered to, whether through the privileging of personal knowledge and experience, differing attitudes to risk and danger, or the inequalities of training and resources that characterize the journalism industry around the world as well as the differentiated risk positions occupied by staffers and free-lancers, stringers and fixers, and national and international journalists.

We have also heard the journalists' views on the rapidly transforming communications environment in which they work, and how this now enters into their reporting practices and affects the nature of the risks and dangers which they must confront. Sometimes, this is indirect and derives from the wider sea changes in communications accessibility and the capacity of belligerents as well as citizen journalists and activists to bypass mainstream news media channels and send their own messages direct to their preferred audiences on their own terms and with their preferred images. This, according to many of our respondents, has increasingly undermined the earlier dependence of conflicting parties on news journalists, and has thereby positioned journalists, in their eyes at least, as relatively redundant and therefore possibly without value. But so too has the digital revolution produced highly portable equipment that can easily and universally connect with wider networks and transmit images and words, events and ideas, around the globe in near real-time.

The advent of social media now promises to make greater inroads into production processes, sensitising and informing journalists of the different views and values, identities and interests, in contention, and equipping them to produce better informed and better grounded accounts and story treatments (Pantti et al. 2012, Hänska-Ahy and Shapour

2013). But so too does the digital revolution and its enhanced surveillance capacity not only empower journalism and the civil sphere to monitor unfolding conflicts and human rights abuses, but also potentially affords malevolent social and political forces to monitor, disrupt and potentially intimidate or worse target journalists' communications and their sources (Cottle 2011, Morozov 2012).

As all our interviewees have suggested, the changing communications environment is neither simply benevolent nor malevolent, nor is it simply advantageous or disadvantageous to journalists working in dangerous and difficult situations; it can be both, depending on how the opportunities that it facilitates as well as the new challenges that it poses become leveraged in practice and by whom. The field of journalism safety and security will undoubtedly become increasingly technologically shaped and informed. In the future, the journalism industry will need to factor into its thinking and practices new and novel ways in which this technology can be put to work in keeping journalists if not safe, certainly safer, in the dangerous and vital work they do in shining a world spotlight on the dark crises and dangerous crevices of inhumanity around the globe.

References

Cottle, S. (2011) 'Media and the Arab Uprisings 2011: Research Notes', *Journalism: Theory, Practice & Criticism*, 12(5): 647–659.

Hänska-Ahy, M. and Shapour, R. (2013) 'Who's Reporting the Protests? Converging Practices of Citizen Journalists and Two BBC World Service Newsrooms, from Iran's Election Protests to the Arab Uprisings', *Journalism Studies*, 14(1): 29–45.

Morozov, E. (2012) *The Net Delusion: How Not to Liberate the World*. London: Penguin.

Murrell, C. (2010) 'Baghdad Bureaux: An Exploration of the Inter-Connected World of Fixers and Correspondents at the BBC and CNN', *Media, War and Conflict*, 3(2): 125–137.

Murrell, C. (2015) *Foreign Correspondents and International Newsgathering: The Role of Fixers*. New York and London: Routledge.

Pantti, M., Wahl-Jorensen, K. and Cottle, S. (2012) *Disasters and the Media*. New York: Peter Lang.

Part IV
From Protecting to Safeguarding

8
Protecting Journalists: An Evolving Responsibility

Richard Sambrook

The Newseum in Washington DC, run by the Freedom Forum, lists 69 reporters killed during the Second World War and 66 in the ten peak years of the Vietnam War. In Iraq in 2003, the (Committee to Protect Journalists) says more than 70 were killed. Both organisations recognise those numbers may be under-reported. However, the correlation between casualties in a global conflict over six years, and a regional conflict lasting just weeks indicates the increase in risk for journalists over the intervening 60 years. If you include the subsequent insurgency in Iraq during the following eight years, the figure rises to more than 200 – the vast majority Iraqi – according to the CPJ (Smyth 2013).

Journalist casualties in Chechnya in the1990s were, according to the CPJ – 13; in Somalia – 15; in Bosnia – 25. Again, the majority of them were local journalists. The figures for the Syrian conflict, including 'citizen journalists', runs into the hundreds. The International News Safety Institute (INSI) estimates that in the decade from 2004–2014 almost 1,500 journalists died – 50 per cent more than in the previous decade (CPJ 2015). The figures reveal that more journalists are being killed now than at any time since records were kept.

Journalists have always taken risks to report the most extreme events in the world – particularly conflict. From William Russell in the Crimea in the nineteenth century, to the Spanish Civil War prefiguring the Second World War, to Vietnam, the Falklands and the Middle East, there are many examples of well-known correspondents paying the ultimate price in doing so. Nicholas Tomalin, correspondent for *The Sunday Times*, killed in the Yom Kippur war in 1973; David Blundy, correspondent for the UK's *Sunday Correspondent*, shot by a sniper in El Salvador in 1989; Dan Eldon, a 22-year-old photo journalist, beaten to death in Somalia in 1993; BBC Correspondent John Schofield, shot

171

in Croatia in 1995; Daniel Pearl of the *Wall Street Journal*, beheaded in Pakistan in 2002; ITN's Terry Lloyd, killed in southern Iraq in 2003 – the list is extensive. But the list of less well-known local journalists killed is far longer.

As we saw in Chapter 3, recording accurate casualty figures is still a rough science. In the early and mid-twentieth century, there was no central organisation collating them globally. Today, there are several, but they all employ different criteria and offer slightly different figures. Some record only journalists employed by a professional news organisation; others include freelances; some record 'citizen journalists' separately; some include camera-operators, producers or translators – others don't. Increasingly, the different groups recording casualties are being more transparent about how and what they record – which allows greater coherence if not entirely common tallies. However, the relentless upward trend is clear.

This increase in risk is due to the factors we identified earlier – particularly the increasingly blurred lines between citizens and professional journalists, and the changing character of global conflicts. In these circumstances, the journalist's responsibility to bear witness, seek multiple viewpoints and challenge what they are told places them in even greater jeopardy than in the past.

However, the industry's response to these changing circumstances has been in many respects slow and fragmented. A long-established journalistic culture initially resisted attempts to professionalise its response to conflict and risk, baulked at the cost, and competitive and other factors militated against concerted action. In many ways, this fragmented approach persists.

For much of the twentieth century, news organisations accepted that the still rare death of a journalist was a hard but unsurprising price of newsgathering. Many industries face casualties. However, in the news industry there was little serious attention – or others might argue responsibility taken – until the scale of risk became unignorable.

This happened in the 1990s – largely due to the civil wars in the Balkans and in Chechnya. These were the first major conflicts in Europe since the Second World War, and grew directly from the end of the Cold War between East and West in 1989. A new nationalism was born with the characteristics of insurgency, fluid lines and allegiances that we have had to adjust to in the intervening years.

In 2007, INSI published a report – *Killing The Messenger* – into what then was the bloodiest decade in history for journalists – 1996–2007 – in which more than 1,000 journalists and media workers lost their lives. Nearly two-thirds of them were murdered. (As noted earlier, that rate has increased by some 50 per cent since.) This was the decade in which the news industry – large newsgathering organisations like the BBC, CNN, AP and Reuters – began to take safety seriously. They developed and introduced safety training for conflict zones, started to provide equipment such as armoured cars, helmets and flak jackets – sometimes against the wishes of their staff who felt self conscious with what might have been interpreted as a quasi-military approach (see Chapter 7). *Professionalisation* of newsgathering in conflict was a new and in some quarters controversial approach. Until then, journalists had learned on the job and relied on luck or judgement to keep themselves alive.

The BBC's Jeremy Bowen recalls his first assignment to El Salvador:

> In the next few days other journalists with more experience told me how to try to look after myself and the people with me. Don't look like a soldier, don't run fast, make sure you always look like a journalist, a non-combatant. Most journalists covering urban wars in the 1980's did not have flak jackets or helmets, because the theory was it was better to look like a civilian. On the streets in El Salvador the custom was to wave white flags and yell '*periodista*', Spanish for journalist, in the hope the gunmen would not shoot ... the only special equipment I had in El Salvador in 1989 was a pair of running shoes: I thought I might need to run away. (Bowen 2006, p. 446)

But by the mid-1990s, journalists, once used to wandering wherever they liked, were now being targeted by insurgents and militias, and were losing their lives in increasing numbers.

The lead was taken by Chris Cramer – then Head of Newsgathering at the BBC (and later to work for CNN, Thomson-Reuters and the WSJ). He recalls that in the early 1990s in the UK, new legislation was introduced making employers liable for where they sent their staff and the support they provided:

> The wake-up call for me came when BBC newsmen covered the siege of Dubrovnik in October 1991. The team I had assigned there decided the situation was too dangerous to stay. The city was under constant bombardment and their lives were at risk. They told me they were leaving.

> I was furious, knowing that our media competitors were going to sty and, as it turned out, produced remarkable coverage which won several broadcast awards.
>
> How could my staff do this to me? How could they leave a story of such magnitude when the world needed to know what it looked liked and how it felt to the people who lived there?
>
> Then – my epiphany. How could I react this way? ... Since I had deployed staff to a war zone ... then I was legally – and for that matter morally – responsible for their safety. Everything else was secondary. (Owen & Purdey 2009, p. 169)

This was backed up by the BBC's then safety officer, Peter Hunter, who strongly advocated serious training and awareness, arguing that the media should be no different from other professions that have to put themselves in harm's way – taking training, safety awareness and first aid seriously by adopting a professional approach.

So Cramer led a programme of change through the BBC, with support from senior management and the Board of Governors, for developing training, offering equipment, providing insurance (including for freelances) and setting a criterion that no-one would be deployed to a conflict zone without battlefield first-aid and awareness training. Other major organisations were arriving at similar conclusions at this time. But the BBC, with its global reach and reputation, took a decisive lead.

Staff were not entirely happy, arguing that flak jackets were too heavy, or likely to get stolen, or that such equipment distinguished them unhelpfully from the local population, or that training was simply unnecessary. The BBC implemented and stuck to its policy, and slowly attitudes changed.

There were other initiatives on the ground as well. The BBC correspondent Martin Bell, recalls the 'Sarajevo pool' – an unprecedented collaboration between competitive newsgathering organisations designed to reduce risk. It meant only one cameraman a day would go out and risk the shelling and snipers, with all news organisations then sharing the coverage:

> It made arithmetical sense. But it wasn't popular. It penalised the brave. It rewarded the indolent, who need not leave the hotel or their bunkers at the TV station, as many did not and yet were feted as heroes in their home countries. It went against the traditional grain of winner-takes-all journalism. And the news agencies' managers did not approve at all, at least at the outset. One called his producer and

demanded an explanation .... 'What's got into you guys? Have you lost your killer instinct?' (Bell 1995, p. 64)

The pool eventually broke down under competitive pressure from the news agencies, but it was an important initiative offering unprecedented collaboration between competitors and establishing safety as a higher priority than scoops.

During this period, hostile-environment training courses were developed working with ex-military advisors. Typically, these courses would cover situational awareness in conflict zones, awareness of risk, familiarity with the capability of different armaments and battlefield first aid. They would include some role-playing of passing through hostile checkpoints or being taken hostage. These courses were widely adopted by broadcasters and news agencies around the world, allowing numerous providers to develop businesses based on training the media. Print organisations were less swift to adopt such training as standard practice, although that too gradually changed as the training became better established. Later, as the risks continued to rise, these safety-training providers would also offer ex-military advisors to escort journalists on location in hostile areas.

However, this approach is still open to debate. In 2013, the BBC's Afghanistan correspondent, David Loyn, wrote:

There is a 'triangle' of ownership of risk in news organisations – involving safety advisers, news managers and journalists in the field – and the pendulum has swung between them over the years. ...

But challenges still remain, and the balance is now shifting so that both managers and journalists increasingly want safety advisers to take more control, which the best of them are resisting. At it's worst, this development has led to risk assessment being a box-ticking exercise, an insurance policy or comfort blanket for managers. And handing over control – outsourcing safety decisions to security advisers in an almost mystical belief in the quality of ex-soldiers – has led to a generation of journalists growing up who have had personal responsibility trained out of them. (Loyn 2014)

News organisations, trying to adopt a professional approach and accept appropriate duty of care, have to balance that against the importance of journalistic independence and editorial-led decision-making on the ground. Trying to define best practice and manage it across diverse organisations and journalistic communities in a wide range of volatile situations has often proved problematic.

In 2000, after the first years of establishing a new safety culture, the BBC, Reuters, APTN, CNN and ITN agreed a set of safety guidelines designed to establish best practice:

1. The preservation of human life and safety is paramount. Staff and freelancers should be made aware that unwarranted risks in pursuit of a story are unacceptable and must be strongly discouraged. Assignments to warzones or hostile environments must be voluntary, and should only involve experienced newsgathering practitioners.
2. All staff and freelancers asked to work in hostile environments must have access to appropriate safety training and retraining. Employers are encouraged to make this mandatory.
3. Employers must provide efficient safety equipment to all staff and freelancers assigned to hazardous locations, including personal issue Kevlar vest/jackets, protective headgear and properly protected vehicles if necessary.
4. All staff and feelancers should be afforded personal insurance while working in hostile areas, including cover against death and personal injury.
5. Employers are to provide and encourage the use of voluntary and confidential counselling for staff and freelancers returning from hostile areas or after the coverage of distressing events. (This is likely to require some training of media managers in the recognition of the symptoms of Post Traumatic Stress Disorder.)
6. Media companies and their representatives are neutral observers. No member of the media should carry a firearm in the course of his or her work.
7. Media companies should work together to establish a data bank of safety information, including the exchange of up-to-date safety assessments of hostile and dangerous areas. (Owen & Purdey 2009, p. 172)

There are a number of notable points about this first set of common guidelines.

Firstly, and most obviously, it was the initial example of a cross-industry group seeking to collaborate and establish a new benchmark of best practise. News is a highly competitive arena and collaboration is therefore always difficult. However, there was broad recognition that safety should not be a competitive issue. Coordination amongst news providers – and amongst support NGOs – remains a key issue, however, in addressing more fully the problems surrounding journalist safety.

Secondly, this first set of guidelines recognised issues which were to develop and become crucial areas of sometimes heated debate in the years ahead. For example, the duty of care towards freelances: that these major organisations ought to both accept responsibility for the freelances they used, including with insurance, but in doing so help professionalise the freelance community through encouraging safety training and awareness.

Insurance became a difficult issue, with some employers refusing to accept liability for non-staff journalists and insurance companies unwilling to insure those setting out into hostile environments without the full and explicit support and training a major organisation can provide. And some news editors believed some freelances took unacceptable risks and exposed commissioners to unfair liability. As a result, they refused to accept freelance work.

Following the death of Marie Colvin in Homs in 2012, *The Sunday Times* refused all photographs and copy of the Syrian conflict submitted by freelances as they did 'not wish to encourage freelancers to take exceptional risks'. In a statement, *The Sunday Times'* parent company News International said to CBS: '*The Sunday Times* foreign desk does not believe that freelancers, many who have had no training and have no insurance or back up, are the best people to place on the front lines'. Other major UK broadsheets have revealed they back *The Sunday Times* approach and all have initiated similar policies.

In due course, many in the freelance world felt the industry had an over-developed sense of 'duty of care' which was prohibiting them from making a legitimate living from freelance journalism.

Vaughan Smith, founder of London's Frontline Club, and in the 1990s the Frontline News agency, has sought to help freelances better represent their interests with the major news organisations. He set up a Frontline Freelance Register as a first step in organising freelance journalists around the world. He believes freelances should take responsibility for being professionally trained, but then news organisations should accept them as a core and trusted part of any news operation:

> There has to be a universal minimum bar of entry into war journalism for those that travel to join it and that bar must include the maintenance of appropriate first aid skills. We have the right to expect that if we are injured and can be saved then our colleagues will have the skills to do so. We should correct negative assumptions about freelancers. In truth their content is now indispensable. In

fact, freelance operators have become, on the whole, more experienced in covering conflicts than their employed colleagues. As way of example, freelance content dominates international news coverage of Syria. Without freelancers, reports would be reliant on material from activists, fighters and other local observers.

Freelancers have a surprising potential to collaborate and organise themselves to improve their collective safety and there is long-established freelance practice in mentoring. Freelancers lack resources but the very many serious ones have no lack of integrity or commitment. (Smith 2014)

At the same time, the definition of a freelance journalist, set against a citizen journalist, became more complex and intractable with the availability of cheap digital equipment lowering barriers to entry and allowing anyone to easily produce digital content. This too argued for the professional freelance community to organise themselves and set some minimum expected standards.

Also identified in those early guidelines, the principle of never carrying arms came under pressure during the height of the post 2003 Iraq insurgency. Bluntly, it was impossible for news teams to operate in some areas without armed protection. Some organisations withdrew, others employed, selectively, armed security advisors making the key distinction between journalists being armed and those paid to protect them being armed. It is not a topic which any organisation was comfortable discussing, but as Mark Wood, former Editor in Chief of Reuters, explained in 2004:

In Baghdad, like most media organisations we always have security people alongside our teams now. It's one of the big expense items. And the big debate in the last few weeks has been around whether the security men should be armed or not ... the situation in Iraq is that travelling in and out is clearly so dangerous. One or two news organisations have stared to review that. A lot of the security guards now won't work unless they are armed. (Tumber and Webster 2006, p. 138)

CNN certainly believed that armed security escorts saved their teams' lives on more than one occasion (Owen & Purdey 2009, p. 184), but other organisations were less comfortable in accepting armed escorts. By and large, news organisations have held the line against newsgathering alongside private, armed security. But the nature of current conflicts means it is an issue that is likely to return.

Finally, the recognition of post traumatic stress disorder (PTSD) and counselling as an aspect of responsible management of staff were prescient. If professionalising physical safety was difficult, establishing the importance of emotional health was more controversial. The myth of the hard-bitten hack who shrugs off the troubling scenes they witness had a firm grip on the profession. It took years of discreet but persistent work for journalists and their managers to recognise that reporters are no more immune to the effects of what they witness than anyone else.

Mark Brayne is a former BBC correspondent who retrained as a psychotherapist specialising in PTSD among journalists. He makes the point that understanding trauma makes for better journalism. Much of journalism is about reporting on others who have experienced trauma – as much as it is reporters directly experiencing traumatic events:

> In the immediate aftermath of a traumatic event or experience, many of those involved will experience PTSD-like symptoms including intrusive recollections, numbing, avoidance and hyper-arousal … Just as flesh wounds take a couple of weeks to heal and bones a couple of months, there's a natural cycle to recovery from emotional trauma. (Owen et al. 2006, p. 204)

Training news-desk editors to recognise stress and support staff suffering from PTSD were other major steps in professionalising the news industry's attitude to safety and deploying staff to dangerous environments.

So, from the earliest attempts to establish some common principles of safety in news, a number of contentious issues emerged which continue to rumble unresolved in spite of the considerable progress which has been made.

These early, pan-industry principles were built upon in establishing the International News Safety Institute after the 2003 Iraq War. Although other news safety charities existed, INSI was differentiated by being an initiative which was driven *within* the industry by a growing concern for journalists safety

The International Federation of Journalists and The International News Safety Institute

In 2002 the International Federation of Journalists (IFJ) and the International Press Institute put forward a proposition to launch a new journalism safety body.

The proposal, at the International Press Institute's (IPI) annual congress in Ljubljana, said:

> Currently, only larger and well-resourced media organisations are providing systematic safety training for staff – Reuters, CNN, The BBC, Associated Press – these organisations have developed their own code of conduct on the issue which is being taken up by other broadcast media. Significantly, not one single press body has signed up.
>
> The problems are as follows:
>
> a) safety training is very expensive (up to 500$ a head per day) as is the provision of basic equipment (flak jackets and helmets)
> b) many of the journalists most in need are freelance;
> c) most of the victims of violence are local, without the capacity to receive in their own languages even basic training on safety issues;
> d) very little information exists on the establishment of a health and safety programme for media staff embracing risk awareness, stress and trauma counselling, etc.
>
> To combat this the IFJ proposes that media professional organisations (employers and trade unions) should establish a non-profit independent institution. (Appendix 2, IPI 2002)

With initial financial support from the IFJ, the organisation was launched on World Press Freedom Day, 2003 in the aftermath of the Iraq War.

Coming out of that conflict, one of the initial issues INSI and its members faced was an apparent high level of antagonism (or carelessness) between the military and the media (Paterson 2014). One of INSI's first successes was to engage with the British Ministry of Defence in the drafting of a new version of the 'Green Book' (INSI 2013, MoD 2013), which sets out arrangements for the media with UK armed forces at times of conflict. Critically, it established formal recognition that the media are entitled to work independently from the armed forces as well as on an embedded basis.

Attempts to engage the Pentagon in similar negotiations were unsuccessful, however. Nor could INSI or its members establish from the US armed forces explanations for the killing of a number of media staff (Paterson 2014).

INSI went on to launch a global inquiry into the factors behind journalists' deaths – *Killing The Messenger* – establishing that 1,000 journalists had died in ten years – most of them murdered (INSI 2007). As a consequence of that finding, and the continuing misgivings over the number of media casualties in Iraq, the organisation turned to the issue of impunity.

A letter from the IFJ's then Director, Aidan White, to the UN's Secretary-General Kofi Annan in August 2005 put the case:

> Altogether and counting all essential media staff including drivers and translators, we have registered some 95 journalists and media staff who have died in the Iraq conflict.
>
> The toll is appalling, with many of our colleagues helpless victims of a conflict in which there will be, inevitably, unavoidable casualties.
>
> However, some of these deaths could and should have been avoided.
>
> The United Nations has a responsibility to ensure that international law is enforced and the rights of victims in this conflict are properly protected. It is time, we believe, for the UN itself to demand that there is justice and respect for basic humanitarian rights on the part of democratic countries involved in this conflict. (Appendix 3, White 2005)

Later that year, at the U.N Information Summit in Tunis, the text of a draft UN resolution was discussed. A year later, on 23 December 2006, it was adopted as Resolution 1738.

Resolution 1738 (2006)

This was adopted by the Security Council at its 5,613th meeting, on 23 December 2006, on the question of the protection of civilians in armed conflict (United Nations Security Council 2006).[2]

The Security Council,
Bearing in mind its primary responsibility under the Charter of the United Nations for the maintenance of international peace and security, and underlining the importance of taking measures aimed at conflict prevention and resolution,

Reaffirming its resolutions 1265 (1999), 1296 (2000) and 1674 (2006) on the protection of civilians in armed conflict and its resolution 1502 (2003) on protection of United Nations personnel, associated personnel and humanitarian personnel in conflict zones, as well as other relevant resolutions and presidential statements,

Reaffirming its commitment to the Purposes of the Charter of the United Nations as set out in Article 1 (1–4) of the Charter, and to the Principles of the Charter as set out in Article 2 (1–7) of the Charter, including its commitment to the principles of the political independence, sovereign equality and territorial integrity of all States, and respect for the sovereignty of all States,

Reaffirming that parties to an armed conflict bear the primary responsibility to take all feasible steps to ensure the protection of affected civilians,

Recalling the Geneva Conventions of 12 August 1949, in particular the Third Geneva Convention of 12 August 1949 on the treatment of prisoners of war, and the Additional Protocols of 8 June 1977, in particular article 79 of the Additional Protocol I regarding the protection of journalists engaged in dangerous professional missions in areas of armed conflict,

Emphasizing that there are existing prohibitions under international humanitarian law against attacks intentionally directed against civilians, as such, which in situations of armed conflict constitute war crimes, and *recalling* the need for States to end impunity for such criminal acts,

Recalling that the States Parties to the Geneva Conventions have an obligation to search for persons alleged to have committed, or to have ordered to be committed a grave breach of these Conventions, and an obligation to try them before their own courts, regardless of their nationality, or may hand them over for trial to another concerned State provided this State has made out a prima facie case against the said persons,

Drawing the attention of all States to the full range of justice and reconciliation mechanisms, including national, international and 'mixed' criminal courts and tribunals and truth and reconciliation commissions, and *noting* that such mechanisms can promote not only individual responsibility for serious crimes, but also peace, truth, reconciliation and the rights of the victims,

Recognizing the importance of a comprehensive, coherent and action-oriented approach, including in early planning, of protection of civilians in situations of armed conflict. *Stressing*, in this regard, the need to adopt a broad strategy of conflict prevention, which addresses the root causes of armed conflict in a comprehensive manner in order to enhance the protection of civilians on a long-term basis, including by promoting sustainable development, poverty eradication, national reconciliation, good governance, democracy, the rule of law and respect for and protection of human rights,

Deeply concerned at the frequency of acts of violence in many parts of the world against journalists, media professionals and associated personnel in armed conflict, in particular deliberate attacks in violation of international humanitarian law,

Recognizing that the consideration of the issue of protection of journalists in armed conflict by the Security Council is based on the urgency and importance of this issue, and recognizing the valuable role that the Secretary-General can play in providing more information on this issue,

1. *Condemns* intentional attacks against journalists, media professionals and associated personnel, as such, in situations of armed conflict, and calls upon all parties to put an end to such practices;

2. *Recalls* in this regard that journalists, media professionals and associated personnel engaged in dangerous professional missions in areas of armed conflict shall be considered as civilians and shall be respected and protected as such, provided that they take no action adversely affecting their status as civilians. This is without prejudice to the right of war correspondents accredited to the armed forces to the status of prisoners of war provided for in article 4.A.4 of the Third Geneva Convention;

3. *Recalls also* that media equipment and installations constitute civilian objects, and in this respect shall not be the object of attack or of reprisals, unless they are military objectives;

4. *Reaffirms* its condemnation of all incitements to violence against civilians in situations of armed conflict, further reaffirms the need to bring to justice, in accordance with applicable international law, individuals who incite such violence, and indicates its willingness, when authorizing missions, to consider, where appropriate, steps in response to media broadcast inciting genocide, crimes against humanity and serious violations of international humanitarian law;

5. *Recalls its demand* that all parties to an armed conflict comply fully with the obligations applicable to them under international law related to the protection of civilians in armed conflict, including journalists, media professionals and associated personnel;

6. *Urges* States and all other parties to an armed conflict to do their utmost to prevent violations of international humanitarian law against civilians, including journalists, media professionals and associated personnel;

7. *Emphasizes* the responsibility of States to comply with the relevant obligations under international law to end impunity and to prosecute those responsible for serious violations of international humanitarian law;

8. *Urges* all parties involved in situations of armed conflict to respect the professional independence and rights of journalists, media professionals and associated personnel as civilians;

9. *Recalls* that the deliberate targeting of civilians and other protected persons, and the commission of systematic, flagrant and widespread violations of international humanitarian and human rights law in situations of armed conflict may constitute a threat to international peace and security, and *reaffirms in this regard its readiness* to consider such situations and, where necessary, to adopt appropriate steps;

10. *Invites* States which have not yet done so to consider becoming parties to the Additional Protocols I and II of 1977 to the Geneva Conventions at the earliest possible date;

11. *Affirms* that it will address the issue of protection of journalists in armed conflict strictly under the agenda item 'protection of civilians in armed conflict';

12. *Requests* the Secretary-General to include as a sub-item in his next reports on the protection of civilians in armed conflict the issue of the safety and security of journalists, media professionals and associated personnel.

This was the start of a new level of engagement by the UN and UN agencies with the issue of journalist safety, which we will consider in Chapter 9.

INSI has continued to provide safety training around the world and to facilitate cooperation and collaboration between news providers and freelances working in hostile areas. Its remit is now focused on prevention of harm, preparedness, and research and profile-raising for safety issues. It represents a strong example of the news industry self-organising to raise awareness, share best practice and engage politically to address the increased risks to journalists. It is an example built upon by other alliances like A Culture of Safety (ACOS) which brings together 90 news organisations to endorse common safety principles and support freelance journalists. (ACOS, 2015).

While major news providers were developing their practical approach to safety in the field, and negotiating the issues the new safety paradigm raised in a more complex dangerous environment, other NGOs continued to pursue policy objectives. And as the issues shifted through the 1990s, post-Iraq and into the conflicts surrounding the 'Arab Spring', other initiatives and organisations developed (see Appendix 1).

Notes

1. Available from: http://www.un.org/en/ga/search/view_doc.asp?symbol=S/RES/1738(2006) [Accessed September 6th 2015]

References

Bell, M. (1995) *In Harm's Way: Reflections of a War Zone Thug*. London: Hamish Hamilton.

Bowen, J. (2006) *War Stories*. London: Simon & Schuster.

Committee to Protect Journalists (CPJ). (2015). *1141 Journalists Killed since 1992*. Available from: <https://cpj.org/killed/> (last accessed on 6 August 2015).

Henrichsen, J., Betz, M. and Lisosky, J. (2015) *Building Digital Safety for Journalism: A Survey of Selected Issues*. Paris: UNESCO.

International News Safety Institute (INSI). (2007) *Killing the Messenger*. Available from <http://www.newssafety.org/safety/projects/killing-the-messenger/> (last accessed on 6 August 2015).

International News Safety Institute (INSI). (2013) *Media Military Relations*. Available from: <http://www.newssafety.org/safety/projects/media-military-relations/> (last accessed on 6 August 2015).

Loyn, D. (2014) *Newsgathering Safety and the Welfare of Freelancers: Duty of Care*. Available from <http://www.frontlineclub.com/wp-content/uploads/2013/06/Safety-Report_WEB.pdf> (last accessed on 6 August 2015).

Ministry of Defence (MoD). (2013) *Green Book*. Available from <https://www.gov.uk/government/uploads/system/uploads/attachment_data/file/70682/green-book_v8_20130131.pdf> (last accessed on 6 August 2015).

Owen, J. and Purdey, H. (Eds) (2009) *International News Reporting: Frontlines and Deadlines*. Oxford: Wiley & Blackwell.

Paterson, C. (2014) *War Reporters Under Threat*. London: Pluto Press.

Smith, V. (2014) *Newsgathering Safety and the Welfare of Freelancers: Introduction*. Available from <http://www.frontlineclub.com/wp-content/uploads/2013/06/Safety-Report_WEB.pdf> (last accessed on 6 August 2015).

Smyth, F. (2013) *Iraq War and News Media: A Look Inside the Death Toll.* Available from <https://cpj.org/blog/2013/03/iraq-war-and-news-media-a-look-inside-the-death-to.php> (last accessed on 6 August 2015).

Tumber, H. and Webster, F. (2006) *Journalists Under Fire.* London: Sage.

United Nations Security Council (2006) 'Resolution 1738 (2006)'. Available from <http://www.un.org/en/ga/search/view_doc.asp?symbol=S/RES/1738(2006)> (last accessed on 6 September 2015).

9

Safeguarding Journalists and the Continuing Responsibility to Report

Richard Sambrook

For more than 30 years, Colombia has been classified as one of the most dangerous countries for journalists in the world. In 35 years, 142 journalists were killed, largely as a consequence of the drugs trade and accompanying corruption. Alongside the murders there were hundreds of documented cases of threats, attacks, kidnapping and forced displacement.

In 2000, the country decided to implement a mechanism to protect journalists. It was built on the recognition that a free press was an essential element in confronting the country's problems. Today, some 21 national agencies take part in the scheme which handles about 130 requests a year, offering support to some 90 journalists on average. The costs exceed $7million a year.[1]

The system rests on a legal framework which enshrines the rights of journalists to report freely, and offers a set of underlying principles. These allow national agencies to respond with practical assistance. When a journalist asks for help, there is a risk assessment undertaken which determines the most appropriate response and the best agency to lead. Assistance can include an airline ticket out of the country, temporary relocation, bodyguards, provision of technical security equipment, support in moving location, coordinated media coverage and psychological support.

Although not perfect – and the system's site has testimony from journalists with frustrations about its operation – it is deemed to have made an important difference. Journalist casualties in Colombia have dropped significantly in the last 15 years – although not solely due to this project given the other social and political changes which have helped bring about an overall drop in violence in the country.

If nothing more, its existence is an important signal that the authorities are supporting independent journalism, and that those investigating crime are looked after by the state and civil society. In 2010, a similar scheme was launched in Mexico.

This is a strong illustration that coordinated action against violence, threats and impunity can have an impact. Crucially, it rests on a *policy and legal framework* which commits the state to supporting independent journalism and allows *practical measures* of support to follow. It supports these with *monitoring* activities and a commitment to raise *public awareness* about the issue. Equally crucially, it does not demand that the state license journalists or determine who is eligible. The criteria and risk assessment decide the appropriate response based on the nature of the threat.

The scheme has faced funding and resource issues, has encountered some fraud and elements of being 'played' by those who were not under serious threat, but as the schemes' wiki makes clear, its value is as much in its being a public statement of support for journalists at risk.

Those four responses – Policy, Practical Support, Monitoring and Awareness – provide the basis of all civil and political responses to the issue of journalist safety and impunity. They are all components of proper social and political support for the work of independent journalism. We have discussed the practical measures offered by news organisations and safety groups. Different actors take on different responsibilities – and some more than one. To date, the fragmentation of response across different parties has unquestionably undermined overall progress and effectiveness on all four of these responses. Increasingly, however, there are attempts to coordinate between all interested actors across all activities to provide a coherent vision of why and how civil society should support journalism.

Policy

It is clear that journalists rely on state and institutional support to be able to carry out their watchdog function on behalf of society. It requires appropriate legislation, an independent and functioning judiciary, strong state institutions, strong civil society and access to information. Without these, the issue of impunity is hard to address and intimidation of independent journalism can flourish. Without free expression and watchdog journalism, civil society is weakened and more vulnerable to crime and corruption.

The work of international bodies to win recognition of free journalism's centrality to political and economic health builds on the existing international statutes and conventions which offer some protection but which, in the view of many, are insufficient to deal with the scale of the current problem.

Currently, the status and protection afforded to journalists is encapsulated in international law principally through treating them as civilians with the associated rights in war or conflict and through civil human-rights legislation.

The main protection in conflict lies under the Geneva Conventions. First signed in 1864, and updated a number of times since, they are designed to protect civilians, the sick and wounded under the supervision of the International Red Cross. The Conventions are now ratified by nearly 200 states and are globally applicable. Under them, journalists are afforded the same rights and protection as civilians although there is specific mention of journalists.

Under Protocol 1, Article 79, 'Measures of Protection for Journalists', the Conventions state:

> Journalists engaged in dangerous professional missions in areas of armed conflict shall be considered civilian within the meaning of the Conventions;
>
> Journalists shall be protected as civilians provided that they take no actions adversely affecting their status as civilians, and without prejudice to the right of war correspondents accredited to the armed forces to the status provided for in Article 4 (A) (4) of the Third Convention;
>
> Journalists should obtain an identity card. This card, which shall be issued by the government of the state of which the journalist is a national or in whose territory he resides or in which the news medium employing him is located, shall attest to his status as a journalist. (ICRC, Geneva Conventions 2015)

This provision, affording no more or less protection than for civilians, means journalists should be spared from indiscriminate attack or used as hostages or from being the object of deliberate reprisals. If they are, international law can be used to prosecute the perpetrators.

Journalists are also covered by the Rome statute of the International Criminal Court, established in 2002 to end impunity for those responsible for crimes of significant concern to the international community. The ICC has 113 countries as signatories. Article 68 (1) of the Rome Statute says the Court should take 'appropriate measures to protect the safety, physical and psychological well-being, dignity and privacy of victims and witnesses'. Any direct action against civilians (including journalists, although the latter are not specified) shall constitute a war crime whether it occurs in an international or internal conflict.

In some respects, journalists are unlike civilians in time of war in that they actively seek the conflict rather than try to escape. Equally, however, journalists are not combatants and should not be treated as such.

There have been a number of initiatives to suggest journalists should hold some special status in war – identified by an emblem or particular accreditation. These have generally not been successful, largely because in current circumstances clear identification as a journalist may increase rather than reduce risk and licensing of journalists by parties in a conflict is deemed too problematic (although, of course, war correspondents and embedded reporters are generally accredited by one side or the other).

The Geneva Conventions and Rome Statute apply in situations of war or conflict. However the risk to journalists today is as much in countries formally at peace.

The general right to free expression is defined under Article 19 of the Universal Declaration of Human Rights. This asserts that 'everyone has the right to freedom of opinion and expression; this right includes freedom to hold opinions without interference and to seek, receive and impart information and ideas through any media and regardless of frontiers'. Crucially, Article 19 asserts this right as long as it is 'in accordance with the law' – placing a responsibility to abide by the state's rules alongside it.

The Council of Europe, which oversees the European Convention on Human Rights and the European Court, defines its role in protecting journalists more broadly. A paper commissioned by the Council of Europe Steering Committee on Media and Information Society (CDMSI) examined the protection offered to journalists from the case law of the European Court of Human Rights (Leach 2013). It outlines significant case law offering protection of the right to free expression and the right to be protected by the state when threatened. However, it also notes the responsibility of journalists to have acted in an ethical way and to have avoided criminal activity or anything approaching hate speech. As ever, rights are balanced with responsibilities in the greater interests of civil society.

The Council of Europe sees its role to enhance media freedom and the protection of journalists woven into multiple aspects of the Convention on Human Rights:

- Not only Article 10 of the ECHR, but also the number of autonomous rights guaranteed in the ECHR **is** potentially … implicated in issues surrounding the **safety of journalists and the fight against impunity**. Typically, they include: the right to life (Article 2); prohibition of torture (Article 3); right to liberty and security (Article 5); right to a fair trial (Article 6) and no punishment without law (Article 7). The ECHR has read positive State obligations into these rights.

- State obligations to protect the physical integrity of journalists under the European Convention on Human Rights can be simplified to: **prevention, protection and prosecution.**

- Attacks on, and intimidation of, journalists and other media actors inevitably have a very **chilling effect on freedom of expression.** The chill factor is all the more piercing when the prevalence of attacks and intimidation is compounded by a culture of legal impunity for their perpetrators.(Council of Europe, 2013)

Here the Council of Europe clearly identifies state responsibilities to protect journalists and address impunity. (In the US, of course, the First Amendment does not attempt to define the right to free expression or the state's responsibility to protect – it is drafted as a restraint on government interference with the media.)

Although journalists have some protection under these international provisions, many agencies and organisations believe they do not go far enough in offering adequate protection to journalists and free media.

Deeper international support has to start with the value of free media to open and democratic societies. There has therefore been an active debate among international and regional institutions on the importance of independent journalists: as defenders of human rights; in promoting open and accountable government; and in allowing economic and social development. Some governments do not accept this link and believe media should be more directly accountable to state objectives.

The World Bank started to make the connection between free speech and economic development in the 1990s but there were more autocratic members of the international community who resisted making any formal link. Each step in attempting to agree the importance of media freedom and protection for journalists to economic and political heath and stability has been hard fought against the opposition of countries and constituencies less enamoured of an open, Western, media model.

As Guy Berger, the Director of Freedom of Expression for UNESCO, has written:

Development is one thing, and attacks on journalists are another. But there's a link between them, and it's much deeper than many people may think. And because of this link, we can't expect sustainable or equitable development in a society unless journalists are able to do their work in safety.

Everyone knows that one of the worst violations of the right to freedom of expression is when journalists are subjected to threats or physical attacks. But less clear is how this impacts directly on development.

What connects safety and development is 'governance'. Imagine a triangle of 'development', 'journalism' and 'governance'. Optimum performance at each point can contribute to strengthening the others. But weakness in one can also affect the possibilities in the others. (UNESCO, Media and Development, p. 47)

That argument is not always recognised. Since the fall of the Marcos Dictatorship in 1986, there have been 146 murders of media staff in the Philippines – only 15 of which have been solved. A lawyer working for Filipino journalists, Prima Jesusa Quinsayas, suggests this is in part because neither the government nor wider society recognises the scale or implications of the problem:

In December 2012, the President was quoted as saying media killings in the Philippines are 'not a national catastrophe.'

Even the public seems unaware that these attacks against journalists affect their right and access to information, and their ability to engage in the public sphere. There is no outrage at the surge in media killings.

In a way, this is understandable as the country has urgent challenges on many fronts. It has yet to start full implementation of rehabilitation after super- typhoon *Yolanda* and already it has had to deal with other natural disasters. But the killings of journalists that reflect the culture of impunity as being deeply embedded in society, makes all citizens vulnerable. (UNESCO, Media and Development, p. 71)

This debate was reflected in the UN Report of the High-Level Panel of Eminent Persons on the Post-2015 Development Agenda published in 2013. In setting out ways to eradicate extreme poverty it recognised the importance of 'good governance and effective institutions' with two necessary conditions (UN 2013, Goal 10, p. 50):

- 'Ensure that people enjoy freedom of speech, association, peaceful protest and access to independent media and information'
- 'Guarantee the public's right to information and access to government data.'

By putting free media at the heart of the development challenge, it marked a significant advance from the UN Millennium Development goals, which had made scant mention of media. For those concerned with journalist safety, it was an important shift. Free media is essential to good governance, supporting economic and social development. But free media cannot be guaranteed without dealing with the rising threats to journalists and the issue of impunity.

In May 2013, alongside the High Level Panel report, the UN launched a Plan of Action on the Safety of Journalists and the Issue of Impunity. It called for a new UN inter-agency mechanism to assess journalist safety, for greater powers for the UN special rapporteur on freedom of expression, and for help for member states in passing national legislation to prosecute the killers of journalists (UN 2013).

It also encouraged greater cooperation and coordination between the UN and media safety groups, called for emergency response procedures (such as those introduced in Colombia), provisions for press safety in conflict zones and campaigns for global awareness. As part of the campaign objectives, as well as 3 May being World Press Freedom Day, 2 November was identified as the annual International Day to End Impunity to provide an annual event around which to build communications and awareness. (However, this plan also faced opposition before finally being agreed. Pakistan, India and Brazil – which have all had poor records of violence against journalists – initially objected to various provisions.)

The UNESCO plan was supported by the UN Chief Executives Board for co-ordination and was discussed by the Security Council in 2013. Late that year, the UN General Assembly passed another resolution on safety and impunity, calling on governments to protect journalists and bring to justice those who attack them.

In August 2014, UNESCO convened a Global Media Forum in Bali to discuss 'the roles of media in realising the future we want for all.' In a publication stemming from that meeting, UNESCO's Guy Berger said:

> Without safety of journalists, there can be no free, pluralistic and independent media. Safety is essential for the right of journalists to provide information without fearing for their security and life – in other words, for their exercise of the right to press freedom.
>
> Safety of journalists is also about citizens' right of access to information. Journalists often face violent attacks from people who want to keep certain information hidden. Such hostile acts jeopardize the fundamental right of society to be kept informed. When journalists are killed or intimidated, the flow of information dries up – and

development can be delayed or distorted. Conversely, by protecting journalists a society ensures that it can get the information it needs to shape its development. (UNESCO 2015, Media and Development)

The forum published the Bali Roadmap towards media development, which, among other measures, called on governments 'to promote and implement the UN Plan of Action on the Safety of Journalists and the Issue of Impunity'.

In 2015 the UN Sustainable Development Goals (SDGs) were published with agreed performance indicators. Among the 169 targets in 16 goals, is a commitment to 'ensure public access to information and protect fundamental freedoms in accordance with national legislation and international agreements'. This underlined the responsibility of the state in ensuring press freedom and safety. UNESCO, the Office for the High Commissioner for Human Rights, and various advocacy organisations have pressed for including a media-freedom metric, principally measured by progress in regard to the number of cases of attacks, kidnappings and killings of journalists, human-rights defenders and trades unionists. But that will be one of some 32,000 data sets from 193 countries – a daunting task.

The commitment is an important means of ensuring that the role of independent journalism and its contribution to civil societies are fully recognised and supported by the international community, and endorsed at the highest political levels. It further strengthens the pressure and resources for monitoring and confronting violent intimidation and impunity.

However statistics alone can be misleading. In the first part of 2015, France was the country with most journalist-related deaths, purely due to the single attack on the offices of Charlie Hebdo. France is hardly the most dangerous country in which to operate as a journalist. Similarly, an absence of casualties or victims may simply indicate a level of repression which prevents independent journalists from working at all.

Monitoring and awareness

Monitoring and measurement of progress are important components of any civil response to safety and impunity. There are a number of initiatives which also feed into broader awareness-raising of the issue of journalists' safety.

For example, the Organisation for Security and Co-operation in Europe (OSCE), through its Representative on Freedom of the Media, monitors member states and intervenes where it believes free media may be at risk or where journalists are seen to be at risk. The Representative responds quickly and directly with the participating states and other parties through diplomatic channels and public statements. It also offers a Safety of Journalists guidebook, providing practical advice. The Council of Europe has launched an Internet site to promote the protection of journalism and the safety of journalists. Working with partner agencies, it highlights attacks on journalists and infringements of free speech, and disseminates information through social media (CoE 2015).

Other media safety groups and human-rights organisations, such as Article 19, offer similar monitoring operations.

In the US, President Obama introduced the Daniel Pearl Freedom of the Press Act in 2010. Named after the *Wall Street Journal* correspondent who was murdered in Pakistan in 2002, the Act expanded the examination of freedom of the press worldwide reflected in the State Department's annual reports on Human Rights practices. Rep. Adam Schiff, the main sponsor of the act, stated:

> We hope this legislation will help the United States work with other nations to better protect his colleagues serving on the frontlines in the fight for greater accountability and transparency. Freedom of expression cannot exist where journalists are not safe from persecution and attack. Our government must promote freedom of the press by putting on center stage those countries in which journalists are killed, imprisoned, kidnapped, threatened, or censored. (Schiff 2010)

It's a further example of a major power attempting to use its international weight to monitor abuses, raise awareness and encourage an end to impunity.

In addition, the opportunity offered by declaring 3 May World Press Freedom Day, and 2 November 2 an International Day to end Impunity allows the international community to make regular declarations of intent.

One of the strongest examples was the Medellin Declaration on World Press Freedom Day in 2007. Multiple parties assembled by UNESCO in Colombia signed a joint declaration designed to confront the issue of impunity and journalist killings in Colombia. Among many other points, it urged all states:

> To investigate all acts of violence of which journalists, media professionals and associated personnel are victims which have occurred

in their territory or abroad when their armed or security forces may have been involved in them;

To search for persons alleged to have committed, or to have ordered to be committed, a crime against journalists, media professionals or associated personnel, to bring such persons, regardless of their nationality, before their own courts or to hand them over for trial to another concerned State, provided this State has made out a credible case against the said persons; (UN Medellin Declaration 2007)

Similarly, on World Press Freedom Day 2015, the UN Special Rapporteur on Freedom of Opinion and Expression, the Organization for Security and Co-operation in Europe (OSCE) Representative on Freedom of the Media, the Organization of American States (OAS) Special Rapporteur on Freedom of Expression and the African Commission on Human and Peoples' Rights (ACHPR) Special Rapporteur on Freedom of Expression and Access to Information, issued a joint declaration on Freedom of Expression and Responses to Conflict Situations, which included the assertion that:

States have an obligation to take effective measures to prevent attacks against journalists and others exercising their right to freedom of expression and to combat impunity, in particular by vigorously condemning such attacks when they do occur, by investigating them promptly and effectively in order to duly sanction those responsible, and by providing compensation to the victims where appropriate. States also have an obligation to provide protection to journalists and others exercising their right to freedom of expression who are at a high risk of being attacked. (Article 19 et al. 2015)

These are examples of co-ordinated action to raise awareness and bring multiple voices to support a common objective. Cynics might suggest they have little direct impact on the ground. However, by continuing to build awareness and debate over a period of time, supporters would argue they can change the political climate, place pressure on member states and support the introduction of more practical measures.

Awareness-raising, monitoring and policy initiatives need to be matched by more pragmatic responses. The news organisations have sought to professionalise their operations but are sometimes reluctant to publicise journalism casualties and the wider issue in case it appears that they are guilty of special pleading in their own interests.

One exception was the Finnish newspaper *Ilta-Sanomat*, which ran an 80-part series on journalist safety offering case studies from around the world (BBC 2013). The series was later translated by UNESCO into all six official UN languages. The extent to which the media should use its own channels to build support in its own interests by publicising the risks for journalists remains a contentious debating point among editors. However, the UN representative for the Global Forum for Media Development, Bill Orme, who has worked closely on the inclusion of free-media and journalism safety in the 2015 Sustainable Development Goals, is clear that journalists have a responsibility to help themselves:

> Diplomats and staff professionals at the UN who strongly support the proposed SDG 16.10 target have stressed to civil society activists that meaningful transparency and accountability provisions and indicators in the SDGs [Sustainable Development Goals] require sustained public engagement on the issue – and active coverage of the debate by the journalists whose interests a post-2015 access-to-information commitment would help protect. (UNESCO, Media and Development 2015, p. 91)

In an effort to promote collaboration on journalist safety between news organisations, NGOs and other agencies, UNESCO held a conference in February 2016 on the safety of media professionals with a view to strengthening collaboration and reinforcing news organisations involvement in safety. It was recognition that safety is an area where a wide coalition of interests can be brought together. There are other areas in which pragmatic action might make a decisive difference. At a symposium on journalism safety held by the BBC in April 2014, David McCraw, the Assistant General Counsel for the *New York Times*, said he believed there should be a strategic, legal response to the problem of impunity. Drawing an analogy with the US civil rights movement in the 1960s, he suggested there was a need for an international legal NGO which could pursue affirmative litigation. Which courts in which countries can offer a fair trial? Which cases have sufficient evidence to mount a successful prosecution? He suggested that to confront impunity and change the climate in which killing journalists was regarded as low-risk, the international community should identify and go after the winnable cases and build momentum (BBC 2014).

Addressing the problem of journalist safety, and impunity for their killers, is one which, like the civil-rights movement 50 years ago, will require courage, persistence and the determination to move public opinion. There is scope for greater collaboration and coordination between concerned parties, and for further initiatives to close the gap between policy and practice.

Champions of free expression have long argued that it rests on journalists being able to do their jobs safely and without intimidation. It is a strong argument, but one which is failing in many parts of the world. Press Freedom has more battles to fight to be recognised as a basic human right. And there is further to go in asserting the broader civic responsibility to defend independent journalism and the rights and social value of free reporting.

It is a multidimensional problem – but at its core lies recognition that journalism and civil society are indivisible.

Reporting from uncivil societies remains as crucial as it has ever been – but in many places has become more dangerous than it has ever been.

As for the motivation of journalists taking high risks to report from the most dangerous of uncivil societies, we might reflect on the words of Marie Colvin, spoken two years before her death at a memorial service for colleagues who had been killed reporting the news:

> In an age of 24/7 rolling news, blogs and Twitters, we are on constant call wherever we are. But war reporting is still essentially the same – someone has to go there and see what is happening. You can't get that information without going to places where people are being shot at, and others are shooting at you. The real difficulty is having enough faith in humanity to believe that enough people be they government, military or the man on the street, will care when your file reaches the printed page, the website or the TV screen. We do have that faith because we believe we do make a difference. (Colvin 2012)

Notes

1. The system is explained in detail on its official wiki page: <http://journalist protection.wikispaces.com/> (last accessed on 12 August 2015).

References

Article 19 et al. (2015) *Joint Declaration on Freedom of Expression and Responses to Conflict Situation.* Available from <https://www.article19.org/resources.php/ resource/37951/en/joint-declaration-on-freedom-of-expression-and-responses-to-conflict-situation> (last accessed on 15 August 2015).

BBC (2013) *How Journalist Safety and Freedom of Speech Made the Headlines in Finland.* Available from <http://www.bbc.co.uk/blogs/collegeofjournalism/entries/ 866fd335-c152-368f-bbcc-52671d8c08cd> (last accessed on 21 August 2015).

BBC Academy (2014) *'Getting Away with Murder?' How to Fight Impunity through Law.* Available from: <https://www.youtube.com/watch?v=LXgcy_CyqaI& index=6&list=PLom7Q2FZ5qMOWPH4j-y-D-zryDCQYRxx> (last accessed on 10 August 2015).

Colvin, M. (2012) *'Our Mission Is to Report These Horrors of War with Accuracy and Without Prejudice'.* Available from: <http://www.theguardian.com/commentis

free/2012/feb/22/marie-colvin-our-mission-is-to-speak-truth> (last accessed on 10 July 2015).

Committee to Protect Journalists (CPJ) (2014) *Attacks on the Press: Journalism on the World's Front Lines.* New York: Wiley.

Council of Europe (CoE) (2015) *Media Freedom.* Available from: <http://www.coe.int/en/web/media-freedom/home> (last accessed on 12 August 2015).

Council of Europe (2013) *The role of the Council of Europe Bodies to enhance media freedom and the protection of journalists.* Available from: https://www.coe.int/t/dghl/standardsetting/media/1604%20INFO%20DOC%20The%20role%20of%20Council%20of%20Europe%20bodies%20to%20enhance%20media%20freedom%20and%20the%20protection%20of%20journalists_en.pdf (last accessed Januray 29th 2016)

Deane, J. (2013) *Fragile States: The Role of Media and Communication.* London: BBC Media Action.

Henrichsen, J., Betz, M. and Lisosky, J. (2015) *Building Digital Safety for Journalism: A Survey of Selected Issues.* Paris: UNESCO.

Lisosky, J. and Henrichsen, J. (2011) *War on Words: Who Should Protect Journalists?* Oxford: Praeger.

ICRC. (2015) *Geneva Conventions.* Available from: <https://www.icrc.org/ihl/WebART/470-750102?OpenDocument> (last accessed on 12 August 2015).

International Criminal Court (1998) *Rome Statute.* Available from: <http://legal.un.org/icc/statute/english/rome_statute(e).pdf> (last accessed on 12 August 2015).

Leach, P. (2013) *The Principles Which Can Be Drawn from the Case-law of the European Court of Human Rights Relating to the Protection and Safety of Journalists and Journalism.* Strasbourg: Council of Europe (CDMSI). Available from: <http://www.coe.int/t/dghl/standardsetting/media/cdmsi/CDMSI(2013) Misc3_en.pdf> (last accessed on 12 August 2015).

Schiff, A. (2010) *Daniel Pearl Freedom of the Press Act to be Sent to the President.* Available from: <http://schiff.house.gov/news/press-releases/daniel-pearl-freedom-of-the-press-act-to-be-sent-to-the-president> (last accessed on 12 August 2015).

UNESCO. (2014) *UN Plan of Action on Safety of Journalists.* Available from: <http://www.unesco.org/new/fileadmin/MULTIMEDIA/HQ/CI/import/ReviewReportUNPlan_of_Action_on_Safety_of_Journalist_Fin.pdf> (last accessed on 12 August 2015).

UNESCO (2015) *Media and Development.* Paris: UNESCO.

UNESCO: The International Programme for the Development of Communication (2014) *Why Free, Independent and Pluralistic Media Deserve to be at the Heart of a Post-2015 Development Agenda.* Available from: <http://www.unesco.org/new/fileadmin/MULTIMEDIA/HQ/CI/CI/pdf/news/free_media_ post_2015.pdf> (12 August 2014).

United Nations (UN) (1948) *Universal Declaration of Human Rights.* Available from: <http://www.un.org/en/documents/udhr/> (last accessed on 12 August 2015).

UN (2013) *High-Level Panel of Eminent Persons on the Post-2015 Development Agenda.* Available from: <http://www.un.org/sg/management/hlppost2015.shtml> (last accessed on 12 August 2015).

UN (2007) *Medellin Declaration.* Available from: <http://www.unesco.org/new/en/unesco/events/prizes-and-celebrations/celebrations/international-days/world-press-freedom-day/previous-celebrations/worldpressfreedomday2009000/medellin-declaration/> (last accessed on 12 August 2015).

10
Conclusion: Ways Forward

Reporting Dangerously: Journalist Killings, Intimidation and Security has set out a number of arguments about the importance of journalism to civil society which underline the broader responsibility to safeguard independent journalism in the face of today's changing and increasing threats.

Civil society depends upon free access to information and the representation – and, ideally, participation – of different voices, views and values to support democratic institutions and economic development. Good governance benefits from the scrutiny and challenge of independent, critical journalism. At a time in world history when nation-state violence is apparently in decline, we need to explain the seeming paradox of how it can be that increasing numbers of journalists are positioned at risk and more than at any time previously are now losing their lives. Notwithstanding historical trends in respect of the 'pacification of violence' and the seeming 'moral repugnance' displayed in many civil societies toward naked violence, journalism and journalists, we have argued, are bound up in these same historical forces and in ways that position them at increased risk. These now compel many of them to report on the human consequences of conflicts and the brutal injustices suffered by ordinary people living in conditions of violence and precarity around the world. In a world of globalised communications, journalism's capacity to report from unruly, uncivil places has become geographically expanded, culturally deepened and, we suggest, historically and normatively compelled. This is often overlooked in the contemporary world of academic scholarship.

However, we have also argued that the historical tide of globalisation is raising more risks for journalism and for civil society. These need to be better recognised and understood. Collectively, it is the responsibility of

200

all of us to take a keener interest in the difficult and sometimes danger-ous work undertaken by increasing numbers of journalists around the world. News organisations and safety bodies have developed tactical responses to these increasing threats in terms of training, equipment and assessment of risk. The UN and other pan-national organisa-tions are seeking to raise at global level the importance of supporting independent journalism because of its impact on social, political and economic development. However, there is a gap between these two levels of engagement, at national and societal level, where as yet there is inadequate recognition of the important role strong, independent journalism can and should play in the emergence of global, civil society.

Journalism's 'responsibility to report' positions journalists and their craft at the centre of established, emerging and collapsing societies around the world. Journalists witness and communicate conflicts, injus-tices and social and democratic failure, and as such act as the eyes, ears and sometimes conscience of civil society, and may even be instrumen-tal in the development of a transnational or global civil sphere. Today, modern conflicts can be as much for public opinion and the politics of identity as they can be for geographic territory. This places journalists and media in the front line. It exacerbates the mindset of 'you're either with us or against us', which delegitimises any independent or neutral role. Yet it also increases the importance of available, independent, non-partisan information.

This means all of us have a stake in ensuring journalists can continue to enjoy the ability to report freely and openly. The protection of jour-nalists reporting in and from dangerous places cannot be regarded as simply a matter to do only with them – it implicates us all. So we have argued that wider institutional and legal frameworks must be brought into play and robustly enforced if journalists in the future, as well as those currently reporting form uncivil societies, are to be properly rec-ognised and safeguarded. This leads us to a number of conclusions.

The umbilical connection between journalism and civil society needs to be fully recognised and supported

There is now more than sufficient evidence and research to demonstrate the core importance of open access to information, and the ability to both gather and receive it, to the health and successful development of communities and societies. The UN is set to make a significant recogni-tion of this through the 2015 Sustainable Development Goals. However, there will still be governments and other constituencies in whose interest it is to deny this link or to undermine it. The importance of independent information and the representation of a plurality of identities and interests must be recognised and supported. All those concerned with not only free speech and journalism safety, but with the broader issues of social, political and economic development need to support the safe working of journalists, strive to end impunity, and assert that free media is a first-order condition of successful societies. This needs to be monitored, measured and reported on a regular and consistent basis.

Impunity for the death or intimidation of journalists must be tackled at multiple levels

Zero risk in newsgathering is not attainable and should not be pursued as it will necessarily entail pulling back from situations or places which need reporting. However, when journalists necessarily take significant personal risk, or pay with their lives for undertaking the responsibility to report, there should be full accountability for anyone who has sought to deliberately endanger them. Impunity for the killing and intimidation of journalists is a cancer which leads to self-censorship, under-reporting, and allows the conditions for crime and corruption to flourish. Statements of intent at global level, and of protest at NGO or newsroom level, are well and good. But until impunity is consistently pursued at national levels it will continue to exist to an unacceptable degree. The analogy with the civil rights movement of the 1960s is appropriate. There needs to be a well-planned and coordinated, international, legal campaign to bring to justice those who have murdered journalists, and greater international support for local initiatives. Prosecuting some high-profile, winnable cases could help point the way for more difficult cases in future.

In addition, there should be a greater degree of media coverage of impunity. The chances of protecting and safeguarding journalists could be considerably improved by more reporting on the everyday violence, intimidation, crime and corruption that insidiously threaten and undermine 'civil society'.

Journalism is no longer an activity confined to professionals

This is now a statement of the obvious, so we have not sought to explore at length the debate about 'citizen journalism' versus 'professional journalism'. There are, however, complex issues surrounding the blurring lines between activism, eyewitness media and journalism – some of which, as we have discussed, exacerbate the risks journalists face. Activism reinforces the perception of media as partisan. However, journalists are no longer a constituency to be offered protection as the only means of wider communication. An Internet account and camera phone can do the job more directly, and without intermediation of the message. As such, it is the *activity* of reporting which needs to be supported, rather than a professional constituency.

Whether an international correspondent reporting on a global conflict, a local journalist representing the concerns of their community about crime or corruption, or an eyewitness or activist uploading video of an event, they are all contributing towards an informed society and open public debate.

There are many variables in the risk to journalists including age, gender, experience, and role

Our discussion, with the help of a diverse group of journalists, has helped to illuminate how demographics of age and gender, as well as journalist standing and status, whether local or national or international and peripatetic, impact on the field of risk-reporting and how the inherent dangers of reporting from unruly and uncivil places can never be fully mitigated. Such are the unforeseen circumstances and contingencies of risk that often unpredictably position journalists in immanent as well as imminent danger.

We have also heard experienced and less experienced journalists' views and accounts of some of the policies and procedures designed to keep them safe(r), and how and why it is that these are not always strictly adhered to, whether through the privileging of personal knowledge and experience, differing attitudes to risk and danger, or the inequalities of training and resources that characterise the journalism industry around the world as well as the differentiated risk positions occupied by staffers and freelancers, stringers and fixers, and national and international journalists.

Rapidly developing technology has opened new levels of risk for journalists

Journalists have also developed views, as we might expect, on the rapidly transforming communications environment in which they work and how this now enters into their reporting practices and affects the nature of the risks and dangers which they confront. Sometimes, this is indirect and derives from the wider sea changes in communications accessibility and the capacity of belligerents, as well as citizen journalists and activists, to bypass mainstream news media channels and send their own messages direct to their preferred audiences, and within their own terms and with their preferred images. This, according to many of our respondents, has increasingly undermined the earlier dependence of conflicting parties on news journalists, and thereby positioned journalists, in their eyes at least, as relatively redundant and without value. But so too has the digital revolution produced highly portable equipment that can easily and universally connect with wider networks and transmit images and words, events and ideas around the globe in near real-time.

The advent of social media now promises to make greater inroads into production processes, sensitising and informing journalists of the different views and values, identities and interests in contention and equipping them to produce better informed and better grounded accounts and story treatments. But the digital revolution and its enhanced surveillance capacity not only empower journalism and the civil sphere to monitor unfolding conflicts and human-rights abuses, but also potentially affords malevolent social and political forces the capacity to monitor, disrupt and intimidate or worse target journalists' communications and their sources.

The response of the news industry and journalism NGOs has been fragmentary and uncoordinated

Although journalist safety is a common issue for the industry and free-speech bodies, there is a wide spread of organisations addressing the issue and adjacent policy initiatives. The fragmentation of response to safety as a core issue is one of the principal challenges facing those concerned with it. Plurality of interest and action has benefits – but it can also dilute impact. There is growing engagement in journalist safety and impunity from industry and NGOs – but also duplication of effort and fragmented attention. The UN plan of action and the Council of Europe initiative offer some opportunity for collaboration across the sector, but the inherent, independent and competitive culture of news prevents consistent coordination. Addressing the problem of journalist safety and impunity for their killers is one which will require courage, persistence and the determination to move public opinion. There is scope for greater collaboration and coordination between concerned parties, and for further initiatives to close the gap between policy and practice.

The nature of contemporary global society generates new levels of risk for independent journalism

Globalisation generates diverse threats and risks, and these can be unevenly distributed around the globe. Though these are not confined to contemporary forms of warfare, given the globally enmeshed nature of today's ecological, economic and political crises, the changing nature of contemporary warfare nonetheless illuminates how and why it is that journalists are often exposed to increased risk. The 'new Western way of war', 'new wars' and 'transnational and mediatized terror' increasingly embroil civilians and non-combatants. This is disturbing enough, but they also now put journalists at increased risk and, sometimes, in targeted harm's way.

The endemic problems of global interdependency point to some of the most profound challenges confronting humanity and the planet, processes that can all too easily spill over into enmity and violence as much as cooperation and cosmopolitanism. Resource depletion, unsustainable environments, global population movements and contemporary geopolitical inequalities are all set to produce unruly and uncivil places in the future. And here new forms of conflict and violence will exacerbate the precarity of life for many on the planet. Under such conditions, journalists will find themselves compelled to report on the plight of others around the world. Many will thereby also become subject to those same forces of threat and destruction that they seek to expose to wider global attention.

Champions of free expression have long argued that it rests on journalists being able to do their jobs safely and without intimidation. It is a strong argument, but one which is failing in many parts of the world. Free speech and press freedom have more battles to fight to be recognised as basic human rights. And there is further to go in asserting the broader civic responsibility to defend independent journalism and the rights and social value of free reporting.

It is a multidimensional problem – but at its core lies the recognition that journalism and civil society are indivisible. Reporting from uncivil societies remains as crucial as it has ever been – but in many places has become more dangerous than it has ever been. To repeat one last time, it is incumbent upon us all to try to minimise such threats and dangers wherever, whenever and however we can. The responsibility to report, as much as the fledgling world responsibility to protect, applies not only to journalists but to all of us who would inhabit the civil sphere of human society.

Appendix 1

Among the leading NGOs now addressing some issue of journalist safety, in addition to INSI, there are the following.

The Committee to Protect Journalists

The US-based Committee to Protect Journalists was founded in 1981 as an independent, non-profit organisation promoting press freedom globally.

Under its current Executive Director, Joel Simon, it has launched a global campaign against impunity – seeking to ensure those who kill or intimidate journalists face justice. It produces an annual Impunity Index identifying the countries with the worst track records for journalists being murdered and killers going free (currently headed by Syria, Iraq, Somalia and the Philippines).

The CPJ has also led missions around the world confronting governments which in some form are jeopardising free speech and freedom of the press.

It has become the leading global advocacy organisation for press freedom, attempting to 'influence policy and ensure that press freedom is protected and strengthened as a fundamental right for a free, just society'.

The International Press Institute

The IPI was formed in 1950 in New York, still in the shadow of the Second World War when press manipulation had played such a visible role. Its aims were and are:

- The furtherance and safeguarding of freedom of the press, by which is meant: free access to the news, free transmission of news, free publication of newspapers, free expression of views.
- The achievement of understanding amongst journalists and so among peoples.
- The promotion of the free exchange of accurate and balanced news among nations.
- The improvement of the practices of journalism.

It works as a global network of editors, executives and journalists seeking to promote these principles globally with members in more than 120 countries. It produces an annual report on press freedom violations, including violence against journalists.

WAN-IFRA

The World Association of Newspapers and News Publishers was formed in 2009 out of the merger of two trade organisations for the global newspaper industry.

It represents 18,000 titles and 3,000 companies in 120 countries. It sees its first priority as the defence of the freedom of the press and the economic independence of newspapers which is a necessity for that freedom. Although safety is not a primary objective, WAN-IFRA works closely with UNESCO and the Council of Europe on media-freedom issues, including journalist safety.

Reporters Sans Frontières

RSF was founded in France in 1985 as a global non-profit organisation. It now focuses on two priorities – Internet censorship and support for journalists in dangerous locations. It seeks to:

- continuously monitor attacks on freedom of information worldwide;
- denounce any such attacks in the media;
- act in cooperation with governments to fight censorship and laws aimed at restricting freedom of information;
- morally and financially assist persecuted journalists, as well as their families;
- offer material assistance to war correspondents in order to enhance their safety.

It offers direct assistance by making safety equipment available, negotiating insurance, offering a hotline for journalists in difficulty, providing post traumatic stress disorder support and supporting journalists seeking asylum to escape danger. RSF also works closely with UNESCO in Paris.

Human Rights Watch

Human Rights Watch was established in 1978 and investigates human-rights abuses around the world. It recognises journalist safety as central to its work on free speech. and impunity as an issue relevant to its campaign for international justice. As such it undertakes investigations into the killing and intimidation of journalists in different countries, publishing authoritative reports into press freedom.

The Rory Peck Trust

The Rory Peck Trust was established after the death of freelance cameraman Rory Peck in Moscow in 1993. Through a range of fundraising activities, it provides aid to freelance journalists and their families, and training and other support to the freelance community. It helps those who may be imprisoned, threatened or injured, and the relatives of those killed; it offers security advice and training which might otherwise be unaffordable, and professional development resources and advice.

Article 19

Article 19 raises public awareness about impunity and safety of journalists through research, campaigns, advocacy, standard setting, monitoring, and providing legal assistance. Their country reports assess media freedom and offer recommendations to improve freedom of expression.

A Day Without News

A Day Without News is a global campaign launched following the death of the *Sunday Times* correspondent Marie Colvin in Syria in 2013. Its aims are to:

- draw sharper attention to the growing numbers of journalists who have been killed and injured in armed conflict, in some cases as a result of direct targeting by the belligerents;
- develop a public, diplomatic, institutional and legal agenda to combat this more effectively;
- investigate and collect evidence in support of prosecutable cases in this area.

It has worked with the UN to increase the attention given by governments to journalists' safety and impunity, and has a project with a US university to look at how the law and journalism faculties might work together to identify cases where those who have targeted journalists can be brought to justice.

Reporters Instructed in Saving Colleagues

RISC was set up by journalist and author Sebastian Junger to provide free medical training to freelance journalists working in conflict zones. He established the organisation after the death of photojournalist Tim Hetherington in Libya in 2011 from a wound which need not have been fatal if the right medical knowledge had been at hand. Since then, RISC has raised funds to train more than 200 journalists in advanced first aid.

These are the principle international groups addressing journalism safety and related policy issues. There are others, including the Association of European Journalists, PEN International, Freedom House, the Open Society Foundation, Doha Centre for Media Freedom, and the Press Emblem Campaign. Each has a slightly different focus – but with areas of substantial overlap.

Appendix 2

To: Executive Committee

From: General Secretary   May 12th 2002

IPI Congress: IFJ Safety Proposal

The General Secretary addressed the IPI (International Press Institute) Congress in Ljubljana on May 12th and discussed safety of journalists' issues. In the course of the debate the IFJ put forward a suggestion for the creation of an international body to provide safety information, training courses and assistance to journalists and media organisations. This suggestion was taken up. The IPI has indicated its willingness to support this idea.

The proposal arises from discussion within the secretariat and our experience of training and safety work carried out recently in Pakistan and Palestine.

While the safety of journalists and media staff in conflict zones is the inspiration for the proposal, it could point towards a more comprehensive approach to health and safety at work issues for all media staff.

Currently, only larger and well-resourced media organisations are providing systematic safety training for staff – Reuters, CNN, The BBC, Associated Press – these organisations have developed their own code of conduct on the issue which is being taken up by other broadcast media. Significantly, not one single press body has signed up.

The problems are as follows:

a) safety training is very expensive (up to 500$ a head per day) as is the provision of basic equipment (flak jackets and helmets)
b) many of the journalists most in need are freelance
c) most of the victims of violence are local, without the capacity to receive in their own languages even basic training on safety issues
d) very little information exists on the establishment of a health and safety programme for media staff embracing risk awareness, stress and trauma counselling, etc.

To combat this the IFJ proposes that media professional organisations (employers and trade unions) should establish a non-profit independent institution (possible name: the News Safety International) to:

Publish information materials in relevant languages on health and safety issues for journalists and media staff – targeted safety manuals (for TV people, press staff, freelances; leaflets on International Human Rights Law and Geneva Conventions; model collective bargaining clauses, etc);

Promote the organisation of training programmes for journalists and media staff through:

- existing training institutions (journalism schools and colleges)
- mid-career training modules designed to raise awareness of current developments in this area for senior and executive media staff
- crisis intervention: the establishment of a rapid-response unit that, working with national and intergovernmental institutions and appropriate armed forces, could set up a safety unit for journalists and media staff in any region where conflict arises.

Provide access to materials: medical kits, flak jackets and helmets for distribution at local level (we might appeal for "used" materials from national armed forces.

Campaign within the International Community for action on news safety – particularly, ILO, Unesco, Red Cross, NATO etc.

In some countries, Germany and Belgium, for example, only the armed forces provide training for journalists. But this is limited in terms of numbers and in terms of scope. (In Germany there is a course charge of 750 Euro while in Belgium the course is free. In Great Britain, a small, independent group, the Rory Peck Trust, is looking to make a link between safety training and insurance provision.

The IFJ could launch this initiative in the following way:

- Call a meeting in Brussels of relevant groups – IFJ, UNI-Mei, IPI, leading media (BBC, Reuters, Associated Press), European Broadcasting Union and the Committee to Protect Journalists. Other groups may be considered, particularly those that organise memorial prizes (Rory Peck Trust, Kurt Shork Award, etc) as well as leading intergovernmental bodies – the Red Cross and UNESCO, OSCE, for example.
- Establish the mandate of this organisation and set up a regional network for collaboration on this issue.
- Identify possible sources of funding: Unesco, European Union, OSCE, Soros Foundation, International Media Support, national organisations and media organisations. The IFJ could make an initial contribution of, say, 5,000 Euro and ask the other participants to match this initial funding.
- Set up a Steering Committee to take the work forward.

In the first instance the IFJ Safety Fund could be the initiating body and we could allocate an amount from the Fund to support initial actions. I would suggest 20.000 Euro.

We could suggest that next year – around World Press Freedom Day – we organise an international safety event to launch the initiative and invite Terry Anderson and John McCarthy (former Beirut hostages) to participate.

Appendix 3

International Federation of Journalists

From the General Secretary

The Honourable Kofi Annan
Secretary-General
United Nations
New York, NY 10017 - USA
Fax: +1 212 963 2155 / 963 7055
Via email: sg@un.org and ecu@un.org

August 29th 2005

Dear Secretary-General,

Concern over Safety of Media Staff and Deaths of Journalists in Iraq

On behalf of the International Federation of Journalists, the world's largest journalists' group, I am writing to express the strongest possible concern of journalists' worldwide over the perilous situation facing journalists and media staff working in Iraq today.

Yesterday's shooting of Reuter's employee Waleed Khaled in the Hay al-Adil district of west Baghdad, an incident in which cameraman Haider Kadhem was wounded, brings to 70 the number of Iraqi media staff killed since the US invasion in March 2003.

Altogether and counting all essential media staff including drivers and translators, we have registered some 95 journalists and media staff who have died in the Iraq conflict.

The toll is appalling, with many of our colleagues helpless victims of a conflict in which there will be, inevitably, unavoidable casualties.

However, some of these deaths could and should have been avoided. We have noted that 18 of these deaths have been at the hands of US soldiers. In most cases there have been no credible or independent investigations which give thorough explanations, to the satisfaction of friends, family and media organisations, as to why colleagues and loved ones have died. In some cases questions still remain more than two years after the journalists have died.

The number of unexplained media killings by US military personnel is unacceptable. Often it appears that media organisations and journalists' families face a wall of silence and an unfeeling bureaucracy that refuses to give clear and credible answers.

That is why the IFJ is asking you and the United Nations to establish an independent inquiry into the killings of media staff at the hands of US and coalition forces.

The United Nations has a responsibility to ensure that international law is enforced and the rights of victims in this conflict are properly protected. It is time, we believe, for the UN itself to demand that there is justice and respect for basic humanitarian rights on the part of democratic countries involved in this conflict.

I enclose a full list of all of the cases which give us concern. We believe that a full, independent and inclusive inquiry into all of these cases is urgently needed in order to ensure that journalists and media organisations can have confidence that governments are honouring their obligations.

The IFJ acknowledges that many of the incidents may have been unavoidable in the context of a war driven by undemocratic and terrorist groups, but we cannot ignore the fact that in a number of cases answers are still required. So long as this remains the case, there will suggestions of deliberate targeting of media staff.

We need to clear the air. We also consider that in a period of transition to Iraqi authority it is necessary to set the highest standards possible for the investigation and reporting of all incidents in which journalists and media staff are killed.

The IFJ is currently working closely with journalists' groups in Iraq and is in dialogue with groups such as the Iraqi National Communications and Media Commission to try to ensure that the rights of journalists throughout the country are properly protected.

The issue of the safety and security of journalists and media staff must be properly taken up by the international community, which has already responded effectively and decisively on the question of protection of humanitarian staff, including UN personnel.

All losses are terrible to bear, but the numbers of journalists, and local media people in particular, who are now at risk has reached unacceptably high levels.

We ask for you to put this matter before the Security Council and for Member States to be reminded of their duties and responsibilities to protect journalists and media staff, a group of civilians who, like humanitarian workers, have a legitimate right to be present in conflict zones, but whose interests have been ignored for far too long.

With Kind Regards,

AIDAN WHITE

Index

213

Printed by Printforce, the Netherlands